Getting to Peace

Also by William L. Ury

Getting to Yes: Negotiating Agreement Without Giving In
(with Roger Fisher & Bruce M. Patton)

Getting Past No: Negotiating Your Way from Confrontation to Cooperation

Getting Disputes Resolved: Designing Systems to Cut the Costs of Conflict
(with Jeanne M. Brett and Stephen B. Goldberg)

Beyond the Hotline: How Crisis Control Can Prevent Nuclear War

Windows of Opportunity: From Cold War to Peaceful Competition in
U.S.-Soviet Relations (edited with Graham T. Allison and Bruce J. Allyn)

Getting to Peace

Transforming Conflict at Home, at Work, and in the World

William L. Ury

VIKING

VIKING
Published by the Penguin Group
Penguin Putnam Inc., 375 Hudson Street,
New York, New York 10014, U.S.A.
Penguin Books Ltd, 27 Wrights Lane,
London W8 5TZ, England
Penguin Books Australia Ltd, Ringwood,
Victoria, Australia
Penguin Books Canada Ltd, 10 Alcorn Avenue,
Toronto, Ontario, Canada M4V 3B2
Penguin Books (N.Z.) Ltd, 182–190 Wairau Road,
Auckland 10, New Zealand

Penguin Books Ltd, Registered Offices:
Harmondsworth, Middlesex, England

First published in 1999 by Viking Penguin,
a member of Penguin Putnam, Inc.

1   3   5   7   9   10   8   6   4   2

Library of Congress Cataloging-in-Publication Data
Ury, William.
Getting to Peace : transforming conflict at home, at work, and in the world / William L. Ury.
p.   cm.
ISBN 0-670-88758-7
1. Conflict management.   2. Cooperativeness.   I. Title.
HM1126.U79   1999
303.6'9—DC21   99-28121

This book is printed on acid-free paper.
∞

Printed in the United States of America
Set in Minion

For Janice Gray Ury
And her granddaughter Gabriela,
Who, each in her own way,
Have given me life and inspiration

CONTENTS

Author's Note   viii
Acknowledgments   x
Introduction: Can We All Get Along?   xv

I. THE MISSING KEY
1. The Third Side   3

II. A BRIEF HISTORY OF CONFLICT
2. From Coexistence   29
3. To Coercion   57
4. And Back Again?   81

III. THE TEN ROLES OF THE THIRD SIDE
5. Prevent: *Provider, Teacher, Bridge-Builder*   114
6. Resolve: *Mediator, Arbiter, Equalizer, Healer*   140
7. Contain: *Witness, Referee, Peacekeeper*   169

Conclusion: Toward a Co-Culture   196

A Road Map to *Getting to Peace*   208
End Notes   214
Index   241
About the Author   250

AUTHOR'S NOTE

I am an anthropologist, a concerned anthropologist. I am concerned because the tribe I study is in danger. While it is not at all unusual for an anthropologist to study an endangered tribe, this tribe is not foreign. It is my own. It is not a small band of people. It is the human tribe. The danger comes not from the outside world. It comes from the inside—from the human habit of falling into destructive, often deadly conflict whenever a serious difference arises between two people, two groups, or two nations.

This book is a personal as well as a professional quest. As long as I can remember, I have always wondered about the question of how we can all get along despite our deep differences. Perhaps it was being raised with constant quarreling at the family dinner table. Perhaps it was going to school with children from thirty different nationalities and a dozen religions. Perhaps it was growing up under the shadow of the Bomb, speculating with friends whether we had a future at all. The situations varied, but the underlying question remained the same: Are we *humanly* capable of living together without constantly falling into destructive conflict? Is peace a possibility—or a pipe dream?

Not content to remain solely an observer, I became a mediator in order to learn practical ways to resolve conflicts. Over the last two decades, I have served as a third party in disputes ranging from family feuds to wildcat strikes in a Kentucky coal mine and from corporate turf battles to ethnic wars in the former Yugoslavia and the Middle East.

I have also worked on the problem of how to prevent nuclear war, both as a researcher and as a consultant to the White House Crisis Management Center. In discussions with officials and academics, I was often struck that the time frame in people's minds seemed limited to the next five or ten years, not even a human lifetime. Yet, from an anthropological point of view, even a century or a millennium is a brief period. Given the human genius at devising weapons of extraordinary destructiveness, I wondered about how we—and our children and descendants—could learn to coexist on a sustainable basis, free of the threat of annihilation.

Over the years, I have tried to distill in writing what lessons I was learning. A book I coauthored with Roger Fisher and Bruce Patton almost twenty years ago, *Getting to Yes*, proposed a process for negotiating mutually satisfactory agreements. A decade later, in *Getting Past No*, I tried to address the more difficult situations: What if people aren't interested in getting to yes?

This book is a step beyond "Yes" and "No." For the problem we face goes beyond individual transactions and beyond dealing with difficult people. Our present challenge is to change the *culture* of conflict itself within our families, our workplaces, our communities, and our world. It is to create a culture where even the most serious disputes are handled on the basis not of force and coercion but of mutual interest and coexistence. Far from eliminating differences, our challenge is to make the world safe for differences.

ACKNOWLEDGMENTS

There are writers for whom the process of writing resembles farming. They methodically plant, tend, and harvest their crop. And then there are writers for whom the process is more disorderly, somewhat like hunting. They wander in search of scattered game, often going for days without apparent progress before they suddenly spy and capture their prey, an insight or two. I confess I am a member of the latter group. And, as in the hunts of our ancestors, cooperation is essential. This book could not have been written without the advice and support of the members of my intellectual and emotional tribes. I am profoundly grateful to each of them.

I began research for this book almost fifteen years ago by seeking to understand the anthropological roots of conflict. Many scholars generously shared with me their perspectives. I would like to thank in particular C. K. "Bob" Brain, Robert Carneiro, Irven DeVore, Robert Foley, Robert Gordon, Jonathan Haas, David Hamburg, Donald Johanson, Bruce Knauft, William McNeill, Robert North, John Pfeiffer, and Martin van Creveld. Brian Ferguson brought to our many talks his encyclopedic knowledge of the anthropology of war and his rigorous weighing of alternative explanations for prehistoric warfare. Paleontologists Philip Tobias and Lee Berger kindly took me to visit their archaeological sites and patiently tolerated my persistent questions about the earliest evidence for human violence. I learned from conversations with Jane Goodall and Frans de Waal about how the behavior of chimpanzees sheds light on our own.

John Marshall, a passionate defender of the rights of the Bushmen, introduced me to the Ju/'hoansi in Namibia, and Isak Barnard took me to visit a group of Kua in Botswana. I am particularly indebted to the Kua elders Korakoradue, Xamgau, Ramones, Raseukua, and Purana for lengthy informative interviews. Lorna Marshall and Megan Biesele also generously spent many hours with me elucidating the ways in which the Bushmen handle their differences and reach agreement.

For help in understanding clan warfare in New Guinea, I am grateful to Aki Tumi, Ru, and Joseph Anga, among many others, for interviews, as well as to anthropologists Marilyn Strathern and Douglas Young. In Malaysia, Colin Nicholas of the Center for Orang Asli Concerns introduced me to the Semai and their remarkable culture; for insights, I am also much indebted to the work of Clayton and Carole Robarchek. Anthropologist Lye Tuck-Po introduced me to the Batek, a small group of hunter-gatherers, also living in Malaysia.

For partial funding of my research, I am grateful for the generosity of the Carnegie Corporation and the John D. and Catherine T. MacArthur Foundation. Early on, I enjoyed the auspices of the Avoiding Nuclear War Project of the John F. Kennedy School of Government, co-directed by Graham Allison, Albert Carnesale, and Joseph Nye. Throughout I have benefited greatly from the support of my colleagues at the Program on Negotiation at Harvard Law School; in particular, I would like to acknowledge the encouragement of my friend the late Jeffrey Rubin.

I was fortunate to have a series of highly competent research assistants. Cassia Herman diligently helped me dig out the relevant literature on the anthropology of war. Lara Olson did research on a series of relevant topics, offered valuable feedback, and skillfully oversaw the work of four remarkable Harvard students during the summer of 1993—Sami Farhad, Benjamin Moerman, Rupa Roy, and Jeanne Smoot. Over the course of the ensuing two years, Ben proved my most patient and thorough critic. He went over the manuscript line by line and offered a great number of insightful comments and suggestions, which significantly shaped the way my argument was crafted. I am deeply grateful to him.

I am also indebted to Laina Reynolds, who with energy and zeal did exhaustive research on the end notes, offered many useful comments, and made available her invaluable computer wizardry. Finally came Josh Weiss, indefatigable, quick, and ingenious in digging up examples from all domains. He made many fresh suggestions and helped bring the book to the finishing line.

During these years, I benefited as well from the support of a series of extremely capable executive assistants and business managers: Ellen Meyer, Lucia Miller, Linda Lane, Sheryl Gamble, Barbara Hausman, Barbara Drew, Martha Landry, Riana Robert, and Jean Michael. For the last four years, Christine Quistgard helped free my calendar for writing, ever dedicated, protective, and witty.

Then came the writing itself, which benefited enormously from a long series of patient readers, always careful to mix their judicious criticism with encouragement. I owe a particular debt of gratitude to Julie Adams, James Botkin, Francisco Diez, Nicholas Dunlop, Brian Ferguson, Patrick Finerty, Ronald Heifetz, Jill Kneerim, John Paul Lederach, John Naisbitt, Stephen Rhinesmith, Kumar Rupesinghe, Raphael Sagalyn, Alison Sander, Thomas Sander, Benjamin Sherwood, Elizabeth Sherwood, Ed Sketch, Alan Slifka, Mark Sommer, John Steiner, Graciela Tapia, Janice Ury, Joshua Ury, and Mark Walton. I also learned a great deal from consulting Lisa Gray Arback, Edward T. Hall, Ben Levi, Ilana Manolson, and Robert Mnookin.

Writing often required solitude. For offering places of refuge, I thank João Santaella Jr., Paulo Rogerio de Oliveira, Ruth Sporn, Finn Arnesen, and the hospitable people of Glacier View Ranch.

The writing benefited from excellent editing. I am much indebted to Jane von Mehren, always insightful and supportive, who made many valuable suggestions and eliminated needless repetition; to Richard Marek, who honed the text and astutely pointed out sections it still needed; and to my friend Marty Linsky, who helped me craft the conceptual story line and find the right voice.

Words, I learned from Robert Horn, a master of visual language, are best complemented with graphics. His icons, beautifully rendered by Ann Yelin, make the concepts more understandable and memorable.

Agents are indispensable. Joni Evans and Michael Carlisle of the William Morris Agency believed in the project when it was not always easy to do so and, with their infectious enthusiasm, pushed for the book to become more accessible. The reader is the beneficiary.

The support of good friends, I have found, is critical. All were helpful, but three, in particular, had a special influence on this book. Mark Gerzon accompanied the project from its start with wise writerly advice and warm support. Kentyn Reynolds debated many of the book's arguments during countless hikes in the mountains of New Mexico and proved a fearless traveling companion in the Highlands of New Guinea. David Lax, faithful friend, served as adviser *extraordinaire* during our weekly conversations, which have continued now for twenty years.

A book is composed of one yes and a thousand nos. I never could have gotten to this "yes" without the understanding of my colleagues and, most of all, without the warm support of my family. My sons Christian and Thomas proved very patient despite their incredulity that a book could take so long and their belief that I would be better off writing books for children. More than to any other person, however, I am grateful to my wife, Lizanne, unwavering supporter, honest reader, and brave traveling companion to Malaysia. In more ways than she will ever know, she enabled me to get to the peace I needed to write *Getting to Peace*.

William Ury
Boulder, Colorado
April 17, 1999

Introduction

CAN WE ALL
GET ALONG?

At the turn of the millennium, no more critical challenge faces each of us, and all of us together, than how to get along. How can we learn to live together, and deal constructively with our deepest differences?

The challenge exists on the smallest scale and on the largest. Of all the factors influencing the success of a marriage, psychologists report, the single most critical one is the ability to resolve conflicts cooperatively. The same holds true in every other relationship—between friends or business partners, neighbors or nations. So much depends on our ability to get along—our happiness at home, our performance at work, the livability of our communities, and, in this age of mass destruction, the survival of our species.

More than ever, we need to learn how to cooperate. For centuries, we have relied on top-down decision making to get things done. Now the old hierarchies are tumbling down; the father, the boss, the chief, the king cannot simply give orders anymore. Increasingly, we cannot compel others to do what we want; we depend more and more on their voluntary cooperation. We have little choice but to learn how to make our decisions jointly. And yet this is no easy task.

We scarcely know how to do so in groups of six, let alone six hundred, or six billion.

The single biggest barrier to cooperation is destructive conflict. Every time we enter a hospital, our health depends on effective cooperation between nurses and doctors. When their conflicts turn destructive, patient care suffers and people die. Similarly, the health of our families, our businesses, our societies, and our natural environment depends on intricate webs of cooperation among individuals, organizations, and nations—all too often disrupted by quarreling and violence.

The dance of destructive conflict is all too familiar. The husband wants to do fewer chores at home; the wife wants him to do more. One ethnic group wants control over a certain territory; so does another. The language of conflict is universal: "I want it." "No, *I* want it." "I'm right." "No, *I'm* right! *You're* wrong." Soon we are enmeshed in strife, deciding who is right by who is left.

Unfortunately, strife abounds. It tears families apart, causes companies to founder, ruptures communities, and destroys nations. The April 1999 killing rampage at Columbine High School in Littleton, Colorado, which took the lives of fourteen young people and one teacher, was an extreme example, but not unique, unfortunately. Every year in the United States alone, twenty thousand people are murdered; almost a million girls and women are assaulted or raped by a current or former partner; more than fifteen million lawsuits are filed and more than a hundred and fifty billion dollars are spent on legal costs.

On the world stage, the wars in the former Yugoslavia, with their tens of thousands of casualties and millions of refugees, are also, tragically, not unique. At the turn of the millennium, more than two dozen full-scale wars are raging in the world, as are dozens of other violent intergroup conflicts. Even in the absence of war, there is terrorism. If the van that blew up parts of the World Trade Center in New York City in February 1993 had contained a grapefruit-sized nuclear bomb, whose basic design may be found on the Internet, it would have killed everyone within a radius of three miles. Everyone, everywhere, is vulnerable.

The challenge of getting along is all the greater because we are living in the age of the human family reunion. All six billion human beings alive today are descended from the same small group of people, our common grandmothers and grandfathers, who lived several hundred thousand years ago on the African savanna. While humanity has always been biologically united, it is now becoming socially united. Over the last ten thousand years, there has been one fairly steady trend in our history: the ingathering of the tribes of the earth, their incorporation into larger and larger groups, the gradual unification of humanity into a single interacting and interdependent community. For the first time since the origin of our species, humanity is in touch with itself.

Never before in human evolution have people faced the challenge of living in a single community with billions of other human beings. Anthropologists have identified more than fifteen thousand distinct ethnic groups on the planet. Far from bringing a lessening of conflict, the ingathering means, in the short run at least, a heightening of hostilities as people are forced to confront their differences, as jealousies and resentments over inequities flare up, and as identities are threatened by different customs and beliefs. Coming together can produce more heat than light, more conflict than understanding. Family reunions are often far from peaceful and this one is no exception.

Everywhere I go, in speaking with political leaders and taxi drivers, business executives and schoolteachers, I almost always find profound pessimism about our ability to work out our differences. I once participated in a meeting of academics and policy analysts in which the principal speaker advanced an ambitious proposal for preventing wars in the Third World. She called for the superpowers to withdraw all their troops from outside their borders. The audience stirred uncomfortably, taken aback by this bold, seemingly unrealistic proposal, until one scholar was able to articulate his objection: "But wait a minute. You can't stop war. It's human nature!"

When I ask people why peace seems so impossible to them, I hear, in different ways, three deeply ingrained beliefs about human conflict:

- *"When push comes to shove, there's no other way."* When it comes to serious disagreement, we have no alternative but to give in or go to war. Battle, with words or weapons, functions as the final resort, the ultimate arbiter in human affairs.
- *"Besides, it's human nature. Humans have always made war and always will."* Destructive conflict, violence, and war are inherent and inevitable. Life is strife.
- *"Anyway, there isn't much a person can do."* The best approach then when others fight is to stay out of it. "What can I do anyway?" we ask ourselves. If we meddle, we will just get hurt.

Any one of these beliefs constitutes sufficient grounds for pessimism; together, they make a seemingly all-powerful case. There is, it seems, little chance of changing such a fundamental and deep-rooted pattern of human behavior. Destructive conflict, which disrupts our homes, work organizations, communities, and world, is thus widely accepted as an inevitable and prominent part of human existence.

If by chance these assumptions about conflict were mistaken, however, we would never know it for they are insidiously self-confirming. When you don't believe there is much you can do to stop the fighting, you don't do much. The impulse to end the carnage in Bosnia or Rwanda, for example, was continually deflected by the refrain "But these people have been fighting for centuries." The implication was that they would go on fighting for centuries and therefore we bystanders could not really do anything to change the pattern. Fatalism paralyzes our will to act.

Given our daily news diet of wars, street violence, strikes, lawsuits, and political battles, the conventional picture of human beings as naturally prone to violence is understandable. It misses, however, one fundamental point: *Most of the time, most people get along.* Although we may not give it much thought, we know this from personal experience. Despite differing temperaments, habits, and communication styles, most husbands, wives, and children manage to live together. Although they may disagree on basic values, most neighbors succeed in living side by side. Despite opposed interests, labor and management work together most of the time. Even with all their disputes, most nations are at peace with one another. The great majority of relationships among individuals, groups, and nation-states are characterized far more by coexistence than by ongoing destructive conflict. Even in this most deadly of centuries, most people around the planet have lived most of their lives in a condition of peace, not war. Peace is the norm.

It is time, then, to stop thinking of peaceful coexistence as merely a vision. It is a reality. This is not to belittle the existence or importance of strife and war; far from it. It is just to remind us of the prosaic preponderance of peace. It also makes one wonder why, if human nature is so violent, people do not kill one another much more than they in fact do. All the police and armies in the world could not keep people from doing what comes naturally.

Seeing human life as peaceful conflict resolution interrupted by periods of strife, rather than the other way, around transforms the challenge from the negative one of ending war to the positive one of extending the peace. Our task is not to change one absolute—war—into another absolute—peace. It is not to go from zero percent peaceful interaction to a hundred percent, but rather to go from something like ninety percent to something like ninety-nine percent.

In his late eighties, the economist John Kenneth Galbraith took a fall and ended up in the hospital for a major operation. Naturally, his family and friends were worried as the operation appeared risky for a man of his age. As Galbraith was wheeled into the operating room on a gurney, with eyes closed and presumably sleeping, his voice was unexpectedly heard. "I'm taking the optimistic view," he rumbled.

Like Galbraith's condition before the operation, the fate of the human tribe enmeshed in conflict can sometimes seem grim. Working as I have over the past two decades in interminable ethnic wars, bitter labor strife, and family feuds, I have often felt fatalistic myself. Sometimes obstacles have seemed so insuperable, setbacks so frequent, and progress so glacial that it seemed impossible to make any difference at all. By experience, I should be particularly pessimistic then. Nevertheless, like Galbraith, I take the optimistic view.

I take this view not just out of faith but with some solid reasons for hope. For, in the midst of all the strife, I have seen signs of change. At work, many unions and management groups, previously antagonistic, are forging unprecedented partnerships. Many corporations, previously bitter competitors, are finding ways to cooperate—through strategic alliances and joint ventures—as they continue to compete. In many schools, children are learning to mediate among their peers, stopping quarrels and fistfights. Many gangs in the streets are reaching truces—to "squash the beef," as they put it.

Despite devastating conflicts still in the headlines, similar signs of hope are appearing on the international scene. When I began work in the field of conflict resolution in the mid-1970s, the conflicts my colleagues and I addressed were widely considered intractable and permanent: the Cold War, the Arab-Israeli conflict, apartheid in South Africa, and sectarian strife in Northern Ireland. A quarter of a century later, the Cold War is over. In South Africa, after decades of apartheid and civil strife, blacks and whites have accomplished an almost miraculous transformation of their political system. In Northern Ireland, Catholics and Protestants are learning to coexist. Even in the Middle East, Arabs and Israelis are making progress—slow, painful, and marked by frequent setbacks, but progress all the same.

All these seemingly discrete disconnected events do not herald an age of harmony, but they do highlight the potential for change. They raise the question of whether our fatalistic assumptions are, in fact, correct. They speak to the future possibility of preventing most harmful conflict in much the same way we prevent many diseases and most epidemics today.

What if all those innocent children, women, and men dying from a stray bullet on our streets, from a terrorist bomb or an air raid— what if they were dying needlessly from a disease as preventable as smallpox or tuberculosis? What if destructive conflict were preventable—and we simply did not know it? *What if the biggest obstacle to preventing strife lay in our own fatalistic beliefs?*

If, in fact, we could transform our conflicts into constructive dialogue, the payoff for each of us individually—and for all of us together—would be enormous. Our families would be happier, our workplaces more productive, our neighborhoods more congenial, and our world a good deal safer. Since, however, the possibility of peace is negated by so much conventional wisdom, I cannot expect anyone to accept it at first. Hence this book.

This book addresses, in turn, each of three fatalistic beliefs about human conflict. Part One suggests a potentially powerful approach, other than coercion, for handling serious differences when negotiation is not enough. Part Two examines the roots of conflict, presenting a more accurate and more positive story of our human past than the one most of us have been told. Part Three offers ten practical roles each of us can play in order to help ourselves and others get to peace.

In short, this book is about *how* and *why* we may *now*, if we choose, learn to get along. It is intended for all those who, like myself, have ever had a moment of despair about the battles around us, who have ever questioned whether it was all really necessary, who have ever wondered whether we might someday be able to stop the destructive fighting, and, if so, how.

Part One

THE MISSING KEY

THE MISSING KEY

The philosopher Hannah Arendt may have been right when she suggested, shortly after the conclusion of World War II, that the chief reason warfare persists is neither a secret death wish of the human species nor the profits of arms makers, but simply because warfare serves as the ultimate arbiter of differences among nations.

Certainly the parties in any dispute, large or small, between individuals or between groups, can try to talk it out, but what happens if they do not agree, cannot agree, will not agree? However costly, an adversarial contest serves as the ultimate arbiter. Coercion and force have the advantage of being a language understood by everyone. One side loses and the conflict is settled, at least for the time being.

What prevents us from getting to peace, then, perhaps more than anything else, is the lack of an alternative to coercion when conflict turns serious. That is the missing key.

Chapter 1

THE THIRD SIDE

Is this a private fight or can anyone get in?
— Old Irish Saying

 A friend of mine, Herman Engel, was out for a walk with his wife in Lower Manhattan. As the couple was crossing the street at the corner, a speeding car screeched to a halt, missing them by inches. In fear and rage, Engel slammed his fist on the hood of the car.

Furious, the young man driving the car got out, shouting, "Why'd you hit my car?"

Engel shouted back, "You nearly killed my wife and me!"

A crowd gathered. Engel was white, the driver was black, and suddenly the scene took on racial overtones. As people began to take sides, it looked as if the situation might escalate into a full-scale brawl.

Then Engel noticed behind him an onlooker, an older black man. The man's hand, palm down, was slowly moving up and down, as if to say to the young driver, "Okay, now, cool it." The young man visibly struggled to control himself, then suddenly walked back to his car, got in, and drove off without another word.

There are many reasons why conflict escalates. As in this altercation, people may be prompted by anger and fear. Each may believe that he or she is firmly in the right. One or both parties may think they are stronger than the other and will prevail in a fight. Other people may gather around and begin to take sides. In no time, a private vendetta can turn a peaceful neighborhood into a war zone.

The dispute between Engel and the young driver did not end in violence *because* someone intervened, a third party bystander emerging from the crowd. Although unknown to either party, he had the ability to communicate in a manner that commanded respect. Without saying a word, he spoke up against violence. He was an archetypal "third side."

REIMAGINING CONFLICT AS THREE-SIDED

I caught my first glimpse of the third side as a systematic nonviolent alternative to force on a research visit to a group of Bushmen in early 1989. The Bushmen live deep in the Kalahari Desert; traditionally, they are nomadic hunters and gatherers, although this way of life is fast disappearing. Living in small groups of about twenty-five embedded in larger networks of about five hundred, the Bushmen are relatively egalitarian and have no formal leaders. As a !Kung Bushman named /Twi!gum responded to the anthropologist Richard Lee when persistently asked whether they had headmen, "Of course we have headmen! In fact, we are all headmen. Each one of us is headman over himself!"

While the Bushmen are perfectly capable of violence—each man has hunting arrows coated with a poison deadly to humans—they do a good job of controlling harmful conflict. I wanted to find out what, in the absence of a centralized government, stops every dispute from escalating into violence.

Conflict Resolution in Simpler Societies

The secret of the Bushman system for managing conflicts, I discovered, is the vigilant, active, and constructive involvement of the surrounding members of the community. "All of the friends and relatives are approached in a dispute and asked to have a calming word with the disputants," explained Korakoradue, a Kua Bushman elder, as we were sitting around his campfire. The entire community gets involved.

When a serious problem comes up, everyone sits down, all the men and women, and they talk and talk—and talk. Each person has a chance to have his or her say. This open and inclusive process can take days—until the dispute is literally talked out. The community members work hard to discover what social rules have been broken to produce such discord and what needs to be done to restore social harmony. A *kgotla,* which is what they call their discussion, serves as a kind of people's court except that there is no vote by the jury or verdict by the judge; decisions are made by consensus. Unlike a typical court proceeding where one side wins and the other loses, the goal is a stable solution that both the disputants and the community can support. As the group conversation proceeds, a consensus about the appropriate solution gradually crystallizes. After making sure that no opposition or ill will remains, the elders voice this emergent consensus.

If ever tempers rise suddenly and violence threatens, the community is quick to respond. People collect the poisoned arrows and hide them far away in the bush. Others try to separate the antagonists. And the talking begins.

The Bushmen will not rest until the dispute is fully addressed. "Under no conditions," a Kua elder named Ramones informed me, "will a person be allowed to go away until the problem is resolved. We will go and fetch someone if he leaves before the dispute is settled. People do not usually stay angry afterward so they do not move away."

"What if a dispute occurs between people from different groups?" I asked.

"We'll send for the person from the other group. If he doesn't come, our group will go to his group and we will have a talk there."

Seven years later, I visited the Semai people deep in the Malaysian rain forest. The Semai, who have the reputation of being perhaps the most peaceful culture on earth, also make ample use of the community in resolving their disputes. When conflict emerges, people zealously seek to avoid taking sides even when—indeed, especially when—it involves their close relatives or friends. "It is not proper behavior to take sides," one Semai man explained. What is proper is to urge one's relatives to resolve their disputes.

Like the Bushmen, the Semai have long community talks, called *bcaraa'*. I was told of a *bcaraa'* convened to discuss the behavior of a father who had hit his four-year-old son for uprooting plants in the field. It is just not done, people explained. They do not believe in striking children, or forcing them to do something, or even admonishing them. The lesson transmitted through the *bcaraa'* is not only the disapproval of force, but the approval of alternative ways of dealing with the issue through talking and apology.

A *bcaraa'* is organized not just for disputes among adults, but for conflicts among children as well. When a Semai child strikes another, the adults, instead of punishing the child, will call a children's *bcaraa'*. All the children sit down in a circle, discuss what happened, and talk about how to resolve the issue and repair the injured relationship. Everyone thus profits from the dispute by learning the lesson of how to handle frustrations and differences peacefully.

The Challenge in Modern Societies

Our highly populated, urbanized, and technologically complex societies could not be more different from simple societies like those of the Semai and the Bushmen. But, in at least one crucial respect, we face the same challenge. As modern families, workplaces, and political systems become less hierarchical and more horizontal, our great challenge is to learn, as simpler societies have, to handle our differences cooperatively. Our task is not to copy their *kgotla* and *bcaraa'* but to devise our own ways to mobilize the community in helping to resolve conflict.

In our societies, conflict is conventionally thought of as two-sided: husband vs. wife, union vs. employer, Arabs vs. Israelis. The introduction of a third party comes almost as an exception, an aberration, someone meddling in someone else's business. We tend to forget what the simplest societies on earth have long known: namely, that every conflict is actually three-sided. No dispute takes place in a vacuum. There are always others around—relatives, neighbors, allies, neutrals, friends, or onlookers. Every conflict occurs within a community that constitutes the "third side" of any dispute.

The third side is the surrounding community, which serves as a *container* for any escalating conflict. In the absence of that container, serious conflict between two parties all too easily turns into destructive strife. Within the container, however, conflict can gradually be transformed from confrontation into cooperation.

A good analogy for the third side is the body's immune system. When a cell is attacked by a virus, it sends out a chemical alarm awakening the dendritic cells that lie dormant in every tissue of the body. The dendritic cells, in turn, mobilize the T-cells, which come to the rescue. If the T-cells correspond roughly to the police and peacekeepers of the world, the dendritic cells correspond to the surrounding community that must be aroused in order to stop destructive conflict. The third side thus serves as a kind of *social immune system* preventing the spread of the virus of violence.

In the coal country where I used to work as a mediator and arbitrator, there was a famous union song whose refrain went, "Which side are you on?" It was an eloquent call to join up rather than do nothing. The Bushmen and the Semai would wholeheartedly agree with the appeal not to stand aside passively in a dispute, but they would disagree that, in any conflict, there are only two sides to take. To the song's challenge, "Which side are you on?" they might reply in their own language, "The third side."

FROM THE NUCLEAR FAMILY
TO THE HUMAN FAMILY

Spending time in other societies often has the effect of giving one new eyes with which to view one's own culture. That is what happened to me after my visits to the Bushmen and the Semai. Everywhere I looked, from the dinner table to the boardroom, and from the town hall to the courtroom, I began to see traces of the third side in action. What I saw went far beyond the activities of professional mediators such as myself. This was the *community* itself—in the form of neighbors, relatives, and friends—acting as third parties to facilitate the prevention and resolution of conflict. While these examples are still exceptions in our modern societies, they suggest what the third side could accomplish if one day it became strong and these kinds of interventions became the norm.

In the Family

"One night, my mother and her boyfriend got into a silly argument about where they were going to go out," recounts eighteen-year-old Marquise Johnson, who had been trained as a peer mediator at school in one of Cleveland's toughest neighborhoods. "I had to sit them down. That was the hardest thing because he just stared at me when I told him to sit down. But I said, 'I'm going to help you solve this problem—could you sit down, please?' Afterward, we were all sitting there laughing. I was proud. When I finish college, I want to be a social worker or psychologist."

While American customs for dealing with domestic conflict differ greatly from those of the Semai, they are shifting away from passivity toward the active intervention of the surrounding community. Abused children and battered spouses are no longer treated, as they traditionally were, just as a "family matter." Neighbors sound the alarm and social workers, police, and court officers step in. Shelters for battered women offer refuge and counseling.

At the same time, a "Yes" to dialogue is being voiced. Support groups, marital counseling, and family mediation are becoming much more common, and not just among the wealthier classes. Twelve-year-old Jane's parents were so busy arguing that they forgot about how *she* felt. "After they had been to mediation," she recalls, "they listened to each other more, and to me."

"Without family mediation," her father adds, "I feel we would still be battling it out and spreading the damage over a much wider field."

Just as the Bushmen insist on resolving a dispute amicably before letting the parties go their separate ways, so more and more divorces begin with an intense effort to settle the economic and child custody issues in a collaborative fashion through mediation—in order to preserve a working relationship between the parties. This can happen even if the children are already grown; as one divorcing wife explained, "We're going to have to be grandparents together."

In the Workplace

In the workplace, torn by interdepartmental rivalries, corporate lawsuits, strikes, employee grievances, and unexpected violence, there are also signs of the third side at work. "When my sales representatives create conflicts, they're often over customers and territories," says Michael Rosenberg, president of a home food-delivery service. He asks the quarreling salespeople to exchange customers or to work as a team. "This way," he explains, "they're forced to help each other for the good of the company, rather than worrying about protecting their own turf."

Thousands of businesses and government agencies have appointed "ombudspersons," people whose full-time job is to help employees, sometimes on a confidential basis, resolve their disputes with management and one another. Once confined to settling union-management contractual disputes, mediation is increasingly being used to resolve employee and customer grievances. Many businesses are also binding themselves in advance to use mediation and arbitration rather than court to resolve their disputes with customers, suppliers, and partners. Of the one thousand largest corporations in America, nearly ninety percent report having used mediation to settle a dispute in order to save money, achieve a more satisfactory agreement, and preserve a good relationship.

Inside many organizations, facilitators are working with cross-functional teams to overcome interdepartmental issues. Managers are learning to mediate among their teammates, their employees, and often their multiple bosses. The success of a company is coming to depend on the ability of its people to resolve the innumerable conflicts that crop up between manufacturing and marketing, sales and headquarters, employees and supervisors, and to seek a "triple win"—a solution good for each side and for the company as a whole.

In the Community

In the early 1990s, teenage violence in Boston seemed out of control. There was a shooting every day and a half, a tripling of the rate over the course of ten years. A nine-year-old boy out trick-or-treating on Halloween was killed by gang crossfire, as was a teenager walking to an anti-drug meeting. Yet after more than twenty youngsters died from firearms in 1992, the rate fell to zero in 1996.

The key, according to Boston Police Commissioner Paul Evans, was "collaboration." The entire community was mobilized. The police worked closely with teachers and parents to search out kids who had missed school or whose grades had dropped. Local government agencies and businesses provided troubled youth with counseling, educational programs, and after-school jobs. Social workers visited their homes. Ministers and pastors mentored them and offered a substitute family for kids who almost never had two and sometimes not even one parent at home. Community counselors, often ex–gang members, hung out with gang members and taught them to handle their conflicts with talk, not guns.

Boston is not alone in making good use of the third side. All across America, community disputes of all kinds—from barking dogs to landlord-tenant problems to conflicts over children's toys left on the sidewalk—are increasingly being mediated by trained community volunteers. "I would recommend the process [of mediated negotiation] to any dispute that looks insoluble," proclaims Judge Clarence Seeliger after mediation resolved an almost-quarter-century-old bitter dispute in Atlanta over the placement of a highway through local neighborhoods. "They [the third parties] probably kept us from pulling out guns and shooting each other across the table," says Hal Rives, leader of one of the disputing sides. "I don't think it [the agreement] would have happened without them."

As among the Semai, the young too are learning to mediate. "If we don't get mediation, I'd fight her," says Alisha, a sixth-grader at Martin Luther King School. She had asked a fellow pupil, Elizabeth, a simple question, she said, and Elizabeth had responded by calling her names and "getting in my face ugly." Instead of fighting, however, Alisha and Elizabeth stomped down to the Center for Conflict Resolution on the ground floor of the school to ask for help from a fellow student trained in mediation. "They resolved the problem by agreeing they would try to get along and not get smart with each other," explained Patrice Culpepper, the eleventh-grader who mediated the case. "There was follow-up afterward, and they were doing fine."

In more than five thousand schools across America, children are being trained as peer mediators. They do not wait for problems to come to them; they go into the playgrounds and corridors where the problems are. Typically working in pairs, a boy and a girl, the young mediators approach children who are arguing or fighting and ask them if they want to talk it out. Some simple ground rules are stated: Agree not to interrupt, talk about your feelings, agree to look for a solution. The success rate is high. At Melrose Elementary School in Oakland, for instance, the mediation program was credited with substantially reducing violence and cutting suspensions fiftyfold.

This trend of consensual dispute resolution is not limited to the United States. It is occurring around the world, often building on the traditions of mediation indigenous to each society and culture. The Hawaiians have a tradition of *ho'oponopono;* the Palestinians call it *sulha;* and the peoples of the Caucasus use their elders as mediators. Spreading from one society to another, benefiting from local traditions, mediation is becoming a worldwide movement.

In a Warring World

It started as a conversation involving professors and peace activists. Norwegian sociologist Terje Rod Larsen and diplomat Mona Juul, a husband-and-wife team, set up a series of direct unofficial secret peace talks between Israelis and Palestinians in Norway. The first Israeli representatives were two scholarly peaceniks, Yair Hirschfeld and Ron Pundik, with links to the Israeli leadership. Representing the Palestine Liberation Organization were economist Abu Alaa and two aides, Hassan Asfour and Maher el Kurd. The talks eventually ended up becoming official and produced the 1993 Oslo Accord, captured for the world in a televised handshake on the White House lawn between PLO leader Yasser Arafat and Israeli President Yitzhak Rabin. Although only one step along the tortuous path toward Middle East peace, it was the biggest breakthrough in decades of violent conflict.

The third side is increasingly stepping in to help resolve international disputes that once only warfare would have settled. The Vatican averted a war over the Beagle Channel islands between Argentina and Chile by mediating a mutually acceptable division of territory. Mediation by the international community has ended wars in Namibia, Mozambique, Cambodia, Nicaragua, and Guatemala.

Nor is it just governments that intervene. As in the Oslo talks, more and more nongovernmental organizations and private citizens are working in parallel with official diplomats to bring parties together and facilitate talks. The Community of Sant'Egidio, an assembly of Christian communities, is credited with facilitating an end to the war in Mozambique.

The third side sometimes goes further and intervenes forcefully to stop aggression and war. With the world public continually appalled by massacres and rapes of defenseless Muslims in Bosnia, international forces finally intervened, destroyed Serb arsenals, and helped Muslim and Croat armies redress the balance of power to the point where the Serbs were ready to talk. The ensuing peace settlement, forged by international mediators, is being enforced, as this is written, by armed peacekeepers from twenty-four nations.

Across Domains

The third side cuts across domains. What children learn at school, they begin to apply in the family. As fifteen-year-old Makita Moore, a peer mediator, recounts, "Before [my training], when my mother would come in and talk to me, I used to get real mad, but now I know how to listen. And when I don't get loud, she listens to me. So we get along better." What black and white South Africans learned in labor negotiations during the 1980s contributed substantially to the breakthrough political negotiations during the 1990s that ended apartheid. Violence is not the only contagious phenomenon. So is cooperation.

WHAT EXACTLY IS THE THIRD SIDE?

The third side is *people*—from the community—using a certain kind of *power*—the power of peers—from a certain *perspective*—of common ground—supporting a certain *process*—of dialogue and nonviolence—and aiming for a certain *product*—a "triple win."

People from the Community

Unlike the ultimate arbiter in the form of a king or authoritarian state, the third side is not a transcendent individual or institution who dominates all, but rather the *emergent will of the community.* It is an impulse that arises from the vital relationships linking each member and every other member of the community.

It may be hard to grasp how such an amorphous entity could prevent serious strife. People naturally look to superior authority to police their conflicts, yet genuine coexistence cannot be imposed from above. Ultimately, it can emerge only from the parties and those around them. Just as a central planning authority cannot run a complex and dynamic economy efficiently by decree alone, as the failure of Soviet communism so clearly demonstrated, so a top-down response to complex and dynamic conflict would be vastly inadequate. Just as in the free market, the initiative needs to come from anywhere and everywhere, from private citizens and institutions as well as government. Just as the free market is the creation of a host of individuals and organizations freely interacting with each other, so too is the third side. People can contribute to the third side, but no one commands it. Like the market, it is *self-organizing,* with its own natural laws. As each person contributes his or her bit, a powerful phenomenon materializes.

Using the Power of Peers

In one of Aesop's fables, the North Wind and the Sun were arguing about who was more powerful. They finally agreed to a contest: Whoever could strip a wandering shepherd boy of his cloak would win the argument. The North Wind went first, blowing with all his might, but the harder he blew, the more tightly the boy held on to his cloak. It was the Sun's turn next; she warmed the boy with her rays. In no time at all, the boy had decided to cast off his cloak and bathe in the sun.

If the North Wind is the traditional approach of superior force, the Sun is the approach of the third side. It uses the power of persuasion. It influences the parties primarily through an appeal to their interests and to community norms. The third side possesses the power of peer pressure and the force of public opinion. It is people power.

A simple experiment will reveal, in its most elementary form, the influence of the third side. Introduce a neutral third person into any argument between two people. Even if the third person does not talk, the parties' tone will usually begin to moderate and their behavior will become more controlled. If the third person commands special respect, the effect will become even more pronounced.

In every conflict, there usually exists not just one possible third party but a multitude. Individually, people may not prove very influential. But collectively, they are potentially more powerful than any two conflicting parties. Organizing themselves into a coalition, they can balance the power between the parties and protect the weaker one. "Do you see these sticks in my hand?" Tsamko, a Ju/'hoan Bushman, once asked his group. "One stick alone breaks easily, but if you pick up lots of sticks like this, you can't break them."

In the end, power comes not from government, not even from superior force, but from people who choose whether or not to give their obedience to the government or their respect to superior force. If the will of the people can be mobilized, it can prevail.

From a Perspective of Common Ground

A senior executive attending one of my negotiation classes re-counted a story of how, one day on a four-lane highway, he failed to notice a driver behind him trying to pass. The frustrated driver finally passed on the right, blared his horn, and made an insulting gesture. The executive became enraged, sped up, and began to overtake the other car on the right. As he was passing it, he rolled open his window to shout a response; the other driver did the same. As the executive looked at the other driver, suddenly the words popped out, "I'm sorry!" The other driver was speechless, then he too replied, "*I'm* sorry!" Each ended up motioning the other to go ahead: "You first!" "No, you first!"

"What happened to your anger?" I asked the executive.

"I don't know," he replied, "I guess I just suddenly saw how ridiculous the conflict was."

That is a third-side perspective—and it is available, as the story illustrates, even to the disputing parties themselves. While most issues in contention are presented as having just two sides—pro and con—there usually exists a third. From this third perspective, the truth of each competing point of view can be appreciated. Shared interests often come to loom larger than the differences. People remember that they all, in the end, belong to the same extended community.

Third parties can help disputants achieve this sense of perspective. "Within minutes the mediator had me and the person I fought with laughing together," reports one New York high school student. "I knew that if I could talk and act calmly instead of getting upset, I might never have to fight again!"

Supporting a Process of Dialogue and Nonviolence

In the midst of a firefight in the rice paddies between American soldiers and the Viet Cong early in the Vietnam War, six monks walked toward the line of fire. "They didn't look right, they didn't look left. They walked straight through," remembers David Busch, one of the American soldiers. "It was really strange, because nobody shot at 'em. And after they walked over the berm, suddenly all the fight was out of me. It just didn't feel like I wanted to do this anymore, at least not that day. It must have been that way for everybody, because everybody quit. We just stopped fighting."

Like the monks walking across the rice paddy or the older man on the Manhattan street corner, the third side, silently or loudly, says "No" to violence. Conversely, the third side says, "Yes" to dialogue. As among the Bushmen and the Semai, thirdsiders urge disputants to sit down and talk out their differences respectfully. Thirdsiders, in other words, focus on the process. To them, *how* people handle their differences is just as important as *what* outcome they reach.

Aiming for a Product of a "Triple Win"

The dispute had lasted nine years and gone all the way to the U.S. Supreme Court without resolution. The Georgia Department of Transportation wanted to put an elevated parkway through a historic Atlanta neighborhood. The local neighborhood residents opposed it. The wider community wanted the dispute solved and a solution implemented before the Olympics came to town. Two mediators went to work and, in nine meetings, helped the parties hammer out a solution: a four-lane surface street with a substantial expansion of parkland. Everyone—the parties and the wider community—pronounced themselves satisfied.

As in this case, thirdsiders strive for a resolution that satisfies the legitimate needs of the parties *and* at the same time meets the needs of the wider community. The goal of the third side is, in other words, a "triple win."

WHO IS THE THIRD SIDE?

For decades, South Africa was the leading example of racial injustice on the planet. On my first visit, in early 1989, I found almost everyone I interviewed expecting the repression, terrorism, and guerrilla warfare to continue far into the future. My own experiences only seemed to confirm this. A few days before I was to meet anthropologist David Webster, a determined opponent of the apartheid system, he was assassinated on his doorstep in front of his wife by a government-backed death squad. A few weeks after I spent a long evening conversing with Anton Lubowski, a political opponent of South African government in Namibia, he too fell to the bullets of a death squad. The conflict appeared irreconcilable.

Six years later, on a return visit to South Africa, I felt as if I had entered a different country. Nelson Mandela, who had still been in prison on my last visit, had become president. The former president, F. W. de Klerk, was now serving as second deputy to Mandela. Blacks and whites, previously isolated from each other across a seemingly unbridgeable chasm, were reaching out to find ways to work together for a peaceful and prosperous South Africa. Bullets had given way to bridges.

While the transformation of the conflict in South Africa seemed almost miraculous at the time, it actually resulted from the coordinated practical actions of the third side—in three forms:

Outsiders

"You must believe," declared South African Archbishop Desmond Tutu, "that this spectacular victory [over apartheid] would have been totally, totally impossible had it not been that we were supported so remarkably by the international community." The outside world strongly opposed the institutionalized racism of the apartheid regime. Governments imposed economic sanctions. Sports federations ostracized South African teams. The United Nations provided political and economic support to Mandela's African National Congress. Intergovernmental organizations dispatched groups of eminent statesmen to mediate. Churches mobilized the public conscience and university students carried out protests. Under intense pressure, universities and corporations in the United States made decisions to stop investing in South Africa. From ordinary citizens to governments, outside third parties came together to support a democratic community.

WHO IS THE THIRD SIDE?

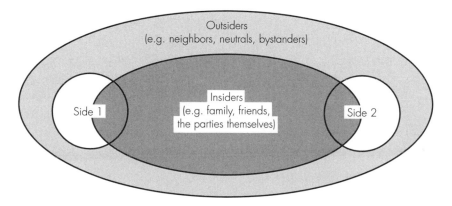

The third side is made up of both outsiders and insiders.

Insiders

Even more critical were insider third parties. While Nelson Mandela and F. W. de Klerk were solidly rooted in their own groups, fighting hard to protect their interests, they also played the curious role of third parties seeking a nonviolent resolution. Indeed, a pair of insiders, one from each side, can often make the most effective third party; while separately neither would be perceived as neutral, together they may be seen as balanced. As an outsider neutral, I find myself impressed by the considerable virtues of insider third parties. In contrast to outsiders, insider third parties possess intimate knowledge of the conflict and its players. They also are more likely to work on a conflict all the way through implementation of a settlement.

Working with Mandela and de Klerk were thousands of other insiders determined to reach across the chasm of color. Church and business leaders came together with the white government, the African National Congress, and other political groups to devise the National Peace Accord, an unprecedented countrywide network of dispute-resolution committees at the local, regional, and national levels. The committees, made up of people from the different communities who had never talked or worked with each other before, succeeded in defusing a great many violent confrontations between white police and black citizens, and provided a training ground in grassroots democracy.

Thus emerged a critical mass of insider third parties, a strong new center capable of withstanding the polarizing pressure of the extremists on each side. Outsiders helped, but, in the end, it was the insider third parties who did the real work.

An Inner Third Side?

Imprisoned for twenty-seven years, treated harshly by whites, Nelson Mandela somehow found it within himself to forgive his white captors, the oppressors of his race. I was impressed, when I heard him speak about his white adversaries, that his voice and demeanor betrayed no rancor. And while this inner change of heart was the solitary soul-searching act of an individual, it did not stop there. For, in the hope of reconstructing a South Africa in which both blacks and whites could live together in peace and prosperity, Mandela succeeded in persuading first his colleagues, and then his people, to tread the same difficult path of forgiveness and reconciliation. An individual act of spirit thereby became an emotional shift among millions, a political force with far-reaching effects.

On the other side of the divide, F. W. de Klerk, previously an arch defender of the apartheid system, came to realize it had been a terrible mistake, resulting in unfair discrimination and the domination of the majority by the minority. In acknowledging the error publicly, he helped his own people, rigidly attached to the old ways, accept the painful necessity of surrendering much of their power and privilege to the black majority.

The surprising magnitude and speed of transformation in South Africa cannot be explained by a change of mind alone; a change in heart and spirit was required. Because it is not as tangible as an outsider or an insider, the "inner third side" is harder to describe. However nebulous, its power cannot be denied because, in the final analysis, deep-seated conflict is resolved largely through the emotional, psychological, and spiritual work of the parties. The third side manifests itself as a kind of conscience within the single individual engaged in conflict. It is the voice that urges us to heal old grievances; it is the capacity to listen to the other side and show empathy; it is the impulse to respect the basic human needs of all.

The inner third side instinctively values life and abhors violence. In World War II, the U.S. Army was astonished to learn that at least three out of every four riflemen, trained to kill and commanded to do so, could not bring themselves to pull the trigger when they could actually see the person they were about to shoot. Amazingly, this held true even when the individual rifleman himself was in danger of being shot. The riflemen refrained from shooting as long as they thought they were not being observed by their commanding officer.

Psychiatrists found that the chief cause of combat fatigue was not fear of being killed, but fear of killing. Colonel S. L. A. Marshall, who interviewed the infantrymen, concluded:

> It is therefore reasonable to believe that the average and normally healthy individual—the man who can endure the mental and physical stresses of combat—still has such an inner and usually unrealized resistance towards killing a fellow man that he will not of his own volition take life if it is possible to turn away from that responsibility. Though it is impossible that he may ever analyze his own feelings so

searchingly as to know what is stopping his own hand, his hand is nonetheless stopped. At the vital point he became a conscientious objector, unknowing.

The inner resistance to violence is a well-kept secret, for interestingly, when interviewed, each rifleman believed that he was the *only* one disobeying the orders to shoot. While this resistance to violence can obviously be weakened, it can also be strengthened. Therein lies the potential of awakening the inner third side.

All Together

Outsiders empower insiders, insiders mobilize outsiders, and both are inspired by an inner third side. Working together, they can transform even an intractable conflict such as South Africa.

THE THIRD SIDE IS US

In the spring of 1987, I visited the headquarters of the U.S. Strategic Air Command (SAC) based in Omaha, Nebraska. On the tour, my academic colleagues and I received a thorough briefing on every aspect of American preparedness for a nuclear war with the Soviet Union. Our military guide led us into the underground headquarters and showed us how one could communicate with every missile silo and bomber base in America. At the end of our visit, he took us on board the giant aircraft that the U.S. president would use during a nuclear attack. The plan, our guide explained, provided for the president to lift off in the plane to escape the attack and continue to direct the war. The plane was jam-packed with communications gear and trailed a huge antenna so that the president could communicate even with a submarine commander submerged in the depths of the Pacific Ocean. Everything was planned down to the last detail—and a trained crew of eighty stood ready to take to the skies at any time of the day or night.

When our guide paused for questions, I raised my hand. "Not to be presumptuous," I asked, "but if I were in the president's shoes in the middle of a nuclear crisis, the first person I'd want to talk to would be the Soviet premier so that we could figure out how to stop the war. Do you have a communications link on this plane to the Hot Line and a Russian translator on board?"

The Department of Defense official looked me straight in the eye and answered, "Communicating with the Russians is not *our* job. It's the job of the State Department."

The same attitude of "not our job" is pervasive when it comes to dealing with the destructive conflicts around us. Our first instinct when a dispute erupts is often to stand aside on the grounds that it is none of our business. Or we take sides. Either way, we contribute to the escalation of the conflict. To paraphrase Edmund Burke, the only thing necessary for the triumph of force is for good people to do nothing.

But the job of getting to peace is too important to be relegated to others. It cannot be assigned to extraordinary leaders such as Mandela or to the authorities. As simple societies like the Semai have long recognized, it is everyone's responsibility to prevent harmful conflict. "You have to help resolve a dispute," one Semai explained. "If you don't intervene and something happens between the two disputants, you are accountable." "Friends for life don't let friends fight" is the slogan of a successful media campaign against violence in Boston. That could be the motto of the third side.

Taking the third side is not an easy responsibility. It consumes time and energy. Those who step into the middle can find themselves criticized by one party or both for "interfering" or "meddling." Taking the third side may not always be easy, but as conflicts jeopardize the happiness of our families, the productivity of our workplaces, and the safety of our communities, it is in our self-interest. We are all stakeholders in the conflicts around us.

We may not think of ourselves as third parties—in fact, we

generally don't. Yet each of us has the opportunity to serve as a third party in the conflicts around us—either as outsiders or as insiders. We constitute the family, the friends, the colleagues, the neighbors, the onlookers, the witnesses. Even when no third party is present, each of us has the opportunity to mediate our own disputes by taking the third side.

In short, the third side is not some mysterious or special other. It is us. The missing alternative to force and domination is in our hands.

THE POTENTIAL OF THE THIRD SIDE

In one sense, the third side is nothing new. It is in action all around us. It is just not self-aware yet. There has been no specific name for it. There is not much recognition of its potential. Nor is there much acceptance of common responsibility for the conflicts around us.

Although I have not always thought about it in these terms, all my professional life as a mediator and writer, I have been a student of the third side. Yet I feel I have only begun to grasp its extraordinary possibilities.

A story from World War II captures the third side's potential for me. In the heart of Nazi-dominated Europe, when millions of Jews were being torn from their communities and dispatched to the death camps, one community of three thousand farmers took it upon themselves to offer sanctuary to Jewish refugees until they could be spirited to safety. For four years, the villagers of Le Chambon risked their lives defending innocent people against the Nazis and their hirelings. The number of refugees protected was not small. Twenty-five hundred Jews, mostly children, were estimated to have been rescued.

Le Chambon's efforts did not escape the notice of the authorities. The village was not far from Vichy, whose officials made a number of determined efforts to get the villagers to surrender their guests. They sent policemen and buses, but the people of Le Chambon refused to cooperate with the police and hid the refugees. When the Nazis took direct control of the region, the Gestapo conducted a raid and caught a few children, whom they deported, along with their local host, to the death camps. The Gestapo also sentenced Dr. Roger Le Forestier, a local leader, to death as an example to the villagers. But even with their lives and their families' lives under direct threat, the villagers refused to turn in their guests.

Indeed, the villagers' courage helped change the minds and move the hearts of several of their opponents. The Vichy government's efforts to carry out the Nazi directives eventually turned perfunctory. Later, the German military commander of the region, Major Schmehling, moved by Dr. Le Forestier's testimony at his trial, attempted to explain to the Gestapo chief, Colonel Metzger, why it was useless to fight the villagers: "I told Metzger that this kind of resistance had nothing to do with violence, nothing to do with anything we could destroy with violence." Metzger was not persuaded and insisted Schmehling use massive force. But Schmehling kept delaying the plans, and eventually France was liberated and the lives of the Jewish refugees were saved.

Why should the villagers have cared about a group of strangers? When asked this question decades later, Roger Darcissac, a local pastor, explained, "It all happened very simply. We didn't ask ourselves why. Because it's the human thing to do . . . something like that. That's all I can tell you." An elderly peasant echoed his explanation: "Because we were human, that's all." In her analysis of the pedestrian and bureaucratic ways in which the Nazis proceeded to exterminate millions, Hannah Arendt coined the phrase "the banality of evil." The villagers of Le Chambon exemplified "the banality of decency."

Most remarkable of all was that, to them, their behavior seemed unremarkable. There was not much to say. They did not think of themselves as heroic. They weren't being modest; it was almost as if it had never occurred to them to act differently. When people commit murder and mayhem, it is tempting to look for explanations in human nature. And it is true that such acts of violence fall well within the range of human behavior. But so do such altruistic actions to prevent violence as the decisions of the villagers to protect their guests from certain death. The example of Le Chambon suggests that we humans may be capable of making the villagers' protective behavior as habitual as we have made violence and war. That is the potential of the third side.

Part Two

A BRIEF HISTORY OF CONFLICT

If the third side were fully mobilized, it could help us realize the dream of living together without massive amounts of strife and violence. It is clear, however, that we are far from this point. The third side resembles a sleeping giant, capable of great things, but lost in slumber.

Perhaps the single biggest obstacle to mobilizing the third side is our fatalistic acceptance of destructive conflict as part of human nature. Underlying our hopelessness is the story we commonly tell ourselves and our children about our past. People have been warring with one another since the beginning of time. Scratch the veneer of civilization and you will get a Kosovo. People regress all too easily.

Anthropologists call this an "origin myth." It tells us about who we are and where we came from. The time I had spent with simpler societies like the Bushmen and the Semai made me question whether we have the story entirely right. So I set out to reexamine what is known and not known about our collective past. A story very different from the conventional one began to emerge, one that holds surprising hope for all of us today.

Chapter 2

FROM COEXISTENCE

If people do not like each other, but one gives a gift and the other must
accept, this brings a peace between them. We give to one another always.
We give what we have. This is the way we live together.

—Demi, a !Kung Bushman

 In the winter of 1995, I visited the Gladysvale archaeological site in South Africa, where paleontologist Lee Berger and his students were uncovering remains of early humans. As far as the eye could see, there stretched beautiful rolling grasslands. Giraffes were grazing over here, antelope over there. The skies were darkening. I could smell the sweetness of the approaching rain. In the distance, lightning was striking. It was easy to imagine a troop of hairy two-legged chimpanzeelike creatures walking with a rolling gait across the landscape. Three million years ago, of course.

The land that lay in view is one of the birthplaces of humanity. Fully forty percent of all early human fossils have been found within a few kilometers of this spot. If human evolution is a drama, this was its stage. This was where our brains grew, where we began to learn to walk upright with locked knees, where we evolved into modern humans. These valleys and hills, with their enormous diversity of fauna and flora, served as the cauldron out of which emerged the human species.

The Gladysvale cave itself is so rich with fossils, Lee Berger explained, that it would take twenty lifetimes to excavate it. I could see the bones literally sticking out of the rock walls. He and his team had already found fossils of australopithecines—popularly known as ape men—two and a half million years old, of *Homo habilis* a million years old, all the way along the evolutionary chain to the first modern humans, a hundred thousand years old. They had also uncovered evidence of humans living in the cave nine thousand five hundred years ago as well as a dung floor with four-thousand-year-old Iron Age remains. This one cave has been involved in virtually the entire evolution of humanity. "Never will you stand," Berger declared, "in a place with so much human history!"

While in the Gladysvale cave, I tried to imagine all the thousands of generations of humans who had inhabited this place, who had used its shelter, who had returned to it from their hunting and gathering expeditions, who had sat around their campfires cooking their food, chattering, joking, crying, and singing—all the people for whom this place had been home. How did they deal with their differences? I wondered. Did they live "in a war of every man against every man," as the philosopher Thomas Hobbes supposed? Was Sigmund Freud right that "under primitive conditions, it is superior force—brute violence, or violence backed by arms—that lords it everywhere?"

Trying to reconstruct what happened in places like this is a speculative venture but a necessary one. We have based our beliefs about human nature largely on our knowledge of the last five thousand years of history. Yet, just as no one would pretend to know what a book was about from reading the last page, or write a history of the millennium solely from the record of the last decade, so one cannot base suppositions about human nature on the last one percent or less of the human story. We need to understand what happened during the first ninety-nine percent.

THE ARCHAEOLOGICAL PUZZLE

In 1948, three years after the conclusion of the deadliest war in world history, the eminent anthropologist Raymond Dart discovered what he believed to be the explanation for such bloody carnage. In a cave a few hours' drive from Gladysvale, Dart uncovered what appeared to him to be the kitchen garbage heap of a group of our antecedents, the australopithecines. Ominously, among the jumbled bones of antelopes, giraffes, bears, hippos, rhinos, elephants, lions, hyenas, and baboons, Dart found the bones of australopithecines. "The most shocking specimen," he later reflected, "was the fractured jaw of a twelve-year-old son of a man-like ape. The lad had been killed by a violent blow delivered with calculated accuracy on the point of the chin, either by a smashing fist or a club. The bludgeon blow was so vicious that it had shattered the jaw on both sides of the face and knocked out all the front teeth. That dramatic specimen impelled me in 1948 and the seven years following to study further their murderous and cannibalistic way of life."

Citing the mutilation of the skulls of the australopithecines and baboons as evidence, Dart asserted that the cave dwellers had been professional headhunters. In a series of highly influential papers, he elaborated a theory that human beings had evolved as killers and cannibals. In Dart's own evocative language, "The blood-bespattered, slaughter-gutted archives of human history, from the earliest Egyptian or Sumerian records to the most recent atrocities of the Second World War, accord with early universal cannibalism . . . in proclaiming this common bloodlust differentiator, this predaceous habit, this mark of Cain." Like it or not, Dart suggested, our murderous nature enabled us to survive and thrive as a species. Killing, in short, is what made humans human.

The American writer Robert Ardrey trumpeted Dart's conception of humans as "killer apes" around the world in a series of best-selling books, which I remember reading as a boy. They served to confirm the already widespread belief that violence and war lay at the core of human nature. Indeed, theories about the bloodthirsty origins of humanity seemed strangely comforting in the wake of several world wars and genocides. How else could one account for such terrible happenings when modern civilization, we believed, had become more humane than all the others preceding it? If war was embedded in human nature, however, then it was understandable that we couldn't act much differently. Not only did this explain our behavior, but it relieved us of feelings of guilt and shame. The fault, after all, lay not in our intentions, but our instincts.

While in South Africa, I took the opportunity to visit Dart's old offices at the Medical School of the University of Witswatersrand. A vault there contains many of the great fossil finds of paleontology, including Dart's "shocking specimen." Lee Berger handed me this three-and-a-half-million-year-old skull, and I examined closely the crack in the jaw. Dart's interpretation seemed quite plausible.

Plausible but wrong, as it turned out.

The rebuttal came from a scientist with the peculiarly appropriate name of Brain. Over dinner one night in Johannesburg, Bob Brain told me that he admired Raymond Dart but found him a trifle "bloodthirsty," calling to mind one occasion during an intellectual argument when Dart brandished a bone at him menacingly, shouting, "See, I could kill you with this!" What we read into the past, Brain was suggesting, depends in no small measure on our own personality.

As a young man in 1955, Brain heard Dart expound his theories and decided to test them if he ever got the opportunity. His chance came a decade later. In a research project that ended up taking ten years, Brain found a cave similar to Dart's with the same kind of bone heap and proceeded to examine each bone in order to determine exactly how it had ended up where it did. Through painstaking detective work, Brain was able to demonstrate that the signs of crushing Dart had attributed to protohumans had resulted mostly from compression over time by the layers of rock, dirt, and bones resting on them. That damage which was clearly produced by violence turned out, moreover, not to be the work of australopithecines.

In a dramatic demonstration, Brain took a protohuman skull with two neat holes in its base about an inch apart—signs Dart had interpreted as deliberate mutilation for ritual purposes—and showed how the lower canines of a leopard skull found in the same stratum fit exactly into the two holes. Far from being the kitchen garbage heaps of our ancestors, the caves proved to be the lairs of big cats, a reminder that we humans have not always been at the top of the food chain. Our ancestors, it turned out, were not the hunters but the hunted.

So careful and measured was Brain's analysis that Dart himself gracefully conceded the point, explaining that he had put forth his theory in such strong terms precisely in order to provoke a debate.

The Startling Absence of Evidence

Brain's refutation of Dart's evidence for the killer ape hypothesis was not an exception. For there turns out to be little conclusive evidence in the archaeological record for the story of pandemic human violence during the first ninety-nine percent of human evolution.

For the last ten thousand years—during the last one percent of human evolution—there exists clear and often abundant evidence of organized violence and warfare. Archaeologists have found bones with spearheads or arrowheads embedded in them or with breaks in the forearm, as if the person had tried to ward off a blow. Mass graves point to warfare; graves with a relative absence of adult male skeletons suggest that the men may have died in battle elsewhere. Remains of fortifications, defensive sites, and settlements destroyed violently provide further evidence, as does the discovery of weapons specialized for killing humans, such as swords, daggers, maces, and battleaxes. If more were needed, much ancient art depicts scenes of war and carnage. Much of the evidence of violence antedates "civilization"—defined as the building of cities, the invention of writing, and the birth of the state—as the archaeologist Lawrence

Keeley has persuasively demonstrated in his 1995 study *War Before Civilization*. There can be little doubt that violence and war leave clear traces in the archaeological record.

It is all the more surprising, then, that convincing evidence of organized violence becomes so sparse before ten thousand years ago. In the period from ten thousand to fourteen thousand years ago, there are two credible if controversial sets of evidence of small-group violence, a cemetery in Jebel Sahaba, Sudan, and rock paintings in Arnhem Land, Australia; both instances seem to have occurred in the wake of catastrophic ecological change. Beyond that, there is evidence, in at least nine skeletons, pointing to scattered individual killings stretching back across time, but little or no evidence of war itself.

In 1969, the archaeologist Marilyn Roper surveyed the archaeological evidence of warfare and concluded that "warfare cannot be documented in the Paleolithic . . . with the possible exception of Site 117 as reported by Fred Wendorf." More recently, during the 1980s, the paleontologists Timothy White and Nicholas Toth carried out a survey of known hominid fossils in order to sum up the evidence of prehistoric human violence. In specimen after specimen for which the claim of violence had been made, they reviewed the evidence and found alternative explanations equally or more persuasive. In one case, for instance, they showed that what had been assumed to be cut marks on bones was actually the result of damage during the archaeological preparation of the bones.

An even more recent (1996) survey of the archaeological evidence, *Troubled Times: Violence and Warfare in the Past*, edited by Debra Martin and David Frayer, confirms the existence in considerable detail of prehistoric violence for any who might question it. Almost all of it falls within the last eight thousand years, less than one percent of human evolution. In the closing chapter, which reviews the known archaeological evidence worldwide, Brian Ferguson concludes that "individual killings seem rare and organized killing nearly absent throughout most of our collective past."

The eminent paleontologist Philip Tobias, a former student and colleague of Dart's, has offered one possible explanation. He was showing a group of us around one day at the Sterkfontein site in South Africa, where he has been excavating for thirty years. He described how australopithecines and two species of early humans—*Homo erectus* and *Homo habilis*—are known to have shared the same habitats in Africa from two and a half million years ago to a million and a half years ago, yet the fossil record reveals no evidence of violence having occurred between them. They may well have left each other alone. "Think about it," Tobias exclaimed, "a million years of peaceful coexistence!"

Tobias's hunch is just that, of course. Not enough is known yet and the absence of evidence cannot be conclusively taken as evidence of absence. But it is nevertheless a tantalizing hypothesis. For it involves not just a lifetime or two, but a period two hundred times as long as recorded history. If true, it would demonstrate that it is not impossible for different kinds of people to live alongside each other on a continuing basis without constantly murdering one another.

A TIMELINE OF HUMAN CONFLICT

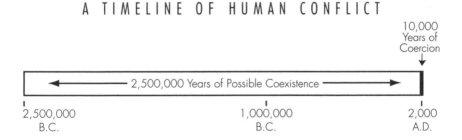

Interestingly, the far more recent archaeological record of modern humans, from a hundred thousand years ago until ten thousand years ago, does not contradict Tobias's hypothesis. For over a century, scholars have speculated that our Neanderthal cousins died in a series of bloodbaths at the hands of our ancestors—*Homo sapiens sapiens*—but no archaeological evidence has yet emerged to substantiate this notion.

Nor does an examination of prehistoric weapons suggest anything different. A clan warrior in the Highlands of New Guinea once explained to me how certain arrowheads were designed specifically for war as opposed to hunting; they were shaped to cause maximal damage when pulled out of the body. Given the technological talents of our prehistoric ancestors, it is at least curious that archaeologists have yet to find specialized weapons of war much older than the eight-thousand-year-old daggers and maces from the Middle Eastern city of Catal Huyuk. Similarly, the earliest fortifications uncovered are the walls of Jericho, dating back almost ten thousand years ago; even these, archaeologist O. Bar-Yosef has suggested, might have served the purpose of flood protection rather than defense.

The impression one receives from prehistoric art is equally suggestive. Archaeologists have identified thousands of cave paintings, rock carvings, and sculptures. Some are as old as thirty-five thousand years. As in the celebrated paintings of Lascaux and Altamira, the vast majority of images are of bison, ibexes, horses, and other animals. Many of the animals have arrows and spears embedded in them. While the art reveals a good deal about hunting and ritual life, it offers few indications of armed combat. Only when one approaches the ten-thousand-year mark do the exceptions begin to appear—in the Spanish Levant and in Arnhem Land, Australia. Even these, archaeologists J. D. Lewis-Williams and J. H. N. Loubsher argue, might be depictions of combat in the spiritual, not material, world. Whatever the case, if violence and war were central preoccupations of our early ancestors, it is curious that for so long they chose to neglect them in their art. For contrast, one need only look at the wall paintings and sculptures from Sumeria and Egypt of four thousand or five thousand years ago in which bloody battle after battle is richly depicted.

The Puzzle

The puzzling prehistory of human conflict reminds me of the Sherlock Holmes murder mystery in which Holmes draws Colonel

Ross's attention to "the curious incident of the dog in the night-time." Ross protests, "The dog did nothing in the night-time." To which Holmes answers, "That was the curious incident."

The "dog" here is organized violence and war. The "curious incident" is the *scarcity* of conclusive archaeological evidence of organized violence during the first ninety-nine percent of human history. Just as Sherlock Holmes was able to solve the murder mystery by paying attention to the dog that did not bark, so we may be able to shed light on the puzzle of prehistory by trying to understand this scarcity of evidence.

It remains possible, of course, that anthropologists just have not found the extensive confirmation yet. Indeed, given the clear human capacity for violence, it would be surprising if archaeologists did not someday discover more signs of interpersonal violence and, indeed, of intergroup combat before ten thousand years ago. The critical question, however, is the amount and proportion. Considering that modern academic theories posit a death rate in "primitive" war of at least a quarter of all adult males, one would expect to have already found a great deal of evidence. And we have not.

A second possible explanation is that human nature is essentially peaceful, as the philosopher Jean-Jacques Rousseau proposed two centuries ago. Before civilization spoiled it, he posited, humans lived in harmony with one another. Yet, the archaeological record of violence *before* the dawn of civilization five thousand years ago suggests that this is not right, either.

If neither of these explanations is particularly satisfactory, what other might there be? Perhaps the most promising way to find a credible explanation lies in examining what we know about how humans lived in the simple societies that existed for most of human history.

THE COOPERATIVE APE

When I first walked in the open African savanna, still inhabited by lions, tigers, leopards, cheetahs, and elephants, I remember how completely vulnerable and physically deficient I felt. We humans are comparatively weak creatures, after all, slow-footed and lacking natural defenses like sharp teeth and claws. I wondered how our ancestors managed to survive, competing for food with and protecting themselves against predators who were, if anything, bigger and more ferocious than they are today.

Cooperating to Compete

One key to human survival was the ability to cooperate—to work together in pursuit of common goals such as protection and food. Indeed, our brains—as well as language itself—may have evolved as tools for managing the increasingly complex cooperation that lay at the heart of our ancestors' hunting and gathering economies. Instead of consuming the food they found on the spot, as is the usual habit of other primates, our ancestors began to carry it back to their home base and share it with their mates, their offspring, and other members of the group. The extensive sharing of food and the cooperative division of labor were breakthrough innovations, greatly increasing the group's ability to feed themselves dependably.

Cooperative hunting increases the chances of bagging a significant prey and ensures that meat will not be wasted or scavenged by other animals. Three or more heads and pairs of hands also prove better than one. I once observed a group of Bushman hunters at work. As we were traveling through the desert, one man suddenly spotted a plant that a certain beetle liked to eat and began digging underneath it looking for beetle larvae, which could then be distilled into a paralyzing poison used to coat the tips of hunting arrows. Another man spotted the tracks of a steenbok, a small antelope, and we followed them until they came to a bush where we found a slight rubbing mark on the bark and a tiny tuft of fur. Here the steenbok had marked its territory. Knowing it would return to the same spot in a day or two, the hunters began to make a trap by bending a nearby branch, planting it into the ground, and tying a loop around it with a piece of rope I had seen them fashion from a reed the day before. Then they covered their trap with brush and went on. Returning the next day, they found the steenbok. While their bows and arrows may have been flimsy, they had valuable knowledge and the ability to cooperate.

In such small-scale nomadic societies, the pervasive habits of cooperation, sharing, and reciprocity extend outward to include the surrounding groups in an open network of interdependent ties. As anthropologist Richard Lee notes, the !Kung Bushmen "consciously strive to maintain a boundaryless universe because this is the best way to operate as hunter-gatherers in a world where group size and resources vary from year to year. At the //Gakwe=dwa grove, if one year the Dobe people eat their way farther east, then the !Kangwas will eat their way farther west the next ... Among the !Kung and other hunter-gatherers, good fences do not make good neighbors."

Small bands gather together regularly in order to find mates, trade, mount a large hunt requiring many hunters—or simply to socialize and carry out collective rituals. Forming close ties with other groups is not just useful and enjoyable, but essential to survival. If a drought occurs or a seasonal imbalance in game, plants, or water, people can go visit relatives and friends, who would share their territory and food. The following year, the visitors could reciprocate and receive the hosts of the previous year. One revealing estimate from studies of the !Kung is that fully two-thirds of their time is spent visiting or being visited by friends and relatives.

An Expandable Pie

Scattered plants and animals are an expandable pie. Hunting and gathering cooperatively, and sharing the yield, typically ensure that there will be more for everyone. This may help explain why groups such as the !Kung, despite their "subsistence living," feel as if they live in a world of abundance. When asked by Lee why they did not plant food, one !Kung man pointed to the nutritious mongongo nuts and exclaimed, "Why should we plant when there are so many mongongos in the world?" Even when one type of food proves scarce, the mobility of hunter-gatherers and the cooperative relationships they forge with one another allow them to move around and adapt.

Remember too that the number of mouths to be fed remained stable. For hundreds of thousands of years, human population grew very slowly. From one million years ago until ten thousand years ago, the average rate of population growth probably stayed far below one percent a year. A nomadic life of constant exercise may have helped control population; lowered levels of body fat may decrease fertility and delay the onset of puberty.

The Most Successful Way of Life—Yet

Anthropologist Claude Lévi-Strauss once observed that, if a Martian anthropologist visited the earth in the wake of a cataclysmic nuclear war, he would conclude that humans had had only one truly sustainably successful way of life in their long history—hunting and gathering. All the rest of human history, from the Agricultural Revolution to the present, the Martian would treat as an aberration at the end leading to self-destruction. A way of life easily dismissed by us as "subsistence living," hunting and gathering enabled our ancestors to survive against high odds in the savanna. It made possible a remarkable journey out of Africa into almost every kind of environment imaginable, from boiling deserts to freezing mountains. Without this way of life, we would not be here today. And the key to its success lay in our ancestors' highly developed ability to cooperate. A more fitting name for our species than the "killer ape" would be the "cooperative ape."

THE LOGIC OF COEXISTENCE

The practice of daily cooperation and the expandable nature of the basic resources meant that, when it came to conflict, people would have been drawn to cooperative rather than coercive means of handling it.

Cooperation Does Not Exclude Conflict

As any family member knows, the more people are dependent on each other, the more potential conflict they face. Judging from the behavior of contemporary hunter-gatherers, our ancestors undoubtedly bickered about who got what share of the meat, who was doing what amount of work, or who was off with whose mate. People, after all, are merely human. While most conflict probably occurred between individuals, some must have arisen between groups. With frequent fluctuations in the availability of food, there must have been at least occasional tensions between groups over prized resources—a favorite grove of nut trees, a valued water hole, or an animal shot by one group but who wandered over to the territory of another.

When trying to establish how our ancestors dealt with their conflicts, it is critical to distinguish among three separate but easily confused meanings of the term "conflict." The first refers to the underlying conflict of *interests*—people's needs and desires. Where a scarcity of food exists, one person's interest in eating may be considered in conflict with another's. A second meaning is a conflict of *positions*, a clash of concrete demands motivated by the underlying interests; one person may announce she wants that piece of meat while another claims it too. The third meaning refers to a *power* struggle; people may start fighting to obtain the piece of meat.

Just because there is a conflict of interests, however, does not necessarily imply a conflict of positions. Where the norm was to share food and access to territory, many potential conflicts of interest would not have become overt conflicts of position. Nor do conflicts of position necessarily produce power struggles. The habit of cooperation would have helped people find ways to avert escalation by, for instance, negotiating a fair division. Humans, in short, have a choice—they can handle their conflicts cooperatively or coercively. Far from being the opposite of conflict, then, cooperation becomes a prime way to deal with conflict.

Little Place for Coercion

It is easier, in fact, to imagine cooperation than coercion. If one person tries to coerce another in a simple, nomadic society, the victim can simply pick up his or her few possessions and go join kin elsewhere. Or the victim can recruit allies. A bully may be more powerful than any one person, but not more than a group. The use of force would, moreover, undermine the valuable cooperative ties that sustain the bully along with everyone else.

What about war, then? With tempers running high and deadly weapons always available, it is not difficult to imagine an occasional bout of impulsive violence or even, in some communities, a compensatory homicide, a carefully measured slaying as a form of justice for the murder of one's own kin. But war in the sense of *organized* violence *between* groups for *group goals* such as land, possessions, power, or prestige is another matter. Since its consequences are so serious and since it requires cooperation from many individuals, war tends to be preceded by a process of rational decision making. To make war, war usually has to make sense.

Putting oneself in the place of our ancestors for a moment, imagine trying to persuade the group to fight another. What benefits could one cite? What is the great use of taking their territory if people moved around all the time and couldn't practically defend it? Besides, it was not land people lived off—it was scattered plants and roving animals. As for seizing the possessions of others, hunter-gatherers have little property to steal. Nor would it make much sense to enslave others, if only because they could escape so easily. And when it came to the sheer thrill of fighting, defending against predators and hunting big animals provided plenty of that.

In a decision to go to war, the group would also have had to weigh the heavy costs. In a fight at close quarters, someone in the group might get killed. Even a disabling injury would spell almost certain death in a nomadic society. A death would not only be a calamity for the family and friends, but the loss of even a single hunter in an average group of twenty-five people would mean the loss of one-fifth of its hunting capacity.

An appreciation of this logic led even the most ardent propagator of the "killer ape" hypothesis, Robert Ardrey, to admit in a debate about human aggression with anthropologist Louis Leakey:

> In the old hunting days we were too busy making a living. . . . And you didn't really have that much energy left at night for going out and quarreling with a neighbor. Maybe in a cave, with your very close neighbor. But going fifteen miles away to get into a battle—nonsense. You might lose someone you needed for getting the next day's hunt. Very important!

As Ardrey rightly points out, the population density was low—on average less than one person per square mile—and groups were widely scattered. The spacing alone would have made war difficult to organize.

Even if one's group were able to win the fight, one would remain vulnerable to retaliation. Among the Bushmen, the poison-tipped arrows often take days to kill a person, long enough for the victim to exact vengeance. In a society where men leave their families to go off for days on a hunt, moreover, revenge would be easy to take against women and children. Ages before the Cold War, our ancestors would have come to appreciate the reality of mutual deterrence. As one Bushman put it, "I want to hunt eland, kudu, gemsbok [types of antelopes], but hunting man is what gets you killed!" Similarly, when asked, "Why don't you hit another person?" one Semai tribesman replied, "What if he hits back?"

In an interdependent network, moreover, fighting would usually mean killing kin or the kin of kin. One would be destroying the one real wealth that hunter-gatherers have—personal relationships. The people one would attack might very well be those whose help one might need in hard times. Assuming one won, what kind of victory would it prove to be if they and their relatives and friends in the wider network stopped sharing?

The ready availability of the exit option as an alternative would have made organized violence seem all the more unnecessary. When tensions reached the boiling point among the Hadza, a hunter-gatherer group in East Africa, one of the groups in contention would "suddenly realize that the berries were better elsewhere" and that would be it.

Trying to persuade one's kinsmen to go into battle against another group would thus have been a difficult task. I can easily imagine them reacting much as a group of Bushmen did when I showed them pictures of war from *Time* magazine. They were incredulous and disapproving, finding it hard to understand the motivation for such a brutal method of handling conflict.

As a modern analogy, think of the relationship between the United States and Canada, whose border stretches for three thousand miles. Their past relationship has not always been peaceful, but if anyone today were to suggest that Americans go to war against Canadians as a way of resolving serious disputes over fishing grounds and acid rain, the response would be laughter. It has become unimaginable.

Learning the Logic

In my negotiation courses, I often use a simple, well-known exercise, called by game theorists the "Prisoners' Dilemma." I divide participants into teams of five and pair each team with another. The objective of the game, I explain, is for each team to maximize their own score, regardless of how the other does. The game has ten rounds. In each round, I give each team three minutes to choose X or Y. The teams sit separately and are not allowed to communicate with one another unless otherwise instructed. X means cooperation and Y means refusal to cooperate, an action called defecting.

If both teams independently select X—in other words, decide to cooperate—both win three points each. But if one team selects Y while the other selects X, the defectors win six points and the co-operators lose six points. If both teams defect by selecting Y, each team loses three points. The game's structure mimics life; there are benefits in choosing to cooperate, but if you do, others may take advantage of you.

At the end of each round, I inform both teams of the other's decision so they can tell how their strategy is working. Before rounds five, eight, and ten, bonus rounds in which more points than usual can be won or lost, I allow the teams to negotiate through a designated representative for three minutes to see if they can reach an agreement. At the end of the game, each team tallies up its accumulated points, and we discuss the choices they made on the various rounds and how they obtained the score they did.

I have run this game dozens of times all over the world with widely varying types of participants—European diplomats and UN military officers, American businesspeople and Indonesian engineers, Soviet parliamentarians and Canadian factory workers, Argentinian executives and African university students. The results differ from game to game, but not a great deal. Some of the teams begin immediately to cooperate with each other and continue the pattern of cooperation to the end, achieving a good score for both sides. Other teams begin competitively, choosing to defect while the other side cooperates. Stung by the loss, the other side usually starts retaliating so that both sides lose points. While occasionally both sides continue to defect and lose until the end of the game, usually they agree to start cooperating after the designated representatives meet. Not everyone keeps their agreements, however, especially in the last round when they believe the game is coming to an end.

What strikes me most about watching these games is the steady if tortuous pattern of human learning. Eventually most people learn that defection just breeds defection and they find ways to break out of the trap of distrust. Through communication and negotiation, they learn to cooperate with the other team. The logic of cooperation gradually overcomes the distrust, competitiveness, and outright antagonism between groups.

The logic of cooperation experienced by our hunter-gatherer ancestors must have been, if anything, stronger than the logic inherent in the Prisoners' Dilemma games. Faced with the challenge of survival, everyone could benefit from cooperation while everyone would usually lose from fighting. While, in the games, some teams justify their continued choice to defect on the grounds that, as poorly as they score, the other team's score is worse, our ancestors would not likely have taken much consolation in the fact that, even though they were starving, the other group was starving even more. While, in the games, moreover, some teams break their agreements in the last round, there was *no* last round in the life of our ancestors. Relationships were long-term, which only strengthened the incentive to cooperate.

I suspect that our ancestors learned to handle their differences cooperatively in much the same tentative way participants in the Prisoners' Dilemma games do—by making occasional mistakes and experiencing the costs of fights. When their conflicts became acute or the temptations too strong, some hunter-gatherer groups may have succumbed to fighting, but as long as the logic of cooperation remained strong, those groups who discovered war would eventually have rediscovered the virtues of coexistence.

An analogy to modern times can illuminate this process of learning. At the height of World War I, French and British soldiers faced their German adversaries across the trenches, often for months or years at a time. In order to survive, many opposing units learned to cooperate in flagrant disobedience of orders from headquarters. If they did fire their guns, they would do so at precisely the same time and at the same target so that the other side could take cover. As one

British old-timer explained to a recent arrival, "Mr. Bosche ain't a bad fellow. You leave 'im alone; 'e'll leave you alone." One incident related by a British officer illustrates how far the practice went:

> I was having tea with A Company when we heard a lot of shouting and went out to investigate. We found our men and the Germans standing on their respective parapets. Suddenly a salvo arrived but did no damage. Naturally both sides got down and our men started swearing at the Germans, when all at once a brave German got on his parapet and shouted out, "We are very sorry about that; we hope no one was hurt. It is not our fault; it is that damned Prussian artillery."

If, even in the midst of a brutal war, humans found a way to cooperate when cooperation made sense, one can imagine our ancestors learning to do the same.

A CONFLICT MANAGEMENT SYSTEM

A logic of coexistence and cooperation may explain *why* our ancestors could have gotten along, but it does not explain *how*. The "how" appears particularly puzzling because they did not have a superior centralized authority that could keep the peace. Without formal government, Thomas Hobbes postulated, they must have lived in a state of war, by which he meant a condition of permanent enmity.

Unfortunately, conflict resolution leaves no material traces for archaeologists to uncover. To discover this alternative mechanism requires looking for clues among simpler societies who have survived until modern times. So we come back to groups such as the Bushmen and the Semai. Since each simple society, indeed each group, differs and each changes over time, and since each was studied in a period of at least some contact with more complex societies, it would be a mistake to extrapolate directly from one or two groups at a certain point in time to our prehistoric ancestors. We can use our knowledge of these simple societies, however, to speculate about what conflict management mechanisms our ancestors might have had at their disposal.

When visiting with different groups of Bushmen, it did not take me long to observe that harmony is not their natural state. Conflict is. The Ju/'hoansi, in fact, describe themselves as the "owners of argument." There are constant jealousies and tensions over such issues as the equitable distribution of food, mates and potential mates, and hunting and gathering rights. "It is natural for human beings to have disputes," Korakoradue, one of the Kua elders, explained.

As perhaps their principal mechanisms for averting violence, the Bushmen use a combination of the third side, as already discussed, and the exit option.

If a dispute arises, they are quick to ask others to intercede. When I asked what happens if a person from one group hunts on some other group's territory without seeking permission, Korakoradue explained, "The injured party [one of the "owners" of the territory in question] will then call *three* people as witnesses and he will show them the offender's footprints. Then they all go and talk to the offender and admonish him not to do it again."

"Supposing the man does it a second time, what happens?" I inquired.

"This time, the aggrieved will get *four* witnesses. Now they speak very loudly to the offender and tell him not to do it again."

"What if he does the same thing a third time?"

"No one," Korakoradue pronounced, "would ever have *dared* to violate the norms and offend others like this."

The Bushmen are a truly interdependent society: They are socialized from birth to be acutely aware of and sensitive to one another's needs. Since every individual depends on the community for his or her material needs and psychological well-being, it is rare for an individual to deliberately flout the communal will. Social discipline is strong. Isak Barnard, my companion and guide for one of my visits, told me that he had once left a tin of tobacco at his campsite near the Bushman camp and, although the people prize nothing more than a good smoke, he found the tin untouched when he returned a year later.

The community intervenes to contain conflict that threatens to escalate. One !Kung Bushman described to anthropologist Richard Lee what would happen after an impulsive homicide:

> In the old days the people would bury the dead and over the grave would look at each other with suspicion; there might be whispering of killing another. Then the one who wants to kill would cry out and writhe and tear his hair: "Oh why can't I kill one of them, since my man is dead?" But the elders would take hold of him and forbid further fighting. Then the elders would say, "We see that these people cannot live together properly. You people must separate and each group go into its own *n!ore* [locality surrounding a water-hole] and eat only in its own *n!ore*.

The elders here served as the representatives of the third side, the voice against violence.

Exit serves as a safety valve. "The lesson my father taught me," the Kua Bushman elder Purana told me, "was, 'If you see that you are causing problems, go away from the group for a while.'" In fact, just before I arrived at the Kua camp, seven families had moved away partly because they were afraid of the prospect of disputes. Exit serves to cool the heat of anger and let tensions die down. Exit functions not only as a preventive measure but also as a last resort if all other processes fail to contain the dispute.

As a longtime student of conflict resolution, I was impressed by the informal but comprehensive set of procedures the Bushmen use for dealing with their daily conflicts. It constitutes a kind of "conflict management system," which works first to prevent harmful conflict *before* it arises, then to resolve what cannot be prevented, and finally to contain what cannot be resolved.

It is worth reemphasizing that the Bushmen are not always successful in averting violence. No society is. Indeed, Lee reports the !Kung as having a fairly high homicide rate in this century. At first glance, the !Kung homicide rate from 1920 to 1969 works out to twenty-nine per hundred thousand people per year, less than half the rate of Washington, D.C., but still triple the rate for the United States as a whole. If one does a fair comparison, however, as Lee himself points out, taking into account war casualties and the fact that an aggravated assault which would have led to death without modern medicine is not reported as a homicide, the !Kung rate comes out as less than *one third* that of modern societies. "The balance sheet in this perspective," Lee writes, "clearly favors the hunter-gatherers, who manage to keep their killing rates low even in the absence of our elaborate system of police, courts and prisons."

With deadly weapons in such easy reach, the Bushmen succeed in coexisting relatively well with other individuals and groups; other small-scale societies I have visited, such as the Batek and the Semai of Malaysia, appear to do even better than the Bushmen. These more peaceful groups are exceptional, perhaps constituting only ten percent of tribal societies surveyed, but it is precisely this ten percent whose simple way of life most closely resembles that of our ancestors for the great majority of human evolution. While none of these groups can be used as conclusive proof of how our ancestors managed their conflicts, they do demonstrate that Hobbes was ill-informed. There exists a way of dealing with human differences other than authoritarian government or war: a conflict management system based on the third side.

In the words of a Ju/'hoan woman, Di//Xao=Toma, "When someone says, 'You Bushmen have no government,' we'll say that our old, old people long ago had a government, and it was an ember from the fire where we last lived which we used to light the fire at the new place where we were going."

BUT ISN'T VIOLENCE HUMAN NATURE?

In April 1995, I visited the Yerkes Primate Research Lab outside of Atlanta in the company of primatologist Frans de Waal. De Waal and several of his graduate students were showing me around the enclosures, speaking about their work, when we paused in front of a cage containing an adolescent female chimp. I was asking de Waal about xenophobic behavior, aggressive behavior against strangers, when suddenly a wad of chimp feces came flying through two sets of bars at the one stranger in the lineup, namely myself. Her aim was unerring and the effect messy. I got my answer. I am not one, therefore, to easily doubt the innateness of aggression in primates.

The debate has long raged in and out of anthropology: Humans are naturally aggressive; no, aggression is learned. War is genetically based; no, it is not. The answer is not one or the other, but both.

False Polarities

The polarities turn out to be false polarities. In these questions, there are no absolutes; everything is a matter of degree. In seeing only absolutes, one misses the critical degrees, yet it is in these degrees that lie the answers to the questions of how humanity has gotten along in the past and how we can get along in the future.

The debate, often fierce and emotional, unfortunately obscures where, in fact, scientists and scholars do agree. Few would disagree that humans are both capable of violence and capable of controlling violence. Most would acknowledge that humans sometimes live in a sustained condition of war but also sometimes live in a sustained condition of relative peace.

If human beings were as inevitably aggressive as we are often pictured, I have often wondered, why do we not kill each other far more than we actually do? All the police in the world could not keep people from doing what comes naturally. If war is our natural state, why do the great majority of human conflicts not end in violence? How is it that human societies can live in internal peace and coexist non-violently with their neighbors for long periods of time?

Just because we naturally eat doesn't mean we need to overeat. Just because we like sex doesn't mean we need to rape. Just because some humans like to dominate doesn't mean we need to enslave others. That aggression is innate doesn't mean that violence and war are inevitable. Indeed, there is nothing wrong with aggression in it-self; primate mothers, for instance, use mild forms of aggression to teach their offspring correct behavior. It all depends on how the aggression is expressed and for what purpose.

What About the Chimps?

One of the most widely cited pieces of evidence to prove early human tendencies to make war is primatologist Jane Goodall's celebrated study of chimpanzees in the African rain forest. During the first five years of her thorough, long-term research, Goodall was struck by the relative peacefulness of chimpanzees. In later years, however, she and her students uncovered persuasive evidence of violent attacks by groups of male chimps on individuals belonging to a different group. In one notable case, a group of four to six chimps stalked and over a period of several years appeared to have attacked in sequence at least six members of a breakaway group. All the victims subsequently disappeared or died. The breakaway group was virtually eliminated and the victorious chimps took over its territorial range. Nor was this case an isolated one: The researchers detected similar invasions and attacks by a group of chimpanzees to the south.

Goodall's research clearly shows that chimpanzees are just as capable of violence against their own as are their closely related human cousins. It is not clear, however, what exactly produced the violent attacks. Were they a routine part of chimpanzee life or were they stimulated by artificially changing conditions? Anthropologist

Margaret Power argues that the difference between Goodall's initial and later observations stems from the artificial feedings the researchers provided after the first five years in order to draw the chimpanzees out of the forest for observation; the concentrated food supply, she suggests, greatly exacerbated competition, as did the pressure from the steady encroachment of local farmers on the chimps' territory. As Goodall describes it, "The constant feeding was having a marked effect on the behavior of the chimps. . . . The adult males were becoming increasingly aggressive. When we first offered the chimps bananas, the males seldom fought over their food; they shared boxes. . . . [Now there was] a great deal more fighting than ever before."

Whatever the case, it is intriguing to contrast studies of the common chimpanzee with long-range studies of the other, far less known species of chimpanzee, the bonobos. In some respects, they resemble humans even more than the common chimps. As in most simple hunter-gatherer societies, relations between male and female bonobos are egalitarian—or perhaps even slightly female-centric. Like their human cousins, bonobo females are potentially sexually receptive most of the time. This considerably reduces male competition over access to females. Significantly, bonobos also appear more socially skilled than common chimps, as well as more adept at resolving conflict. The murderous attacks observed among common chimps have not been seen among bonobos.

Indeed, one of the primary ways bonobos defuse tensions that might lead to conflict is through sex. On a research visit to the San Diego Zoo, I once observed a group of bonobos coming in at the end of the day from their outside enclosure into their nighttime eating and sleeping den. Boisterous and excited at the prospect of eating, several bonobo couples copulated vigorously with each other before calming down. Bonobos use sex, Frans de Waal points out, to defuse tensions and prevent conflict over food. Their behavior reminds one of the 1960s slogan: "Make love, not war."

Bonobos also make use of the third side. When a male bonobo chimpanzee gets aggressive with a female, three or more female bonobos have been observed to respond by lining up shoulder to shoulder like linemen on a football team. Slowly they back the offending male away, as if to say, "You've gone too far, big guy. Now behave!"

De Waal has made a prolonged study of peacemaking behavior among chimpanzees and other primates. With thousands of hours of detailed observation, he has been able to document a host of behaviors for preventing aggression, ending it, and reconciling afterward. Along with the capacity for aggressive behavior, he has demonstrated, comes the ability to control aggression. Indeed, it is precisely this ability that permits primates to live closely and continually with one another.

Studies of our closest living cousins offer little grounds, then, for fatalism about immutably violent human nature. What emerges is the sheer variation of behavior among different species, among different groups of the same species, and among different circumstances. Far from being genetic automatons, our primate relatives appear to be social tacticians like ourselves. They have a repertoire of behaviors for dealing with conflict and they appear to choose the behavior most advantageous to their interests. If chimpanzees can exert such a high degree of control, imagine how much more control can be exercised by a creature with an even more developed brain.

Capable of War, Capable of Peace

Human behavior is extraordinarily flexible, as is reflected in the extreme variation in societal rates of violence. Some indigenous cultures like the Waorani of Ecuador manifest levels of violence as much as a thousand times higher than others, such as the Semai of Malaysia. Or consider the contrast between England and Colombia, more than fifty times more violent. Some of us live in societies that more closely resemble England in levels of violence, others in societies that more closely resemble Colombia, and most of us live somewhere in between. The level of variation alone suggests that far more than human nature is at play. One does not find whole societies that eat or make love even ten times more often than others, let alone a thousand times.

The variation derives, in great measure, from how people choose to deal with their differences. Violence is not an autonomous phenomenon, but one choice among many for handling disputes. People are constantly coping with conflicts, their own and those of others, making choices as to which procedures to use. Humans, in other words, are conflict managers.

Our common assumptions about human nature are mistaken. We are not by nature killer apes—one end of the continuum. This does not mean that we are naturally peaceful or harmonious either—the other end of the continuum. Rather, we are capable of both destructive and constructive responses to our differences. As a Semai elder once remarked to me, "Conflict is created by human beings and thus can be controlled by human beings." The answer to the assertion that "War is human nature!" is, "Yes and so is peace."

HOMO NEGOTIATOR

The reason, then, why archaeologists have found so little evidence of organized violence during the first ninety-nine percent of human history may well be the obvious one. We have been maligning our ancestors. They weren't cavemen looking to bash every stranger over the head. Rather, they worked hard at coexisting. They sought to get along with each other and their neighbors. And, by and large, they appear to have succeeded. Conflict was endemic and interpersonal fights, impulsive murder, even an occasional feud undoubtedly took place—but probably very little war to exterminate or conquer another group, the practice that threatens our species today. Humanity evolved in what might be called a "co-culture," where conflict was handled most *co*nstructively—through *co*existence and *co*operation.

The chief explanation for such coexistence does not lie in the inherent peacefulness of human beings. Rather it is that fighting and domination do not make much sense for people living in a flexible interdependent network and roving all over the landscape in search of game and plants. People's livelihood depended on cooperating within the group and with other groups. The benefits of fighting and domination were few, the costs were high, and there was almost always the alternative of exit. One individual or group could just pick up their few possessions and leave.

That our ancestors were quite capable of violence, that indeed they had the ability all along to make war, and that they undoubtedly had many conflicts makes their feat of coexisting all the more remarkable. They had to work hard and courageously to prevent conflicts from arising, to resolve difficult issues, and to contain violent fights. One of the keys to their success, I am persuaded, was a vigilant and active community—a powerful third side. Their peace was not a peace of the weak but a peace of the brave.

Our image for the first ninety-nine percent of human history should be neither of killer apes, nor of naturally peaceful folk, but of human beings prone to conflict and struggling to coexist amid their differences. If anything, we are Homo Negotiator.

Most astonishing of all is just how long our ancestors may have lived in this "co-culture." If all four million years of human evolution were to be telescoped into a single twenty-four-hour day, the period of conflictual coexistence would last through the night, the morning, the afternoon, the evening, all the way, in fact, until just before midnight. The period we call history, filled with violence and domination, wars and empires, would last barely one minute.

Chapter 3

TO COERCION

You go and carry off the enemy's land.
The enemy comes and carries off your land.
— Ancient Sumerian Inscription

With one glance at recorded history, it seems difficult to believe that we humans evolved coexisting with one another. During the last five thousand years, the last one percent of the human story, relationships among individuals and groups appear to have been based more on force than on common interest. Serious conflicts have been resolved through some form of coercion, whether violence, war, or domination.

Why did this change happen? If we are to transform the way we deal with our most serious differences, we will need to understand how most of our societies fell into the trap of destructive conflict.

In search of answers, and in order to challenge my own thinking about the human past, I made a field trip in the fall of 1995 to a place known throughout the world for its "primitive" warfare: the Highlands of New Guinea. The people of the Highlands were the last major population group on earth to come into contact with the modern world. Nobody in the West knew they existed until the 1920s, when pilots flying over the island saw, to their utter surprise, signs of habitation in the lush valleys below. When gold prospectors and government officials finally reached these mountain tribes, they found what they believed to be "Stone Age Man" living in his pristine state replete with stone axes. And they found war, lots of it. Reports and film footage began to trickle out depicting battles fought by hundreds of warriors armed only with spears and bows and arrows. If people needed any confirmation of their beliefs in warlike human nature, here it was.

Clan warfare was still going on in 1995. My very first day in the Highlands, I happened upon a "fight zone." In the midst of a brilliantly green and lush countryside, there were the shells of huts and school buildings that had been burned to the ground. Here and there the orchards had been vengefully destroyed. Trotting down the road were young warriors with brilliantly painted bodies and feathered hairdos, brandishing their bows and arrows. They stopped my companions and me to ask whether we knew where the fighting was that day. The war had begun, they reported, with a quarrel over a land boundary in which one man was killed. His clan had mobilized to exact vengeance—or justice, as they saw it. Thus far, in a period of three to four weeks, three people had been killed on one side, five on the other. The fighting would not stop until the score was even and compensation was paid by both sides.

Rather than confirming assumptions about an innate human drive to fight and kill, however, my visit led me to question those assumptions. In one critical respect, at least, the New Guinea Highlanders differ from our prehistoric ancestors. Our ancestors were nomadic hunters and gatherers. The Highlanders, by contrast, derive virtually all their food from their gardens and herds of pigs. They are sedentary farmers who have been practicing agriculture probably for six thousand years or longer. Their institutions of warfare flow out of the way they organize themselves and structure their lives.

A REVOLUTION IN HUMAN LIFE

Just at the time that evidence of mass violence first appears in the archaeological record, an enormous change was taking place in human life.

Humans Settle Down and Start Farming

After eons of roving across the land, people began to settle down in one place and to exploit the land intensively. Some groups may have settled down by choice because of an abundance of local food—salmon, herring, and deer. But most who settled down in one place probably did so out of necessity. Their world had become full. Hunting and gathering required a large amount of territory; plants were scattered and animals roamed. As the population slowly grew, humans began to approach the carrying capacity of their regions for hunting and gathering. In certain areas circumscribed by water, mountains, or deserts, our ancestors may have experienced a condition of scarcity without the option of moving onto new lands. At the same time, the change in climate may have reduced the supply of wild foods and game. Facing the prospect of famine, some of our ancestors may have taken a gamble and tried to raise their food by planting seeds.

Agriculture was not a sudden invention like the automobile or the computer. Our hunter-gatherer ancestors had probably known for a long time that putting seeds in the soil made it more likely that plants would grow. But with their nomadic way of life, pursuing animals and searching for wild plants, there had never been much incentive to stay around to harvest the crop.

The shift to agriculture did not necessarily mean a better life for those who chose it. To stay in one place after a life of wandering, to invest all your labor and hopes of feeding your family on one plot of land, must have seemed strange, cramped, and insecure. For whatever reason—weather, insects, blights—the plants might shrivel up.

And even if you had a good harvest one season, what about the next? The medical evidence points to the precariousness of the shift: After the introduction of agriculture, people's average heights plummeted and malnutrition and degenerative and infectious diseases increased significantly.

I got a glimpse of the difficulty when visiting one family of Kalahari Bushmen, who were trying to make the giant leap from hunting and gathering to agriculture. They had settled down in one spot in order to start planting a field of millet, but they were having a tough time of it with the uncertain rainfall. Meanwhile, their relatives and friends had chosen to remain together in a semi-nomadic group of four or five families, preferring whenever possible to look for their food the old-fashioned way.

While many of our ancestors probably did not succeed in their initial efforts at farming and animal husbandry, those who did changed the entire course of human evolution. From being part of the natural order like any other living being, our ancestors began to exercise conscious control in order to change that order. What began as a risky experiment by a few would become in a few short millennia the dominant mode of existence for almost everyone on earth. Hunting and gathering, for hundreds of thousands of years the only human way of life, would slowly dwindle in significance until—in this very generation—it has virtually vanished from the earth.

The Population Grows

As the increase in population stimulated the shift to a sedentary way of life, so that way of life, in turn, triggered a further increase in population. Mothers no longer had to carry their babies until the children could walk on their own. Instead of having a child every three years, as hunter-gatherers generally did, these mothers could now give birth every year. Being more sedentary meant having more body fat, which in turn raised fertility rates. Instead of giving birth to three or four babies, of which two might survive into adulthood, the average settled woman might give birth to a dozen, of which five or six might live.

The main limit on population was the amount of food available, a limit steadily pushed upward by improvements in agricultural methods. Within a few thousand years, sophisticated irrigation systems along the banks of the Euphrates and the Tigris, the Nile and the Indus, were creating a large agricultural surplus, making it possible to build the first cities.

Archaeologists estimate that on the eve of the Agricultural Revolution around ten thousand years ago, the human population of the earth was about five million, considerably less than the current population of New York City. A bare five thousand years later, the number had risen ten- or twentyfold to fifty million or a hundred million. Population density soared. Contrast a hunter-gatherer society—with an average of one person per square mile—with an agricultural settlement such as El Amarna in ancient Egypt, whose population density around 1300 B.C. has been estimated at five hundred people per square mile of productive soil.

THE CONSEQUENCES FOR CONFLICT

In the biblical story of Genesis, Adam and Eve live in the Garden of Eden, wandering freely and gathering wild plants and fruits, much as humanity did for most of human evolution. After the expulsion from Eden, Adam and Eve settle down and have a son Cain, who becomes a farmer, and a son Abel, who becomes a herdsman. The first farmer kills the first herdsman. Cain's son Enoch goes on to build the first city, and the killing of men continues by Enoch's great-great-grandson, Lamech.

As the biblical story illuminates in its own way, settling down, agriculture, and population growth were fateful changes—with powerful impacts on the way we live, the way we relate to one another, and ultimately the way we resolve our most acute conflicts even today.

The Expandable Pie Becomes Fixed

When our ancestors settled down and started exploiting the land intensively, the essential resources on which life depended changed from an expandable pie to a fixed one. In contrast to roving animals and scattered plants, land is fixed. The assumption common among simple hunter-gatherers that there could be more for everyone through cooperation gave way to the assumption common in agricultural societies that more for one person or group meant less for another. Whereas the basic resource in life had once fostered cooperation, now it fomented competition.

The shift was not only objective, but subjective. In contrast to hunter-gatherers, many of whom experience a feeling of abundance, agriculturalists often feel a sense of scarcity and insecurity. Unlike nomadic hunter-gatherers, who can vary their food-seeking strategies, farmers depend for their survival on a single resource: a specific plot of cultivated land in which they invest their time and labor. To borrow an apt cliché, farmers put all their eggs in one basket.

While in hunter-gatherer society there had always been day-to-day issues to quarrel about, now there was something critical to daily survival to fight about: land and its agricultural products. When I asked New Guinea Highlanders what they fought about, the answer usually came back the same: "Land, pigs, and women." And women were an issue not only because of jealousy, but because of their economic value as measured in the numbers of pigs needed to pay for a wife. Agriculture often created a surplus, a tangible prize to fight over, that had never existed in simple hunter-gatherer societies, which consumed all they had on the spot. As a motivation for conflict, human need was joined by human greed.

Note that the key factor intensifying conflict was not agriculture in itself but, more broadly, the intensive exploitation of a fixed and highly valuable resource. Thanks to the extraordinarily rich hunting and fishing on their territories, a number of "complex" hunter-gatherer societies, such as the Northwest Coast Indians, lived in large villages and accumulated huge quantities of goods much like agricultural peoples. Like other sedentary peoples, they engaged in warfare over valuable lands and fishing grounds. The Ahousaht and the Clayoquot, for example, fought over salmon streams, herring grounds, and halibut banks.

"Too Many People in the Same Place"

On a trip to Namibia in early 1989, I visited the town of Tsumkwe, where a few decades earlier five hundred Bushmen, deprived of their traditional hunting territories, had been induced by colonial administrators to settle down. As the Bushmen were making the evolutionary shift from nomadic living to a more crowded sedentary existence, more and more fights began to break out, leading one Bushman elder to exclaim, "There are too many people living in the same place."

That is precisely the point. Before five thousand to ten thousand years ago, we humans had never lived year-round in such numbers and in such close proximity. People now faced the unprecedented challenge of coping with the conflicts inherent in large and dense groups.

Crowding can create enormous tension. In one classic experiment among animals, a group of five Sika deer released in 1916 on a small uninhabited island just off the coast of Maryland grew to a herd of almost three hundred, around one deer per acre, by 1955. Then, in the first three months of 1958, half the deer suddenly died. The following year brought more deaths until the population suddenly leveled off at around eighty. In his examination of the carcasses, the scientist John Christian found no evidence of infection or starvation, but he did find vastly enlarged adrenal glands, suggesting that the cause of the mass deaths was high levels of stress. Significantly, the deaths coincided with a freeze that had made it impossible for the deer to continue their habit of swimming to the mainland at night, which may have afforded them temporary relief from the crowding. Similar experiments carried out with Norway rats by the psychologist John Calhoun revealed links between crowding and aggression. In crowded conditions, otherwise peaceful rats engaged in extensive fighting and tail-biting.

Among humans, studies of crowded urban workers and high-rise public housing projects suggest that rates of crime may increase disproportionately with population density. This is not to say that population density directly causes violence—as counterevidence we have the examples today of large cities like Tokyo, where there is surprisingly little violence. Rather, population density can create high levels of stress that, *if not dealt with in other ways,* can lead to violent behavior.

In the New Guinea Highlands, I interviewed Aki Tumi, a historian of the Enga tribe, the largest and perhaps most contentious group in the region. He had painstakingly collected an oral history stretching back ten generations from those tribesmen whose task is to memorize their clan's past. Aki Tumi had found that warfare in the Highlands turned virulent only after the introduction three centuries ago of the sweet potato and the intensive agriculture that went with it. Originally transported from the Andes to Southeast Asia by Portuguese mariners, the sweet potato gradually spread throughout the region. In the Highlands, it greatly multiplied the productivity of the mountain gardens and triggered a sharp increase in the population. Aki Tumi recounted how the oral histories depict much movement of clans at the time and, amid all the social turmoil, a sharp increase in the frequency of warfare.

When our ancestors settled down, the increasing number of hungry mouths created a squeeze on land and food. There was constant pressure to expand the lands under cultivation. As agriculturalists spread out, they came into conflict with others who needed the same land or with hunters and gatherers who saw their game driven off. Even when agriculture normally produced enough food, there were always times of famine. Droughts and shortages tempted groups to attack their neighbors and seize their crops in order to survive. The new way of life thus increased not only the amount but the intensity of conflicts.

The rise in population had one other effect: Whereas a small nomadic hunter-gatherer group could scarcely afford to lose a single hunter in a fight, a large agricultural village, or later a city-state and empire, with their much higher birth rate, had many more young men to spare. The social costs of fighting decreased.

"The Fight Follows You Around"

Not only did too many people live in the same place; increasingly they had nowhere else to go. The Bushmen I visited who had been settled in the little town of Tsumkwe were struggling with a dilemma that our ancestors must have faced countless times during their transition to a sedentary existence. In the words of a Bushman elder, "In the old days, we used to be able to get away from each other. We walked twenty-five kilometers in the hot sun. It would cool off your anger. In Tsumkwe, the fight follows you around."

The importance of the exit option in defusing escalating conflicts in nomadic hunter-gatherer society cannot be overestimated. Once people had settled down, that option became a lot less feasible. People could not leave fields and possessions on which their lives depended. Without the safety valve of exit, conflicts naturally intensified. Society was coming to resemble a pot full of boiling water on which the lid is suddenly closed.

The Third Side Weakens

The other major mechanism for dealing with conflict, the third side, also became less available. When people settled down in one place and then began practicing agriculture, the form of social organization changed from an open network to a relatively closed village. The web of cooperative ties that had linked everyone weakened— and with it the third side.

With so much invested in a particular piece of land, physical boundaries took on critical importance. Boundaries, which for nomadic hunter-gatherers had been relatively porous and open, grew increasingly fixed and closed. The same happened with social boundaries. With agriculture, each group became more self-sufficient and stable in its membership and people's energies began to turn inward, toward their own group. Outsiders came to seem progressively alien—they became "strangers." As tensions arose within the group, it would have been increasingly tempting to project them outward and to blame problems on outsiders. With less mixing between groups, there were fewer potential third parties who understood and had ties to both groups in conflict.

When I run the Prisoners' Dilemma game in my negotiation courses to demonstrate the logic of competition and cooperation, I sometimes vary the rules for purposes of experimentation. If I do not allow groups a chance to communicate with one another, they find it much more difficult to build mutual trust and cooperate. In effect, I am re-creating in the classroom what happened when the open network changed into the self-contained village.

Imagine a hammock with strong strands connecting the knots. This is the ancient network with bonds of kinship, sharing, and co-operation. As the network turns into self-contained villages, the hammock changes: The knots get much bigger and the strands connecting them become thinner and weaker. Now imagine an even heavier person climbing into the hammock. The strands naturally snap and the person collapses to the ground. The fall to the ground was the fall into violence and warfare.

Conditions, Not Certainties

None of this means that the process of settling down and practicing agriculture led automatically to violence and war. It did not. It is worth remembering that ancient Egypt is believed to have experienced a period of fifteen centuries without war with outsiders. Similar claims of peacefulness have been made for early agricultural societies in certain parts of southeastern Europe during the period 7000–3500 B.C.

The point is that, when combined with the rising population that they trigger, the revolutionary developments of settling down and agriculture create the conditions for heightened conflict and at the same time undermine the traditional structures for resolving conflict. The incentives shift. Although some societies may have been able to preserve the peace, most appear to have eventually tumbled into a pattern of recurrent warfare.

THE PYRAMIDS OF POWER

What gave birth to organized violence as a core feature of human life was the dramatic change in the relationship between human beings and their environment, but what turned war into the vast and bloody conquests of recorded history was the change in the relationship between one human being and another. Compulsion replaced cooperation as the dominant form of relating.

From Cooperation to Compulsion

In the early agricultural period, fighting may have served the role of spacing out the growing population as defeated groups fled. With the sharp rise in numbers and the closing of the exit option, however, fighting often became a fight to the death. Since the losers often had no place to flee, the victors had two choices if they wanted the land and its fruit: to exterminate the losers or to incorporate them as a subjugated people. The victors could compel the vanquished to pay tribute in the form of labor, food, and treasure.

For perhaps the first time in human evolution, it became useful to treat other humans in large numbers as slaves, servants, or subordinates. Up until this point, the chief form of human power had been the power to control the environment by using tools to hunt, gather, farm, and herd. Now humans developed a different form of power:

power over others. From relying mainly on voluntary cooperation to meet their needs, people turned increasingly to compulsion.

"Without compulsion no settlement could be founded," an ancient Sumerian inscription explains. "The workers would have no supervisor. The rivers would not bring the overflow." Needing to find ways to feed unprecedented numbers of people living in close quarters, our ancestors may have seen no choice but to order others to work. There was no going back to a simpler and freer existence. Rigid organizations were needed, for example, to construct and maintain complex irrigation systems.

In the new kingdoms the rulers had absolute power, including the power of life and death over every single citizen. I remember an ancient Egyptian wall relief I traced from a history book as a boy of ten. The relief depicted three men holding down a fourth—presumably a slave—while a fifth man towered over him with a heavy stick, about to administer a beating, and a sixth man—presumably the master or foreman—oversaw the punishment. We do not know why the man was being beaten, but the relief captured something of the new relationship between people. Human brutality had undoubtedly always existed, but never in such an organized form. Now force became the organizing logic of society.

In the political realm, the new coercive relations took the form of the state, an institution with a monopoly on the instruments of coercion in a defined territory. The state depended for its existence on coercion. Grain, animals, and labor taken from the peasants made it possible to support an array of full-time specialists—bureaucrats, craftspeople, priests, and warriors. In return for their food and labor, peasants received divine favor and protection from external threats. The relationship between ruler and ruled was half contract, half extortion. Peasants complied out of fear for their lives. The state, in this sense, was a giant "protection racket," put together and held together by force.

Power Becomes a Prize

Power over others became a prize, another central stake to be fought over besides land. Like land, power is a fixed pie, a zero-sum quantity; individuals or groups could gain power only at the expense of others.

Power is an insidious prize. From being a means toward an end, it easily becomes an end in itself. Just as millionaires seek to accumulate more and more money without needing it, so kings and emperors strove to accumulate more and more power, usually at the expense of others. They were spurred not only by ambition and greed, but by the fear that if they stopped, they would be surpassed and conquered themselves.

From Horizontal to Vertical Relations

Somewhat as the enormous pressure of geological forces makes the flat ground buckle up into a mountain, so the extraordinary pressure of conflict forced the relatively egalitarian relationships among human beings into a pyramidal hierarchy of classes and castes in which each group lorded it over the larger group below it. Peasants over slaves, tradesmen over peasants, soldiers over tradesmen, priests and nobility over soldiers, and at the apex the god-king.

Certainly there had always been a degree of hierarchy in human relationships. There were respected elders and later there were chiefs. But the elders and chiefs consulted widely before making decisions, and the decisions they made were typically not enforced by coercion. As the saying goes, "One word from the chief and everyone does as they please." The new hierarchy was something very different, however: a rigid stratification of people based on compulsion.

While every human society is a mixture of horizontal and vertical relationships, the central organizing principle had always been horizontal. People had been organized in networks. Now, however, the main organizing principle in human relations became vertical.

Status and power, not common ties of kinship and interest, came to determine the basic relationships among human beings. The networks of negotiation changed into pyramids of power. It would be hard to imagine a more complete revolution in human relations.

Such a revolution could not fail to utterly change patterns of conflict resolution. With its clear hierarchy, the pyramid was a conflict resolution mechanism, serving the same function as a pecking order among birds. Lower status gave way to higher status. It was an ingenious if inegalitarian way of coping with challenges the human race was facing for the first time. Whereas among simpler nomadic societies the system for resolving conflicts had been communal negotiation in the shadow of exit, now the system became domination in the shadow of force.

THE LOGIC OF WAR

While the pyramids of power controlled conflict by suppressing it, they also bred new conflicts. Almost every hierarchy and state was established out of a struggle for power and, once established, was always open to challenge. Different factions and individuals competed for position inside the hierarchy, and the state was regularly threatened by outsiders. Whether it was charioteers from Assyria or nomadic raiders from Central Asia, the barbarians were waiting at the gates. The state was a valuable prize, a treasure trove of wealth and power. The continuous struggle for control easily and frequently escalated into violence and war.

States Breed Wars as Wars Breed States

Thus began a history-making process of violent coups d'état and conquests by war. A strong city-state conquered other city-states around it and grew into an empire. The Sumerian empire, the Babylonian empire, the Assyrian empire, the Egyptian empire all rose through conquest and fell through conquest. Dynasties were born out of violence, empires out of war.

The state and war—domination and violence—became inseparable. Indeed, the state took on the characteristics of a military organization. As the periods of peace shortened and the frequency of war increased, states became garrisons, machines dedicated to raising tribute and soldiers from the people in order to sustain the capacity to make war. War became the chief preoccupation of the nobility, who served as warriors and military officers, and of the king, who was commander-in-chief. Temporary armies, drafted from the peasantry, gave way to professional standing armies.

Standing armies created the temptation to use them against neighbors to acquire their lands and power, win prestige and glory, or preempt an attack. Instead of having to raise an army, rulers could simply order the army to march with a single command. The more power was concentrated in the hands of a single person, the fewer the constraints on rash and impulsive adventures. It was no coincidence that, in the latter part of the nineteenth century, for example, the explorer Sir Richard Burton observed wars to be far more frequent and ferocious in East Africa, where there were absolute kings, than in West Africa, where there were tribal chiefs guided by councils of elders.

Orders to Kill

Most fatefully, the emergence of the state meant that for the first time in human history, an organization could order a man on pain of death to go into battle to kill or be killed. It may seem commonplace enough to us living today, but it was a revolutionary shift.

The anthropologist Robert Renaldo tells of a conversation he had with a group of Ilonget tribesmen, headhunters who live in the tropical forests of the Philippines. When Renaldo was called up by the U.S. military to go fight in Vietnam, he expected his Ilonget headhunter friends to be supportive.

"We would never ask our brother to sell his body," they protested to Renaldo. "That's unspeakable. How can a human being do that?"

"I thought you guys were into headhunting," Renaldo replied. "Don't you think I should go off to fight the war?"

"War?" they said. "Soldiers sell their bodies."

During World War II, they had witnessed a Japanese officer ordering his "brothers" to step directly into the line of fire. "It's hard to describe how morally appalled they were by this," writes Renaldo. "It was just unthinkable that anyone could do that."

For the Ilonget, it was right to go into battle, to run the risks of injury and death, but only if the *individual* decided to do so. It was wrong, however, to order others into battle to risk their lives on one's behalf while one stood aside and reaped the benefit. It was wrong for one human being to exercise such power over another.

The Ilonget headhunters had a point. War shifted from a fight typically carried out for a personal purpose, such as revenge, to an impersonal battle for someone else's power and glory. The new rulers found the lives of others cheap and the stakes all-important to them personally: land, possessions, prestige, power, and survival. The logic of coexistence may have remained the same as it had always been for the common citizen, but for the king and the noble classes, the logic of war prevailed.

The new rulers ordered more and more lives into battle. The number of deaths ran at first into the hundreds, then into the thousands, then into the tens and hundreds of thousands, and finally, in the present time, into the millions. Fighting for an abstraction like power easily led to unlimited war. Ashurbanipal, king of ancient Assyria, boasted on a stone tablet: "I levelled the city and its houses . . . I consumed them with fire . . . After I destroyed Babylon . . . and massacred its population, I tore up its soil and threw it into the Euphrates."

In societies dedicated to the acquisition and maintenance of power, brute force became the ultimate arbiter. It made kings and unmade them, raised groups up and cast them down, created states and empires and destroyed them. It became the driving thrust of history.

War Is Contagious

The Prisoners' Dilemma games I run in my classes illustrate how contagious competitive behavior can be. Even if one group wants to continue cooperating, as they frequently do, they grow afraid that the other group will take advantage of their goodwill. Similarly, with the new settled agricultural way of life, if a new group or tribe that was used to fighting arrived in the neighborhood, the resident group would have no choice but to defend itself or abandon its lands. And so each group exposed to a warring group would need to learn the art of war or risk their survival. In an environment where it makes sense, war can be highly contagious. War breeds war.

Gradually, organized violence began to spread around the world. Imagine a map of the world roughly divided into a zone of relative coexistence colored blue and a zone of coercion colored red. For the longest time, the map remained largely blue, with perhaps occasional dots of red. Then roughly ten thousand years ago, the red dots started expanding, and perhaps five thousand years ago, the map became mostly red.

Force Makes Sense

Is it any surprise that today the inheritors of five millennia of such bloody history should believe that violence, domination, and war are inevitable and automatic responses of human nature itself? *In truth, however, the violence and domination we have known are the product not so much of human nature but the complex logic of settling down, intensive reliance on land, population increase, the weakening of*

the third side, the closing of the exit option, the development of author-
itarian hierarchies, the growth of the state, and the contagion of war. At
the bottom of this logic is the dependence on fixed-pie resources—
first of land and then of power over other human beings.

The image comes to mind of a gigantic "squeeze." After dozens of
millennia of roaming freely, our ancestors were squeezed into one
spot and resources were often pinched. Human beings began to use
more force because force began to make more sense.

THE DEADLIEST CENTURY

Almost three thousand years after Ashurbanipal, war has not
changed much. Hitler went to war for much the same reasons
Ashurbanipal did: for land and power. Mass slaughter is still the order of the day. We who have lived in the twentieth century like to
think of ourselves as having the most advanced, most civilized, and
most humane societies the world has ever seen. Yet the terrible irony
is that this past century has been the bloodiest century the human
race has ever known. Over a hundred million people have perished
in warfare, and another hundred and seventy million have died
through political violence.

The World Wars

The first major war of the century began in August 1914. When
the war broke out, very few people had any idea of what it would
cost in human life and suffering, of how long it would take, and of
how much of Western civilization it would destroy. And destroy it
did—virtually an entire generation of youth. The historian Barbara
Tuchman cites as a single example a young Frenchman by the name
of André Varagnac, who came of military age in 1914. Owing to ill-
ness, Varagnac was not mobilized in August and found himself by

Christmas the only survivor out of his high school graduating class of twenty-seven. Millions of young men lived like rats in muddy trenches, suffocating to death from poison gas, and mowed down like tenpins by machine guns. It was not the brief glorious adventure people had imagined it would be when they sent their boys off to fight.

After a twenty-year truce, a second world war broke out. In the brief interval, technology had advanced so that this time it could destroy entire cities in a single night of torrential bombing. The death camps, organized as models of industrial efficiency, claimed millions of lives. The war came to an end with the first use of an atomic bomb; a single bomb obliterated the city of Hiroshima and another, three days later, destroyed Nagasaki.

The Specter of Mass Destruction

It was a long path from the one-million-year-old hearth discovered by archaeologist Bob Brain at the Swartkrans cave in South Africa—the earliest sign that early humans had mastered fire—to the radioactive blazes their descendants were able to set off in 1945. In the language of archaeology, a nuclear bomb is just another cultural artifact, another weapon launched by the human hand, the lineal descendant of the rock and the spear. The difference lies in the impact, a billion times greater.

A thousand years from now, if and when schoolchildren look back at this time, they may note very little, but they will remember this signal event in human evolution when human beings acquired the unprecedented ability to put an untimely end to the human experiment. What our natural predators could not do, what our natural competitors could not do, what the ice ages themselves could not do, we can now do to ourselves. What has taken tens of thousands of generations to build up can now be extinguished in an instant. Extinct species naturally evoke associations with the dinosaurs, but the dinosaurs were able to roam this earth for 165 million years.

Humanity is but a few million years old, barely in its infancy, and yet its future is already threatened—by its own creation, no less. From center stage in human politics, war has moved to center stage in human evolution.

The know-how of making nuclear, chemical, and biological weapons continues to spread slowly but relentlessly. So too does the technology of rockets and missiles to carry these weapons; every place on earth can now be reached and destroyed within thirty minutes. While the threat of global nuclear destruction appears to have faded with the end of the Cold War, more than twenty thousand nuclear weapons remain in place, armed and ready for instant use, and anarchy threatens in some of the nations that possess them. Dangerous dictators seek to acquire these weapons or the scientists who know how to make them. The fear that nuclear bombs would be used rationally has diminished, but the possibility of an accident, an act of madness, or the emergence of a new Hitler at the helm of a nuclear power cannot be ruled out. Nor can anyone expect the technological process to stop with the atomic bomb. With advances in genetic research and artificial intelligence, human ingenuity is likely to devise ever more destructive weapons.

A Rash of Ethnic Wars

The end of the Cold War in the late 1980s raised great hopes for peace. Wars that had been supported by one or both superpowers ground slowly to an end in Afghanistan, Cambodia, Angola, Mozambique, Nicaragua, Namibia, and even South Africa. Then in 1991, a savage war—or set of wars—erupted in the heart of Europe in what had been the state of Yugoslavia. Images of concentration camps, of mass rapes, and of wanton slaughter filled the world's television screens. As if this were not enough, a genocide broke out in Rwanda, leaving close to a million dead with its indelible images of hacked-up human bodies floating down the rivers in a gruesome procession. Hopes that the world was entering a new era were dashed.

Just before the turn of the millennium, more than two dozen wars were raging around the planet. None were world wars, yet in total as many people were dying in warfare in the late 1980s as at the height of World War I.

Most of the wars raging around the planet today revolve around the issue of identity—ethnic, religious, or racial. One group fights bitterly with another in an effort to safeguard an identity perceived as threatened. Behind the ethnic animosities, however, lies the old struggle for power and material resources. Seeking to stay in power, demagogic leaders whip up old ethnic grievances and stir up fear and anger. The genocides in both Rwanda and Yugoslavia were directed by governments and instigated by government-controlled media.

War is also increasingly taking the form of terrorism, violence directed mainly against civilians for political purposes. An airliner is blown up over Scotland with the loss of two hundred and seventy innocents. Poison gas spread in a Tokyo subway injures over five thousand people. When future historians look back on this age, they may well remember it as the age of terrorism, of the conscious killing of innocent civilians by guerrilla groups and governments alike. A nuclear bomb and a terrorist bomb have this in common: They do not discriminate.

An image from a trip to the former Yugoslavia in the fall of 1994 sticks in my mind. I was visiting a group of Bosnian refugees camped out in an abandoned village in the no-man's-land between the cease-fire lines. On one side stood the Croatian tanks, on the other the Serbian tanks. Every house in the village sat in ruins, burned out, bombed out, with collapsed roofs and walls. An explosive rocket stuck straight into the trunk of a tree as if someone had been playing a game of darts. Milling around everywhere were children, women, and men. Some people had built makeshift shacks out of furniture or wood that they had dragged out of the bombed-out buildings. My companions and I entered the ruins of what had once been a gymnasium; on the basketball court there stood some wooden shacks, in one of which we found a mother cradling her newborn child. Everyone looked bewildered. Meanwhile, winter approached.

There was nowhere the refugees could go. The Croats would not let them into Croatia, the Serbs did not want them back on what they considered their territory. The fields on either side of the road were mined—not a week went by without someone losing a foot or a leg. The image of these twelve thousand refugees seemed to me a metaphor of humanity caught in the vise of violence. The innocent, young and old, were trapped with no possibility of escape between two warring groups of young men. It made me wonder if anything had changed since the times of ancient Assyria and Babylon.

Yet Signs of Peace

At the same time, paradoxically, there are some intriguing rays of hope in the larger patterns of war and peace.

First, contrary to widely shared expectations during the forty years of the Cold War, the conflict between the United States and the Soviet Union never did erupt into a thermonuclear catastrophe. While the superpowers went to the brink with each other on more than one occasion, they always refrained from using the ultimate weapon. Indeed, not one of the tens of thousands of atomic weapons deployed around the world has been used in war in the half century since Hiroshima. Wherever nations in conflict have developed nuclear weapons, their tendency to go to war has diminished rather than increased. This has proven true thus far not only of the standoff between the United States and the Soviet Union, but between China and the Soviet Union, between China and India, and between India and Pakistan.

Second, since 1945, there have been no wars among the major powers. They have fought wars and proxy wars, but not directly with one another. Time after time in history, when two great powers have confronted each other, the result has been war—the Peloponnesian War between Athens and Sparta, the Punic Wars between Rome and Carthage, the wars between France and England, and between France and Germany. With their strong ideological antagonism and their intense competition for geopolitical power and prestige in the second half of the twentieth century, the United States and the Soviet Union fit perfectly into this historical pattern, yet they did not go to war. The continuing occurrence of smaller wars does not negate this most remarkable development. The current period of peace among the world's major powers is the longest known in recorded history.

Third, for the first time in the five-thousand-year history of states, there are years in which no wars are fought between established states. The state and war are no longer synonymous. Of the two dozen major wars in progress in the world as the century turns, almost all are taking place within states or former states that have recently broken up, such as Yugoslavia. They are internal or civil wars. The pattern applies even among the poorer states of the Third World.

One of the most telling statistics of modern war is the plunging odds of victory for the aggressor. In past centuries, the aggressor in war had at least an even chance of winning. By the mid-twentieth century, these odds had shrunk to thirty percent. By the 1980s, the odds stood at nineteen percent. With odds of winning of less than one in five, it is perhaps not surprising that states are ceasing to start wars with one another.

Finally, war is losing its legitimacy. For millennia, war has been glorified as the noblest adventure of man. A few humanists and theologians through the centuries inveighed against its horrors and a few religious sects believed in pacifism, but right up into the twentieth century, it would be fair to say that aggressive war was considered legitimate in the eyes of every civilization on earth. Now aggressive war is beginning to be seen by the larger community as what it has always been: acts of murder, rape, and theft. In the words of an old French Legionnaire, a veteran of the battle of Dien Bien Phu, "There is no such thing as a war crime. War itself is a crime."

WHICH WAY HUMANITY?

The period we know as history might be appropriately called the Age of Force, for coercion has been the dominant mode human beings have used for handling serious differences. It has been a rough patch and, if the prior picture of the first ninety-nine percent of human evolution is correct, somewhat of an aberration.

Aberration or not, we should not forget the extraordinary social accomplishments of humanity during this evolutionarily brief period. People learned to live in societies thousands of times larger than they had ever lived in before. They learned to cooperate on a scale hitherto unimaginable, spanning the globe with webs of communication and trade. And they invented new ways of dealing with differences, erecting complex hierarchies designed to contain and resolve destructive conflict. It has been a period of adaptation and valuable learning, acquired at a high price in violence and domination.

Whatever the case, this particular chapter in human evolution is drawing to a close. A new chapter, fraught with formidable new dangers and promising new opportunities, has begun. We are living in a time of paradox. One way to interpret the data is that nothing is essentially new when it comes to human conflict. The signs of peace are ephemeral and will pass. An alternative hypothesis holds that the signs of peace point to a possible shift in human affairs. While the centuries-old habits of strife may persist for now, rendered ever more devastating because of developing technologies, a new logic of conflict is forcing people to learn more peaceful ways of dealing with differences.

The first hypothesis is the conventional wisdom; it needs no further explication. The second, more contrarian, more surprising, requires some exploration.

Chapter 4

AND BACK AGAIN?

The idea that if one side wins something in Northern Ireland, the other loses, that's gone. The essence of what we have agreed is a choice: we are all winners or all losers. It is mutually assured benefit or mutually assured destruction.
— British Prime Minister Tony Blair, May 1998

October 27, 1962, may have been the single most dangerous day in millions of years of human evolution. On that day, the two giant superpowers of the planet, armed with nuclear arsenals capable of destroying much if not all of human civilization, stood on the verge of war. The issue was whether the Soviet Union could place nuclear missiles on the island of Cuba, ninety miles away from the United States.

President John F. Kennedy had ordered his navy to encircle Cuba in order to stop the Soviet ships with their cargo of missiles. But the ships kept steaming forward. U.S. intelligence agents detected Soviet diplomats in New York City shredding sensitive documents in anticipation of war. American spy planes were flying every two hours over Cuba, taking pictures of the work in progress on the missile installations. Kennedy had taken a tentative decision to retaliate if the Soviets interfered and shot down an American plane. The U.S. Air Force was ready to attack and the U.S. Army was poised to invade.

Then an American plane *was* shot down and the pilot was killed. Everyone in Washington assumed that the shooting was the result of a decision by the Soviet leadership in Moscow, a deliberate provocation. American bombers prepared to retaliate. In Washington that evening, Robert McNamara, the U.S. secretary of defense, admired the spectacular sunset and wondered whether he would ever see another.

Fortunately, Kennedy hesitated. He decided not to retaliate yet, but to redouble the diplomatic efforts to resolve the crisis. As he had told his advisers a few days earlier, "It isn't the first step that concerns me, but both sides escalating to the fourth and fifth step—and we don't go to the sixth, because there is no one around to do so." The next day, Soviet Premier Nikita Khrushchev saw sense and announced he would withdraw the missiles from Cuba. World War III was averted.

Just how close the world came to nuclear war, no one really knew until twenty-five years later. In the closing years of the Cold War, I was present at a meeting in Moscow of the surviving American, Soviet, and Cuban participants. They were gathered around a conference table to share their knowledge of what had actually happened. Not until this meeting did the world learn of the miscalculations and misunderstandings on both sides. Not until then did the Soviets reveal that the American spy plane had been shot down not on Moscow's command, but by the independent order of a Soviet general on the spot who had made a snap decision during a two-minute window of opportunity. Only then did we learn that the Soviets, unbeknownst to Washington, had already succeeded in smuggling into Cuba a number of nuclear missiles, which they had armed. If American decision makers, in their ignorance, had proceeded with the air and ground attack they had planned, the Soviets might well have responded with a nuclear salvo, and the United States would have felt compelled to retaliate. And so the two adversaries might have come to the fourth and, finally, the fifth step—an all-out nuclear war.

The consequences of such a war would have been incalculable. Certainly tens of millions of us would have perished from blast and fallout. More tens of millions might have died from the resulting economic collapse and environmental damage. "And we call ourselves the human race!" President Kennedy exclaimed.

The Cuban Missile Crisis marked a turning point in the relations between the United States and the Soviet Union. The world's most powerful leaders had been shocked into a realization—that nuclear war made no sense. It was not winnable in any meaningful way; both sides would inevitably lose. To politicians and military leaders schooled in the millennia-old logic of victors and losers in warfare, this came as a bit of a revelation. The new awareness gave impetus to arms control negotiations, which resulted the following year in a limited ban on nuclear testing and the establishment of the Hot Line. It was just a beginning, of course, and the Cold War continued, but a vital lesson had been learned.

As an anthropologist studying the crisis, I wondered where we had arrived in the evolution of human conflict. What did this episode imply about humanity's future prospects for coexistence? Were we now, thanks to our technological genius, facing a countdown to destruction, if not this century, then the next? Or did it suggest a shift in the underlying logic of conflict? Could human beings everywhere, in different arenas, learn the lesson painfully appreciated by American and Soviet leaders in October 1962?

A SHIFT IN THE LOGIC

Humanity is in the midst of a social, economic, and political transformation just as far-reaching as the Agricultural Revolution ten thousand years ago. Just as that revolution utterly changed the way we live and relate to one another, so too does the Knowledge Revolution.

The roots of this transformation go back some five hundred years to the Renaissance in Western Europe. Individual initiative and scientific exploration flourished and gave birth a few centuries later to the Industrial Revolution. New forms of energy such as steam, coal, and oil were discovered and used to power new forms of production and transportation such as the assembly line and the railroad. These inventions, in turn, brought the world to the present Information Age, symbolized by technologies such as radio and television, telephones and fax machines, and, above all, computers. All three eras— the Renaissance, the Industrial Revolution, and the Information Age—are but phases of a single ongoing process that might be called the Knowledge Revolution.

From a Fixed Pie Back to an Expandable One

A shift is taking place in the basic resource of human society— from land to knowledge. Today, almost everything people use to live—from clothing to food and from houses to means of transportation and communication—is produced by scientific knowledge. Whereas land is a fixed pie lending itself to destructive fights over its division, the new basic resource is, as in hunter-gatherer times, an expandable pie. More knowledge for you need not mean less knowledge for me; we can all partake of it. If I give you land, I have less land, but if I give you knowledge, as in this book, I do not thereby have less knowledge. Indeed, we can both benefit from the same knowledge. There are limits to land and material resources, but there are no known limits to learning.

Land is not the only major source of destructive conflict. People and groups also fight fiercely about power. Like land, power over others is a fixed pie. More power for you is less for me. Knowledge represents a different kind of power, one that can be used to satisfy needs and wishes. Knowledge power need not subjugate others, but can be used to liberate and empower them. Contrast the act of driving an automobile with that of being carried in a carriage by a dozen slaves. The ride is not only faster and smoother, but is achieved without mistreating human beings. This new kind of power—power to do things—is not a fixed pie, but an expandable one. Thanks to knowledge power, billions of ordinary citizens with virtually no power over others possess the power to live longer and travel faster and farther than an Assyrian emperor with thousands of minions.

With the Knowledge Revolution, it has become easier to raise production of one's own land than it is to conquer the land of others. It costs less to buy food than it would to enslave people to produce it for you. It is becoming cheaper to synthesize rubber and fibers than to extract them from colonies, cheaper to trade for oil and minerals than to seize them. While it may have made sense to go to war to acquire territory, it makes little sense to go to war to acquire the new prize of knowledge. For knowledge cannot easily be conquered. It is best acquired through learning and cooperation.

In contrast to land, which is typically improved through the act of possession, knowledge is improved through the act of sharing. The core enterprise of the Knowledge Revolution—science—relies on the exchange of theories and information. Scientists compete with one another, as when different teams race to be the first to invent a vaccine, but the competition is mostly in the timing. The fundamental mode is cooperation; no scientist can work effectively without cooperating with colleagues past and present. Through such cooperation and sharing, knowledge as a resource grows more and more abundant for everyone.

Even in the profit-making world, where the competition is fierce and companies often guard their knowledge jealously, the best strategy is often to share one's knowledge—sometimes even for free. Consider the first major software program used for navigating the Internet, Netscape. It consisted almost entirely of knowledge, ones and zeros of computer code. It cost the company next to nothing in the form of labor, machinery, or transport to create an almost infinite number of copies. Indeed, the company succeeded by *giving away* most of its product for nothing on the Internet, thereby allowing it to command eighty-five percent of the market for a period. By positioning itself to sell a host of other products and services to its customers, the company generated enormous value for its investors and was eventually purchased for more than four billion dollars.

From Arrows to Guns

If the Knowledge Revolution makes sharing and cooperating more beneficial, it also makes fighting more harmful. As weapons have become deadlier, they have also become cheaper and more accessible to anyone. Automatic weapons can be purchased on many street corners, land mines can be acquired for a few dollars each, and bombs able to kill hundreds can be assembled from store-bought items. Mass murder and genocide are not new, of course, but they have never been easier.

One of the most telling comments I heard in my interviews with clan warriors in the New Guinea Highlands was: "Arrows are advice. Guns are not advice." By that, the warrior meant that arrows teach people a lesson. If you get an arrow in the leg or ribs, you remember it. It warns you to be careful in the future. Guns, however, are usually fatal, affording no second chance, no opportunity to learn.

For the New Guinea tribesmen, warfare is a matter of logic and proportion. There are costs, but they are calculable and acceptable to the individual warrior. The use of guns did not just enhance one's ability to win the fight; it changed the very nature of fighting, destroying the sense of proportion. In the traditional Great Tourneys, a thousand warriors could fight with bows and arrows for a day with not a single death. With guns, that became impossible.

Like guns in the context of New Guinea warfare, modern weapons change the very nature of what it means to fight. Weapons of mass destruction destroy all sense of proportion. For what political issue is it worth destroying entire societies, not to speak of human civilization? To paraphrase the New Guinea warrior, nuclear war is not advice, it is genocide.

From Win-Lose Toward Lose-Lose

A "win-lose" mentality can wreak havoc in any domain of human life. When husbands and wives seek to control each other, the result is often a bitter divorce. When quarreling neighbors take each other to court, they frequently lose their time and money. When unions and companies fight, everyone can lose their jobs—permanently. Voltaire put it best of all: "I was never ruined but twice: once when I lost a lawsuit and once when I won one."

The Knowledge Revolution only sharpens the "lose-lose" logic of conflict. Partly because the spread of knowledge tends to equalize power, partly because destructive weaponry is increasingly accessible, it is becoming harder to win a dispute in a decisive and enduring fashion.

Consider the history of warfare in the twentieth century. In August 1914, the nations of Europe went to war confident their soldiers would be home by Christmas with a clear victory over the enemy. When the war ended four years later, even the victors had lost. France, the principal battleground, was ravaged, and the British Empire had suffered a blow from which it was never to recover. Even worse, the victory proved to be a mere truce until an even more devastating war erupted twenty years later.

The logic of "no one wins" was clearest during the Cold War. The governments of the United States and the Soviet Union spent hundreds of billions of dollars trying to find a way to make a nuclear war winnable. They came up with weapon system after weapon system, from MIRVs to the neutron bomb, and doctrine after doctrine, from decapitation to first strike. Each weapon and doctrine was designed to make it credible that nuclear weapons could be used to win a war. Some of the best scientific minds of a generation tried to crack this puzzle—to no avail. What became clear over time was that a nuclear war would bring only losers.

Even smaller wars proved hard to win for the powerful nations on earth. The Vietnam War became a cruel education for the United States, as did the war in Afghanistan for the Soviet Union. The spread of advanced weaponry and new ideas of freedom and self-determination, both fruits of the Knowledge Revolution, have made it ever more costly to impose control over others.

This change was driven home for me when I was facilitating peace discussions between Russian and Chechen leaders in the spring and fall of 1997. The vaunted Red Army, which the United States had spent a trillion dollars seeking to contain, had failed to impose its will on tiny Chechnya in almost two years of barbaric warfare. The opposing force that had compelled the Red Army to withdraw consisted, as the Chechen vice president explained, of fewer than seven thousand determined fighters. They obtained much of their weaponry from Russian soldiers and listened in on Russian military radio frequencies to learn their opponents' plans. Thanks to independent media, only recently established, the war became intensely unpopular in Russia; mothers of Russian soldiers traveled to Chechnya to take their sons home. The Chechens' dramatic seizure of hundreds of Russian civilian hostages and the Russian military's violent and ineffectual responses, captured on television, forced the Russian government into negotiations. Unable to fight effectively in an age of information, Moscow withdrew from a devastated Chechnya.

The Knowledge Revolution has accentuated the "all-lose" nature of destructive conflict. One statistic about warfare is particularly telling. In 1900, the ratio of civilian to military casualties in war ranged from ten to fifty percent. Now the average figure is over ninety percent. As in Chechnya, nine out of ten deaths are not soldiers but civilians. It is mostly the innocent who die—elderly shoppers in the marketplace, young children playing in the street, and women huddled in their houses with their babies.

We are all vulnerable. From personal life to business to world politics, people are going through a painful reeducation about the nature of conflict, just as American and Soviet leaders did during the Cuban Missile Crisis. "An eye for an eye" was the old law. The new realization is, in Mahatma Gandhi's words, "An eye for an eye and we all go blind."

From Win-Lose Toward Both-Gain

If the Knowledge Revolution makes it possible for both to lose, it also makes it easier for both to "gain." "Both-gain" does not mean that both parties get everything they want, but rather that they each benefit more than they probably would by fighting. It usually means, furthermore, that the most basic human needs of the parties are met.

Consider the essential need for food. For the last five or ten millennia, food has been an item of scarcity in virtually every agricultural society on earth. Famine and hunger were normal and accepted occurrences. My generation in the United States was admonished to eat all the food on our plates because "children were starving in India and China." Our image of India and China at the time was of teeming millions of people, for whom there would never be enough food. Since the 1950s, however, despite a doubling of their population, India and China have both acquired the ability to feed their own peoples. The Knowledge Revolution in the form of machinery, fertilizers, and genetic breeding has transformed the practice of agriculture. The malnutrition that tragically remains in the world results from economic and political inequity, not from lack of capacity to produce food.

In the global economy, a "both-gain" logic is making more and more sense. Companies are finding it to their advantage to pool their resources for research and development, to share production facilities, and to learn from each other. They are forging strategic alliances and joint ventures, sometimes with their most ardent competitors. The largest company in the world, General Motors, created an alliance with its competitor Toyota; IBM did the same with Fujitsu. Benetton's success comes from its cooperative relationships with its more than seven hundred small entrepreneurial subcontractors. Benetton concentrates on what it does best, buying raw materials, creating colors, and marketing the clothes, while the suppliers do what they do best, making clothes; as Benetton grows, everyone benefits. Increasingly in today's marketplace, a business's ability to compete depends on its ability to cooperate.

The Knowledge Revolution makes possible new solutions to old conflicts. The war between Israel and Egypt, for example, came to an end in a negotiation over the Sinai Peninsula, occupied by Israel during the 1967 Six-Day War. Egypt demanded the return of the entire peninsula, but Israel insisted on retaining a third of the peninsula as a security buffer. No simple compromise was acceptable. It turned out, however, that what Israel really needed most was not the land itself, but knowledge—early warning of attack. Thanks to new technology, both sides were able to agree to demilitarize the Sinai and establish electronic detectors to monitor any threatening movement. Egypt received all its land back and Israel obtained even more of a security buffer than it had been demanding. A negotiated both-gain solution replaced an unstable win-lose solution.

Even an expanded pie, however, still needs to be divided up. Who will get what part? Opposed interests remain. A buyer wants to get a certain product for less; the seller insists on more. An ethnic group wants more autonomy; the state insists on less. While a both-gain logic does not imply an end to the win-lose aspect of conflict, it does sharpen the incentive to handle these opposed interests through negotiation rather than force.

The Example of South Africa

Nowhere has the shift in the underlying logic of human conflict been more dramatically illustrated than in the case of South Africa. In early 1995, I heard Nelson Mandela and F. W. de Klerk, separately, describe the journey each had taken from war to peace. De Klerk spoke about how he had come to realize that, politically and militarily, the white minority could not hold on to power indefinitely in the face of strong black resistance armed with the fruits of the Knowledge Revolution: ideas of equality, modern means of communication, weapons, and international support. South Africa's economy was suffering from international trade and financial sanctions. Only by reaching a peace accord could the white minority hope to retain its quality of life and the Afrikaner tribe protect its identity.

Mandela talked about seeing the country descending into civil strife and economic ruin. While he was confident that the black majority would prevail in the long term, he wondered what kind of country would be left in the end for the blacks to inherit. Only by prospering in the new global economy could they put an end to their poverty and deprivation—and that prosperity could be achieved only by cooperating with the white minority with their technical skills and business experience. The vision of the African National Congress, moreover, had always been a democratic multiracial society. With every passing year of ethnic violence, that vision was fading out of reach.

Both leaders, in other words, realized that the conflict was stalemated. Continuing the violence would spell defeat for everyone. Only through negotiation could both sides hope to meet their needs. If both sides could lose through a spiral of violence, then perhaps both sides could win through a spiral of dialogue. As Mandela put it, "I never sought to undermine Mr. de Klerk, for the practical reason that the weaker he was, the weaker the negotiations process. To make peace with an enemy one must work with that enemy, and the enemy must become one's partner."

To test this theory, de Klerk and other white leaders met with Mandela while he was still in prison, and came away feeling personal respect for the man. Each side came to realize that the people on the other side were not the monsters they had imagined. Gradually, during the course of the negotiations, as Roelf Meyer, the chief negotiator for the white Nationalist government, explained to me, both sides came to believe in the possibility of a new alternative, neither a white victory nor a black victory nor even a split-the-difference compromise. The new alternative they envisioned was a victory for both sides—a peaceful, democratic, and prosperous South Africa that could compete in the new global economy.

Through a process of laborious and continuous conflict resolution, war gradually turned to peace. This peace was not harmony but an ongoing, often conflictual process of seeking to address the basic needs of people for adequate food and shelter, safety, identity, and freedom. For the problems facing South Africa remained enormous. Poverty, malnutrition, and illiteracy were widespread. The economic inequalities were perhaps greater than in any other nation on earth. Crime was rising. Violence between Zulus and other tribes continued. Immigrants from other parts of Africa poured in by the millions. Meeting these challenges depended on harnessing the full potential of the Knowledge Revolution.

None of these problems, however, could detract from the extraordinary political transformation that had taken place. Thanks to the wisdom of the leadership in realizing that neither side could win without the other, what had seemed impossible proved not to be. Irreconcilable confrontation gave way to peaceful cooperation.

BACK TO THE NETWORK

Accompanying the shift in logic is a momentous change in the way people organize themselves in society—with considerable implications for the resolution of conflicts.

The Flattening of the Pyramids

Of all the dramatic changes in the world in the second half of the twentieth century, none was as astonishing as the sudden collapse of the Soviet Union. In less than twenty-six months, the Berlin Wall came down, the nations of Eastern Europe were released from Soviet control, and the Soviet Union itself broke up into fifteen separate republics. The first democratic elections took place and rigidly controlled economies began to give way to free markets. If anyone had predicted a transformation in the Soviet Union of such magnitude and speed, they would have been dismissed as wishful thinkers. The Soviet Union then had the most powerful army in the world. It possessed more nuclear bombs than any nation on earth. It had a highly sophisticated and intrusive apparatus for spying on its own citizens and ruthlessly repressing any sign of dissent. Yet no number of Red Army divisions, no number of nuclear bombs, no number of penal camps could resist the force of the Knowledge Revolution.

The Soviet leadership headed by Mikhail Gorbachev realized they were in a new era. In order to compete economically and militarily in the age of knowledge, they could not remain a closed, hierarchical, highly centralized system. They needed to open up internally and externally in order to release the initiative and creativity of their people. "Glasnost"—openness—became the new catchword.

In the old Soviet Union, all knowledge was controlled. On one academic research visit at a tense time in U.S.-Soviet relations in 1984, my colleague Bruce Allyn and I found ourselves tailed at night by agents of the KGB. They probably suspected us of trying to smuggle out our friend Anatoly Rybakov's long-suppressed novel about the Stalinist period, *Children of the Arbat*. If so, they were wrong. Quite apart from this, conversations with Russian friends had to be circumspect because rooms and phones were routinely bugged. The copying machine at the research institute where we worked was kept under strict lock and key; every copy made required official approval. The fear was palpable and real: Many of our friends had lost family members to Stalin's death camps, where millions were murdered.

Then, a few years later, everything changed. A pyramid of power as great as any the world had ever seen began to collapse. People I had known as closet dissidents ran for office and many were elected to the new democratizing legislature. *Children of the Arbat* was published in Moscow and around the world to widespread acclaim. Academic colleagues of mine went into business and became capitalist entrepreneurs. Computers and fax machines became ubiquitous. The pace of change seemed dizzying, so rapid and dramatic that one

Russian friend boasted to me, "Bill, if *you* want to go to a different country, you have to travel. All *I* have to do is to wake up in the morning."

From an anthropologist's perspective, the collapse of the Soviet Union was part of a much larger trend in human social evolution:

- For millennia, the very symbol of hierarchy was the institution of absolute monarchy. People believed in the divine right of kings. Three centuries ago, absolute monarchy was almost universal. Today, it has all but vanished.
- Two centuries ago, the institution of slavery was widespread and seemed destined to last forever. That some human beings were masters and others slaves was believed to be in the natural order of things. Yet today slavery has been abolished almost everywhere.
- A century ago, the fates of the majority of the world's peoples were controlled by a handful of colonial powers, largely European. Perhaps the most dramatic change in international politics in the twentieth century has been the collapse of the great empires—among them the British, the French, the Portuguese, the Austro-Hungarian, the Ottoman, the German, the Dutch, and, most recently, the Soviet.
- A century ago, half of humanity, the world's women, were socially and legally subordinated to their fathers, husbands, and brothers. In many places, women were treated as the property of men. Almost nowhere did women have the right to vote. The process is still under way, but the women's rights movement has made remarkable progress in overturning male prerogatives and domination.

Almost everywhere, it has become harder for people to use coercion to subjugate others and to resolve conflicts in their favor by squashing dissent. As UN Secretary-General Kofi Annan remarked in 1998, "Dictators who want to suppress the spread of information are going to have nightmares. . . . In quite a few areas, we have had revolutions that have been caused by fax . . . and Internet."

The Return of the Network

What happened in the Soviet Union is taking place in all domains of human life—from politics to the family to the economy. In the place once reserved for the orderly authoritarian hierarchy is emerging something amorphous, seemingly chaotic and messy: the old self-organizing, cooperative network that characterized human life for most of our history.

A network is people sharing information and resources. If a pyramid has the social structure of an army, a network has the social structure of a street market or a town meeting. Whereas pyramids are usually held together by coercion, networks are held together by mutual interest. While pyramids tend to block their members from leaving, networks generally offer alternatives and exits to their members. It is hard to leave an army, easy to leave a street market or to vote for another political party.

Two centuries ago, at the time of the American and French revolutions, it was hard to imagine how societies could be governed without an absolute ruler. How could the rabble rule itself? people asked. Even in the early United States, there was a move afoot to crown George Washington king. Yet the idea of self-government took root and somehow it worked, and on a surprisingly sustainable basis. More than two centuries later, the United States has proved to be one of the longest-running and most stable governments on earth.

In 1776, democracy was very much an exception. Today it is fast becoming the rule. Much progress remains to be made and setbacks are all too possible, even in the most democratic nations. Still, the extraordinary fact is that, at the turn of the millennium, for the first time in recorded history, the majority of states in the world are in some, even if rudimentary, stage of democracy.

No trend has more hopeful implications for the prevention of war. Consider the remarkable constant that, over the last two centuries of the unfolding Knowledge Revolution, no two democracies—liberal representative governments with juridical rights for their citizens—have gone to war with each other. Democracies have made war, to be sure, but with authoritarian regimes. There have been bitter disputes between the United States and Great Britain, for example, over the border with Canada, or between France and Britain over colonial aspirations in Africa, but the democracies involved have always found ways in the end to negotiate rather than go to war.

The changes are taking place in the large and in the small. With the Knowledge Revolution, power relationships are also beginning to flatten in the family. In many cultures, families are moving away from the paternalistic hierarchy where the father was considered the supreme authority, the mother was expected to be subservient to him, and the children subservient to both. With women demanding equality, children are beginning to do the same. The trend is toward a more horizontal, more democratic network where everyone—mother, father, and children—participates in making decisions.

The shift from pyramid to network is just as evident in the marketplace. Businesses that were formerly hyperorganized to establish rigid control from the top down over every activity and expense are now decentralizing into networks. Just as political empires are breaking up into federations and confederations, so too are economic empires. In the late 1980s and early 1990s, Asea Brown Boveri (ABB), a Swiss-Swedish company, at the time the world's largest power-engineering business, employing over two hundred thousand employees, broke itself up into a network of thirteen hundred separate companies, each averaging only two hundred people in size. Each company was linked to the others by electronic communications and through frequent meetings for the purpose of exchanging new ideas. The shift to the network, far from hurting its efficiency, increased its profitability so much so that it became a model to other corporations. Its headquarters staff in Zurich shrank from four thousand people to less than two hundred. "We are not a global business," its CEO Percy Barnevik exclaimed. "We are a collection of local businesses with intense global coordination."

Just as the computer is changing from a box with wires inside it to a network of computers, so the modern organization is changing from a box with people inside it to a network of people and organizations. The organization is the network; the network is the organization.

What is driving the shift to the network perhaps more than anything is the need to capitalize on the new basic resource—knowledge. To survive and thrive in the knowledge economy, organizations of all kinds, from companies to countries, have come to recognize the urgency of breaking down walls of all kinds—communication barriers, tariff barriers, and barriers of rank and status—anything that interferes with the information-sharing process through which new knowledge and wealth are generated. Whereas pyramidal organizations create and reinforce boundaries, network organizations erase boundaries by making connections across them. The tearing down of the Berlin Wall has become a metaphor for what is happening around the globe.

Perhaps the most visible recent sign of the spread of the network is the rise of the Internet. A network of computer networks, the Internet is growing rapidly as a means of communication, conversation, and doing business. If the Age of Agriculture can be symbolized by the pyramids of Egypt, sedentary piles of material, then perhaps the Age of Knowledge can be symbolized by the Internet, a constantly shifting, moving mass of information. Consider the experience of Alberto Villamizar, the Colombian government's anti-kidnapping "czar." In an interview in Bogotá in 1996, he told me how difficult it had always been to communicate with guerrilla groups in the jungle. A letter often took six months to receive a reply. But just that day, to his surprise, he had received a reply to his last letter sent only a few days earlier. The reply he showed me had come via E-mail.

The change from pyramid to network is still far from absolute.

The shift has been gradual and marked by occasional reversals. Pyramidal institutions and pronounced economic inequalities remain everywhere. Indeed, hierarchy as one way of organizing human society will undoubtedly remain. The basic trend is clear, however. The fundamental relationship between human beings is shifting from vertical to horizontal.

No one should be under the illusion that the change means less conflict. Rather, it means more. For horizontal organizations do not suppress conflict, they surface it, which is why democracies often seem so quarrelsome and turbulent when compared with more authoritarian societies. Horizontal organizations, however, do have far less capacity to coerce others and they do have the capacity to transform the increased conflict into constructive negotiations. The potential for preventing organized violence and domination is thereby greatly increased.

THE INGATHERING

One evening during my time with the Bushmen deep in the Kalahari Desert, I was sitting by a campfire listening to one of their songs. I thought I recognized a word or two, so I inquired. The lyrics were translated for me as: "Mama, please buy me an Apollo Eleven." However far from urban civilization, these people had heard the news about the first manned mission to the moon; nomads to the core, they aspired to wander out into space.

This incident underscored for me one other critical change brought about by the Knowledge Revolution. It has extended the network outward until, in the last analysis, it encompasses all of humanity. It has brought about the signal evolutionary event of our era, the ingathering of humanity into one interactive and interdependent global community. Such a dramatic change could not fail but to have consequences on the future of human conflict.

Nowhere is the web of interdependence more obvious than in

daily economic life. Every day hundreds of millions of people from opposite parts of the planet cooperate, directly and indirectly, with one another in the global marketplace. While global trading networks have existed for centuries, today's ties operate on a far greater scale. Few human beings can survive anymore without drawing on the worldwide web of economic links. Every day the network—economic, social, and political—spreads out a little further, encompassing more and more people. Whereas pyramidal institutions grow through the accumulation of centralized power, networks extend themselves through communication and the decentralized initiative of countless individuals and organizations. Humanity is weaving a boundaryless web.

To manage this growing interdependence, the world's nations are experimenting gingerly with various forms of political association. Europe, a collection of warring states at the start of the twentieth century, finds itself increasingly confederated at century's end. NAFTA in North America, Mercosur in South America, and ASEAN in Southeast Asia represent other regional efforts to integrate. At the global level, intergovernmental organizations such as the United Nations and the International Monetary Fund play a larger role in decision making. They are joined by thousands of nongovernmental organizations, which work on every imaginable issue, from security to trade and from the environment to the allocation of the airwaves for telecommunications. From an anthropological perspective, the creation of the European Union and the United Nations is just part of a millennia-long trend in which the different tribes of the earth have been encompassed into larger and larger political units. Humanity may now be in the penultimate phase of its political integration.

More Conflict

Increasing interdependence means more conflict, not less. As any family member can attest, the quarrels among those who depend closely on one another are the most problematic. The more interlinked the world's tribes become, the more they insist on self-determination. European integration has only intensified the activity of separatist movements—the Basques and the Catalans in Spain, the Scots and the Welsh in Great Britain, the Bretons and the Corsicans in France, and the Lombards in Italy. As long as they can share in the prosperity and security of the greater Europe, they wonder, why do they need to take orders from Madrid or London, Paris or Rome?

More Vulnerability

As the web spreads and tightens, it becomes more vulnerable to destructive conflict. Strife comes to hurt not just the immediate parties but people far away. The Middle East war in October 1973 triggered a global oil crisis. A strike in June 1998 by workers at a single General Motors metal-stamping plant in Flint, Michigan, forced factories all over the United States to lay off an estimated one hundred and forty-six thousand workers, and caused economic growth for the entire country to drop almost one percent for a period of six months.

With the communications revolution, destructive behavior spreads more easily across borders. Jet travel and open borders mean that a terrorist can strike anywhere on the planet, even the wealthiest and most secure corners of the world. American politicians invest billions in trying to create a shield over the United States to protect against missiles when a nuclear bomb can be easily smuggled into the country in the back of a pickup truck. The joke among security specialists is that the best place to hide such a bomb would be in a bale of marijuana. No place on earth is completely safe. With the Knowledge Revolution, humanity has reentered an age of vulnerability reminiscent of hunter-gatherer times.

A Potentially Stronger Third Side

Growing vulnerability means greater motivation for the community to take action to prevent harmful conflict. Each person has an interest, not just because war is pernicious, but because peace is precious. A strong third side could potentially emerge from the network of economic, political, and moral ties, just as it has long done among simple societies like the Bushmen and the Semai.

The Knowledge Revolution also creates unprecedented opportunities to mobilize the third side. Thanks to mass media, fax machines, and the Internet, large groups of people spread out across great distances can confer about their common problems. Global conferences and worldwide polling make increasingly possible the articulation of the "will of humanity." For the first time, we have the opportunity to shape in a conscious fashion our destiny as a species. Collectively, we can, if we choose, issue a resounding "No" to violence and coercion and an emphatic "Yes" to coexistence and conflict resolution. People anywhere can act as thirdsiders everywhere.

THE NEGOTIATION REVOLUTION

In response to the new logic of conflict and the flattening of society into a global network, a quiet revolution is taking place in the way in which people make decisions jointly to resolve their differences. The magnitude of this development did not really crystallize for me until the summer of 1994 when I received a phone call from Ford Motor Company.

Ed Sketch and Nanette Des Noyers, from the Ford Executive Development Center, asked whether I could help spread the ideas and skills of negotiation and conflict resolution throughout the company—more than three hundred thousand people located around the world. It seemed an unusual request, particularly coming from an old and well-established business, one of the largest in the world, an icon of the industrial era. "Why conflict resolution?" I asked Sketch and Des Noyers.

Ford, they explained, had always been a pyramidal organization organized along strict functional lines—manufacturing, for example, was rigidly separated from marketing. Decision-making was so vertical and communication across departments so limited that departments were called "chimneys." Moreover, Ford was divided into a host of regionally based organizations in North America, Europe, etc. that made their own different cars. New ideas for making cars better and more cheaply, or for pooling resources, stopped at the walls separating departments and regions; the rest of Ford did not benefit. Decision making, centralized at the top, was slow and inflexible, incapable of responding quickly to the opportunities and dangers in a rapidly changing global marketplace.

The top leadership at Ford, Sketch and Des Noyers continued, had recognized that, if the company was going to remain competitive, radical changes were required. The chimneys had to come down. Alex Trotman, the charismatic president of Ford, had convened a "study team" to design the new twenty-first-century Ford Motor Company. Some two dozen managers from different levels in the organization, from different departments, and from different continents, were brought together for five months in Detroit and instructed to come up with a plan. It was an intense, somewhat chaotic process. Instead of lower-level managers deferring to their seniors, everyone was treated as an equal. In the end, the "network structure" of the team encouraged creative brainstorming and overcame deep-seated departmental conflicts through collaborative negotiation, and both-gain solutions. To the surprise of all, the study team emerged with a unanimously agreed-upon set of recommendations for transforming the old pyramidal Ford into a global network. Trotman and the board accepted the plan and baptized it Ford 2000.

Ford 2000 was one of the largest corporate culture change initiatives in the world. In the new Ford, work was reorganized so that people from different countries, departments, and levels would have to cooperate as teams to achieve their common objectives. A manager in a Brazilian factory manufacturing small cars reported not only to his local boss but also to the manager in Britain responsible for engineering the car's design. Work teams were designed to be "self-organizing" and flexible leaders were encouraged to be "facilitative" rather than authoritarian. Walls between departments and countries were torn down, enabling knowledge to flow more rapidly throughout the entire organization.

As the study team had learned from their own experience, however, none of these changes would work unless people learned how to handle their differences cooperatively. The new network structure generated lots of conflict as people from different departments and countries tried to work together. No longer could they turn to their own separate bosses to resolve their conflicts. Ford therefore wanted their managers all around the world to learn the new skills of collaborative negotiation in order to resolve conflicts quickly and effectively across the barriers of hierarchy, functional specialization, and culture. Intrigued by the challenge, I spent a good part of the ensuing two years working with them, helping to teach tens of thousands of people through leadership seminars, videotapes, and personal coaching.

Negotiation Becomes Ubiquitous

Each profession sees the world through its own prism. Wherever they look, business executives see financial opportunities. Politicians see unconverted voters. Carpenters see houses in need of repair. As a negotiation specialist, I may be guilty of the same distortion, but wherever I look, I see an unheralded revolution happening in business, in the family, in the neighborhood, and in politics. Call it the Negotiation Revolution. As the pyramids collapse into networks, the primary form of decision making changes from vertical—the people on top giving orders—to horizontal—everyone negotiating. We appear to be reverting to our ancestral heritage as Homo Negotiator.

Nowadays, people seem to be negotiating everywhere. It starts first thing in the morning in the family. Who will do the household chores? Who is in charge of the family finances? "We've gone from marriages where very little needed to be negotiated," reports family psychologist Howard Markham, "to ones where nearly everything needs to be negotiated." The process continues at work with co-workers, bosses, and employees. People negotiate with customers and suppliers, with banks, accountants, and lawyers, not to speak of government authorities. We negotiate from the moment we get up until the moment we go to bed.

During the talks I give on negotiation, I usually ask members of the audience how much time they spend negotiating—broadly defined as engaging in back-and-forth communication trying to reach agreement. Whether the audience is managers or schoolteachers, governmental officials or engineers, Americans or Malaysians, the response is invariably the same: The majority of people say they spend over half their waking hours negotiating. Asked if the amount is increasing or decreasing, almost everyone agrees it is going up.

In the 1970s, the subject was hardly a defined field of study and training. Almost no courses were offered in universities. Two decades later, negotiation courses are ubiquitous—taught in most schools of business, government, and law, in most large corporations and many government agencies, and even in elementary schools. The hunger for knowledge about this subject has been overwhelming.

A shift is taking place not just in the quantity of negotiation but in the style of negotiation. Traditionally, negotiation had a "win-lose" quality to it; it was seen as just another form of warfare. Increasingly, however, in response to the gradually shifting logic of conflict, people are searching for methods to arrive at solutions for mutual gain. In my work as a third party consultant, I have had many opportunities to witness hard-bitten union leaders and skeptical managers, for instance, gradually come to see that "mutual gains bargaining" can lead to tangibly better results than shouting at each other and seeking to defeat the other. "I remember the heartburn, the headaches, the sleepless nights," says teacher union negotiator

Arnie Klayman. "This way [mutual gains bargaining] is much less threatening." Instead of trying to divide up an economic pie that is often shrinking with intensified global competition, management and labor seek to expand the pie through innovative ways to increase productivity and share the profits. "Getting along—that's our competitive advantage," one formerly skeptical union leader, Denny Morris of the Paperworkers Union, told me.

Negotiation Becomes a Necessity

The upsurge in cooperative negotiation can be explained, in part, by increasing interdependence. In order to get their jobs done nowadays, people depend on dozens of individuals and organizations over whom they exercise no direct control. They cannot impose a decision; they are compelled to negotiate. Even in the military, the epitome of a pyramidal organization where people are accustomed to give orders and receive instant obedience, the new reality applies. On a lecture tour in Colombia, I was puzzled to receive a request from General Zúñiga, the chief of the armed forces, to give a talk to his generals and admirals. They required negotiating skills, Zúñiga explained, in order to obtain the budget they sought from politicians, the cease-fires they wanted from guerrilla leaders, and the cooperation they needed from their peers. Even with direct subordinates, he added, they could not get the kind of performance they wanted by simple orders; they needed to negotiate for it.

In the corporate world, work is increasingly accomplished in teams and task forces, business is carried out through joint ventures and strategic alliances, and growth is achieved through mergers and acquisitions. Each of these organizational forms requires continuous negotiation—and renegotiation as the business environment changes. Negotiation has become a growth industry.

In the political world, negotiation is the lifeblood of democracy. If every issue had to be decided by voting alone, democracy would quickly become paralyzed. Legislators spend most of their time wheeling and dealing, seeking to reach consensus before they vote. Similarly, if every dispute had to be settled in court, the judicial system would soon find itself overwhelmed. More than nine out of every ten lawsuits filed in court are eventually settled through negotiation. And, contrary to what I learned as a schoolboy, presidents do not sit at their desk simply giving orders; if they did, nothing would happen. Instead, they spend most of their time trying to persuade different constituencies—legislators, interest groups, funders, and voters—to support their programs and their reelection. Negotiation has become the preeminent decision-making process in democracy, just as it has in business and personal life.

Perhaps most promisingly, negotiation has the potential to replace domination and war in the international arena as the leading way to handle serious disputes. As General Lebed, the hard-nosed Russian general who negotiated an end to the war in Chechnya, exclaimed, "I know for sure that all wars, even if they are hundred-year wars, end in negotiations and peace. So, should one fight a hundred years and kill lots of people to come to a negotiated settlement? Perhaps we should start with it."

THE RECURRENCE

What struck me most during the time I was working with Ford Motor Company was how often I was reminded of the Bushmen and other simple societies. Here were the most modern management ideas being put into practice, yet they were reinventions of common practices I had seen among hunter-gatherers. Hunter-gatherers have long used "flexible self-organizing work teams." With their early morning chatter, I have watched the Bushmen spontaneously organize themselves to do the day's work of hunting, gathering, and making simple tools. Eons before it became a corporate fashion, simple societies practiced "facilitative leadership." The leaders led by persuasion, not coercion. And "collaborative decision making" was used to resolve their differences around the campfire.

I came to appreciate how these similar practices emerged from similar working conditions. Modern-day managers and hunter-gatherers both live in a constantly shifting environment, pursuing scattered and mobile resources. For hunter-gatherers, the resources are wild plants and animals; for managers, they are bits of knowledge. Both groups rely on the constant exchange of information. Hunter-gatherers trade tips about weather, the whereabouts of food, and threats from predators; modern-day managers trade data about shifting markets and competitors' products. Both groups are also nomadic by necessity: Hunter-gatherers are always on the move in search of food, while the new knowledge managers are constantly traveling, whether in person or by telecommunication.

The difference between hunter-gatherer communities and the emerging global knowledge society are admittedly enormous—in scale and population, in sophistication of technology, in organizational complexity, and in independence from the natural environment. Yet it was the resemblances that, as an anthropologist, I found striking.

It may be imprudent to describe large historical patterns while in the midst of them, since such patterns usually appear clear only in retrospect. It is hard to distinguish between temporary fluctuations and long-term trends. Nevertheless, let me offer my educated hunch. Humanity is returning to dependence on a basic resource that is, as in hunter-gatherer times, an expandable pie. We are returning to the horizontal relationships that existed among human beings for most of human evolution. The network is once again becoming the defining social organization for the human community. Societies obsessed with territory and boundaries are slowly becoming more open and inclusive. Just as before, the logic of conflict is less win-lose, and more a choice between both-lose or both-win. Just as before, decision-making is increasingly taking the form of negotiation. If ten thousand years ago compulsion began to replace cooperation as a principal

THE RECURRENCE

TYPE OF SOCIETY

		Simple hunter-gatherers	Complex agriculturalists	Knowledge society
C O N D I T I O N S	Basic resource	Expandable pie (wild foods)	Fixed pie (land & power)	Expandable pie (knowledge)
	Basic logic of conflict	Both-gain or both-lose	Win-lose	Both-gain or both-lose
	Basic form of organization	Open network	Closed pyramid	Open network
	Basic form of decision making	Negotiation	Orders	Negotiation
		⬇ COEXISTENCE	⬇ COERCION	⬇ COEXISTENCE?

A Simplified Depiction of History

way of getting needs met, so now cooperation is beginning to replace compulsion. *The pyramids of power are collapsing into the time-honored networks of negotiation.*

There is no certainty that the Recurrence will bring more peace. Conflicts could even get worse, particularly in the shorter term. For we live in a time of transition. The Knowledge Revolution has made available ever more destructive technologies, whereas many human societies are still caught up in old habits of warring over territory and power. Individuals and nations have been learning the hard way about the changing logic of conflict; both sides often end up losing.

We should not expect that peace will suddenly be handed to us. Changing old habits of adversarial disputing will require a great deal of hard work.

With this understood, it remains extraordinarily fortuitous that many of the social conditions that helped our nomadic hunter-gatherer ancestors learn to coexist appear to be reemerging today. *The Knowledge Revolution offers us the most promising opportunity in ten thousand years to create a co-culture of coexistence, cooperation, and constructive conflict.*

Part Three

THE TEN ROLES
OF THE THIRD SIDE

THE TEN ROLES OF THE THIRD SIDE

The big remaining question is "How?" How do we realize our present opportunity to prevent destructive conflict and violence? If the third side is the most sensible alternative to force, what practically can we do to mobilize it?

Our goal cannot—and should not—be to eliminate conflict. For conflict is as natural and as necessary as rainfall. It brings about change. In the form of business competition, it creates prosperity. It lies at the heart of the democratic process. The best decisions result not from a superficial consensus but from surfacing different points of view and searching for creative solutions. Few injustices, moreover, are addressed without serious conflict. We need more conflict, not less.

Like rainfall, however, too much conflict at once can cause huge amounts of damage. Just as we control floods by constructing a series of canals, sluices, and dams to divert excess water, so we may be able to channel conflict into cooperation by employing a series of third-side approaches.

The strategy is to catch conflict as early as possible before it escalates. In Shakespeare's words, "A little fire is quickly trodden out, which, being suffered, rivers cannot quench." Conflict, after all, does not come out of nowhere but typically proceeds from latent tension, develops into overt conflict, erupts into a power struggle, and from there crosses the threshold of destructive conflict and violence. As thirdsiders, our aim is not to suppress conflict altogether but simply to keep the trajectory of escalation below this threshold.

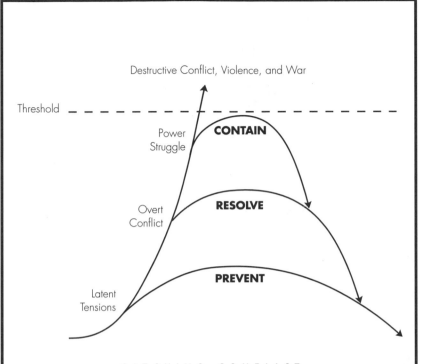

Threshold

Destructive Conflict, Violence, and War

Power
Struggle **CONTAIN**

Overt
Conflict **RESOLVE**

PREVENT

Latent
Tensions

CATCHING CONFLICT
BEFORE IT ESCALATES

*We have at least three major opportunities to channel the conflict's vertical momentum, which leads to destructive struggle, into a horizontal impulse, which leads to constructive change. The first is to **prevent** destructive conflict from emerging in the first place by addressing latent tensions. The second is to **resolve** any overt conflicts which do develop. The third is to **contain** any escalating power struggles that temporarily escape resolution. What is not prevented is resolved; and what is not resolved is contained. The motto of the third side is thus: "Contain if necessary, resolve if possible, best of all prevent."*

Chapter 5

PREVENT

Provider, Teacher, Bridge-Builder

*Confront the difficult while it is still easy; accomplish
the great task by a series of small acts.*

— Lao Tzu

"The greatest lesson my father taught me,"
the Bushman elder Korakoradue told me,
"was, 'Never cause a problem, so that it won't
have to be settled. Try to live in harmony.'"
Every day in such horizontal societies becomes
an exercise in prevention.

We are learning in our modern societies that prevention is the
best cure when it comes to fighting disease. The best way to deal
with heart attacks, for example, better than the most sophisticated
bypass operations, is to prevent them through good nutrition, regular exercise, and medication. As the Bushmen demonstrate, the priority of prevention holds in the arena of destructive conflict too.

Prevention in vertically organized societies generally entails suppression of conflict. In horizontally organized societies, however,
suppression is neither feasible nor desirable. Prevention means addressing the root causes of conflict and laying the foundation for the
cooperative management of differences.

Needs, Skills, and Relationships

Conflict usually arises in the first place from frustrated *needs*. This helps explain why the Bushmen go to such lengths to share food and other resources. Anthropologist Lorna Marshall once studied what happens when Bushman hunters come back to camp with an eland, a large antelope. To her amazement, the eland was divided, in successive waves of gifts to kin and friends, at least sixty-three times *before* it was even cooked, after which the meat was distributed widely yet again. In a Bushman camp no one is allowed to go hungry. The idea of eating alone and not sharing shocks them. "Lions could do that," they say, "but not human beings!" Sharing helps everyone meet their basic needs, thus preventing conflict.

Tensions over conflicting needs can easily escalate when people lack the proper *skills* or attitudes to defuse them. The Bushmen, therefore, carefully teach their children to control their tempers and refrain from violence. Children learn to tolerate and respect others, and to avoid giving offense. They are also taught to share what they have. When two little girls were quarreling over a blanket, Purana, an elder I interviewed, explained how he told the one with the blanket that "she is very lucky that Bise [the good god] gave it to her and, to show her happiness, she should share the blanket with her friend." He was teaching them how to find ways in which both could "win."

Children learn mainly from watching what adults do. The adults place great value on talking as a way to handle problems; indeed, the Bushmen call themselves "the people who talk too much." Go into a Bushman camp and you will hear the steady stream of chatter and joking. The sounds of human voices seem to rise from the very desert, from the early hours of the morning to the late hours of the evening. The constant talk lets people know how everyone is feeling and whether any frictions need to be smoothed or problems hashed out. Listeners continually respond to people's stories, often echoing what they hear. In effect, they are practicing what modern psychologists call "active listening," a technique to defuse negative emotions. Humor and fits of laughter punctuate the talk. People continually express and release their emotions, thus preventing tensions from building.

Good *relationships* are key to preventing conflict. A web of emotional and economic ties among the Bushmen fosters mutual understanding, trust, and clear communication. Through constant visits and the exchange of gifts, they nurture their relationships in other bands as well as in their own. As one !Kung Bushman described the gift-giving custom to anthropologist Richard Lee, "*Hxaro* is when I take a thing of value and give it to you. Later, much later, when you find some good thing, you give it back to me. When I find something good, I will give it to you, and so we will pass the years together." Marshall reported that the necklaces of cowrie shells she gave as parting gifts in 1951 had, by her return the following year, showed up as single shells on people's necklaces throughout a vast region. Such gift-giving cultivates and maintains amicable relationships and reduces envy and friction.

Our aim in modern societies should not be to copy the Bushmen; their circumstances differ greatly from ours and their efforts, in any case, often fall short of perfection. Our challenge rather is to learn to embed prevention in the fabric of normal life as they do. Taking a cue from them, we can enable others to meet their basic *needs,* give them the *skills* to handle disputes, and help them forge *relationships* across lines of conflict. These constitute the three main preventive roles of the third side: the Provider, the Teacher, and the Bridge-Builder.

WHY CONFLICT ESCALATES		WAYS TO PREVENT CONFLICT
Frustrated needs	→	1. The Provider
Poor skills	→	2. The Teacher
Weak relationships	→	3. The Bridge-Builder

1. THE PROVIDER
ENABLING PEOPLE TO MEET THEIR NEEDS

"I've got to check in on America's worst nightmare," announced the Reverend Eugene Rivers. "Ten-year-old kid. His daddy was shot through the head. His mama's got 'chemical' issues. He's a ringleader. You can just see it. He's been getting into trouble—they already caught him with a knife. He'll be packing a Glock before long, unless someone gets to him."

"Hey, Money," Rivers told the boy in a meeting arranged in the school library. "You know what I'm doing here? I'm gonna keep you outta jail." The boy stared at him without expression. "What do you like to do?" Rivers asked. "You like the movies?" Kareem nodded. "What do you want to see?"

Kareem finally spoke. "*Anaconda*," he mumbled.

"Tell you what," Rivers said. "I'll take you to see *Anaconda* if you can stay out of trouble between now and Friday. You know what I'm saying? No more knives. I'm gonna wring your monkey butt, I catch you with a knife."

"I didn't have no knife," he said.

"Oh, yes, you did," Rivers said. "Now I'm gonna be checking up on you. I'm gonna come round your house, talk to your mother after school. Where are you gonna be?"

"Home."

"Home, what?"

"Home, sir."

"Give me five," Rivers said, and Kareem dutifully held out his palm for a slap. "All right! You're the *man!*" Rivers said, standing. Kareem also stood, and the Reverend hugged him close. "You know that I love you, right?" Kareem smiled nervously. "We're gonna keep you out of jail. Go on back to school now. All right? *Oh-kay.*"

Afterwards, Rivers said, "You see that smile? You see the way he lit up? See, he's doable. We can get him. But you got to do an intensive thing with him. He'll go for the love thing, 'cause he's never seen it from a black male before."

Whatever the surface issues in dispute, the underlying cause of conflict usually lies in the deprivation of basic human needs like love and respect. Frustration leads people to bully others, to use violence, and to grab someone else's things. If disputes resemble the matches that light the fire, the frustration of needs is like the flammable tinder.

The most basic human needs include food (and other necessities for living), safety, identity, and freedom. Each provides a form of security—economic, physical, cultural, and political. Put more simply, each person wants to feel well, safe, respected, and free. If we as thirdsiders can help address one or more of these four needs, as Rivers does with Kareem, we can avert much destructive conflict. The role of the Provider is thus fourfold: to share, to protect, to respect, and to free.

Share Resources, Share Knowledge

"What happens if another group comes to hunt on your land?" I once asked a Semai tribesman.

"When other groups are hungry, we let them hunt on our land as if it were theirs," he replied. "If someone in the other group goes hungry, the spirits of the forest will be unhappy and someone might fall sick and die, and we would then be responsible."

The Semai perceive their world as an interdependent one in which the unmet needs of their neighbor will affect them personally. For them, enabling their neighbors to meet their basic needs is simple common sense.

When people feel that there is not enough to go around for everyone, fear and anxiety rise and fights may break out. Hungry people can scarcely be blamed for coveting the food of their well-fed neighbors. Not coincidentally, those societies that share their resources most equitably, such as the Semai or the Scandinavian nations, have relatively low rates of crime and violence. *"Lagom"* is a Swedish expression used when passing food or drink around the table, meaning "Take just enough so that there is enough for everyone."

The Knowledge Revolution creates the possibility of sufficiency even in the poor parts of the world. If a hunter-gatherer group surviving in the wilderness will not let one member go hungry while others have food, surely a twenty-first-century world can do the same. Enough food exists for everyone and the cost of purchasing and distributing it would be a minuscule portion of what is spent on arms and armies. The same holds true when it comes to addressing any of the elementary material needs of human beings such as clean water, warm clothes, simple medical care, and shelter from the elements.

Just as important as sharing scarce resources is sharing knowledge, educating people so that they can meet their own needs. As the old adage goes, "Give a man a fish and you feed him for a day. Teach a man to fish and you feed him for a lifetime." Boston's success in reducing teenage violence stemmed in part from the community, business, and government working together to provide over ten thousand after-school jobs for teenagers at risk, along with educational programs and job training. Churches in Rio de Janeiro aim to do the same by educating poor young men for jobs other than selling drugs.

Jobs enable people to provide for their own needs. In one Fort Worth neighborhood, the crime rate fell by more than half after community activists helped local youth find employment at the airport and elsewhere. The community police officers assisted by distributing job applications. "This was a neighborhood where people wouldn't even talk to the police, and now they were flagging down patrol cars so that they could get a job application from them," reports community activist Deborah Hernandez.

Peace does not require great prosperity. Consider the little country of Costa Rica, not rich despite its name, but with a record of internal and external peace during the last half of the twentieth century that any of the rich nations might envy. The Costa Ricans achieved this record by eliminating their army and using their resources instead for health, education, and development. For many years, Costa Rica spent a larger percentage of its government budget on health than any other country in the world. It had the second highest education budget, proportionally, in the world. While expensive, these social programs were credited with helping head off the immensely more costly social uprisings and revolutions that occurred in almost all of Costa Rica's neighbors in Central America.

Protect

Medieval England had an estimated homicide rate of fifty per hundred thousand inhabitants. Today, England's rate is less than one twenty-fifth of that. One major reason is that people feel safe. Police are present. No one feels compelled, indeed no one is allowed, to carry a weapon. The community provides protection for everyone.

The same lesson is being learned at the international level. During the first half of the twentieth century, the nations of Europe engaged in arms buildups that inflamed fears, triggered arms races, and led to catastrophic wars. Nations sought to make themselves feel more secure by making others feel less secure—and it did not work. In the 1970s and 1980s, European nations began to learn to respect the security needs of others. To reduce fear and distrust, they agreed to exchange military observers and to notify neighbors before carrying out military exercises. No nation, they came to recognize, can feel truly secure unless its neighbors do too. True security lies in common security.

Respect

The filmmaker Steven Spielberg tells the story of how, when he was thirteen, a fifteen-year-old bully at school made his life hell, beating him up and throwing stink bombs at him. So one day he approached the bully and said, "You know, I'm making a home movie about fighting the Nazis and I was wondering if you'd like to play the war hero." The bully laughed at him but a few days later came back and grudgingly agreed. Dressed up in fatigues with a helmet and backpack, he acted the role of hero in the movie. After that, Spielberg says, the bully became his best friend. He had received the recognition and attention that had led him to bully in the first place.

Human beings have a host of emotional needs—for love and recognition, for belonging and identity, for purpose and meaning to their lives. If all these needs had to be subsumed in one word, it might be "respect." People want to be recognized and respected for who they are.

The frustration of these needs creates conflict everywhere. In families, children competing for parental attention fight frequently. In the neighborhood, teenagers join gangs in order to feel a sense of belonging; they regularly kill each other because of a perceived lack of respect. In the workplace, the struggle for recognition and meaning can escalate, sometimes even into violent tragedy. "I enjoyed my job, I loved my job. That's all I lived for, was to go to work," Robert Earl Mack reflected mournfully after he, in a fit of uncontrolled anger, killed his former supervisor and a labor relations specialist for terminating his twenty-five years of service at General Dynamics.

Most of the wars in the world today revolve around identity and respect. As one Turkish Kurd exclaimed to me after describing the suppression of Kurdish language and culture in Turkey, "I want to be able to live like a Kurd, think like a Kurd, and act like a Kurd!" Disrespect for a group's identity—and other basic needs—leads naturally enough to demands for a separate state that will address those needs, demands that in turn can trigger civil war.

By addressing young people's needs for meaning and respect, we as parents, teachers, and community members can help avert violence. In over fifty American cities, midnight basketball leagues use the attraction of the game to draw youth off the dangerous streets to self-esteem workshops and job training for meaningful jobs. In Milwaukee, a midnight basketball program was credited with a thirty percent drop in teenage violence; young men preferred to shoot baskets rather than to shoot each other. Similarly, noting that the hours just after school are peak hours for youth crime, dozens of communities around the United States have organized "homework clubs" that offer young people the chance to engage in stimulating activities after school. In one Florida town, for example, violent crime committed with guns dropped seventy percent in neighborhoods where homework programs operate.

In the workplace, too, the community can honor people's different identities. "We use the word 'inclusion' a lot," says Louis G. Lower, president of Allstate Insurance Company. "I just ask people to think back to times in their lives when they were excluded from something and to recall what emotions they felt. When I think back to those occasions in my own life, it's not something that creates a lot of energy. To us, diversity is bringing everyone into the house and making them feel that they belong and they're valued. It sounds basic and simplistic, but it's a big part of what diversity is for us." Without conscious efforts to respect people's differences, companies find it hard to attract and retain the best people. Respect pays off.

Providing respect also proves critical in reducing ethnic violence. In a world of more than six thousand intermixed ethnic groups, the solution cannot be a state for every ethnic group. Strong national cultures can survive without their own state—but only if the larger community respects their identity and their right to express it—as Catalans in Spain, Tamils in India, and Welsh in Great Britain can attest. When asked why his Bosnian city has enjoyed more ethnic tolerance than so many of its neighbors, Mayor Selim Beslagic explains, "In Tuzla, we have always given priority to respect for human dignity over belonging to a nation or an ethnic community."

The most striking image of mutual respect and appreciation comes from the island of Mauritius in the Indian Ocean with its rich mix of peoples, cultures, and religions—Africans, Indians, and Europeans, and Hindus, Muslims, and Christians. During the 1980s, in the kinds of economic hard times that have produced ethnic riots elsewhere, Mauritians succeeded in coexisting peacefully. The key, in the words of one leading citizen, was that "we consider each group, racial or religious, as a fruit—an apple, a pear, a mango. We don't want to make a marmalade where we mix up everything and have one marmalade with I don't know what taste. Instead we would like to have a fruit salad in which each one preserves its individual flavor and taste."

Free

The need for autonomy, for exercising a measure of control over one's life, runs deep. Even small children want to be able to do things themselves without help from adults. Teenagers struggle to define their identity as separate from their parents. Indeed, many of the wars of the last two centuries have been fought to secure freedom— freedom from feudalism and absolute monarchy, freedom from the grip of colonial powers, freedom from right-wing or left-wing dictatorships, and freedom from the domination of other ethnic or religious groups.

Providing freedom can begin in the family when parents invite young children to make their own decisions whenever possible: "Would you like to wear this outfit or that one?" It can continue at work where companies are learning that getting the most out of their employees requires freeing them to make as many of their own decisions as possible. At Saturn Corporation, a General Motors subsidiary, the old assembly line gave way to self-managed teams that took responsibility for producing a quality car within a given budget. Employees participated in production decisions, pricing decisions, and even capital appropriation decisions. The destructive conflicts so characteristic of employer-employee relations in the automobile industry gave way to constructive collaboration, which enabled the Saturn to become GM's only profitable small car.

Providing freedom can prevent war too. In 1992, Tatarstan, a state in the middle of the Russian Federation, seemed like one of the most dangerous flashpoints in the world. After centuries of Russian domination, Tatars wanted their independence. Despite heavy-handed threats from Moscow, the Tatar leadership held a referendum on independence and sovereignty, which voters overwhelmingly approved. The conflict threatened to turn into a civil war; many feared it would trigger the disintegration of the nuclear-armed federation— with incalculable consequences. In the end, however, reason prevailed. "We were independent for a day," Tatarstan President Mintimer Shaimiev once explained to me. The day after the referendum, the

Tatar government went to work negotiating a treaty with the Russian Federation. Months of arduous and creative discussions produced an agreement granting substantial economic and political self-government to Tatarstan. Civil war was averted.

Open Doors

As Providers, we may not necessarily be able to address others' needs directly. But we may be able to enable people to meet their own needs. Each of us can open doors to resources that others can use to help themselves.

Muhammad Yunus may not think of himself as engaged in prevention, but he is a champion Provider. In 1976, as a young economics professor in the famine-stricken nation of Bangladesh, he met a village woman making a bamboo chair. He asked her how much profit she earned and was astonished to learn that it was only two pennies a day. "Why?" he asked. She explained that she had no bamboo of her own and had to buy it from a trader, who required in return that she sell him the finished chair at the low price he set. Yunus asked how much she needed to be able to buy her own bamboo. "Thirty cents," she said. He loaned her the money and, several weeks later, returned to discover that she had become an entrepreneur with co-workers producing an entire line of chairs.

This experience led Yunus to found the Grameen Bank, which, since its founding in 1983, has provided credit, not aid, to more than two million poor people, mostly women, in tens of thousands of villages. The poor were not "creditworthy," skeptics argued; the loans would never be paid back. The borrowers of the Grameen Bank have proved the skeptics wrong; they have turned out to be far better credit risks than the rich, paying back on average ninety-seven percent of their loans. Now there are Grameen-like banks in over sixty countries, including the United States, enabling the poor to meet their needs with small loans.

2. THE TEACHER
GIVING PEOPLE SKILLS TO HANDLE CONFLICT

"I don't know how smart Heavy was," says Michael Lewis, who taught him conflict resolution in a course given in a maximum-security prison. "He was just a moose of a guy who apparently had a very quick temper, and who in his earlier days had been very quick with his fists. Sometime after Heavy got the training, a fellow prisoner told us, 'I can't believe it. Yesterday Heavy got into an argument and I thought he was going to drop the sucker right in his tracks. Heavy just kept talking to him!' The fellow prisoner was attributing it to the fact that Heavy had learned that he didn't have to drop people in their tracks. He could talk to them and get something out of that."

Sometimes people fight, like Heavy used to, simply because they know no other way to react when a need is frustrated and a serious difference arises. As a prospective husband in a relationship course put it, "The problem with most relationships is you don't have a mechanism to solve the problem as you're going. You know you want to resolve the problem but you don't know how." By helping people learn new values, perspectives, and skills, we as Teachers can show them a better way to deal with differences.

Delegitimize Violence

The first step is to teach that violence solves nothing. The Bushmen, for instance, carefully teach their children about the enormous cost of violence, the pain it causes, and the risks it poses to the entire community. In the United States, by contrast, violence is all too commonly glorified as the manly response to a slight or dispute. The community can help change these attitudes, however:

> Before he began his talk to a room full of teen-age boys, Michael Harrington asked three of them to hop about on one leg. He wanted the

boys to know what the last 25 years have been like for him. Harrington lost his right leg in the Vietnam war. When he returned home, Harrington told the hushed teen-agers, he would sometimes take his anger out on others. The only other sound in the room came from the clicking of Harrington's aluminum crutches. "Physical force has gotten me nowhere," he said. "Talking is the way. Negotiating is the way. Violence isn't."

The Veterans Education Project in Massachusetts deploys veterans of America's wars such as Harrington to schools around the state. By telling their stories about how violence has affected them personally, the veterans get teenagers to talk about the violence in their own lives. "We explain that once you learn to respond violently on the street, it's hard to go home and be a caring son, boyfriend, or father," says veteran Gordon Fletcher-Howell. "That really gets to them because these guys want to be good fathers. Most of them never had one."

In Houston, the Women's Center recruits young men from nearby Rice University and trains them to help high school boys think about the peer pressure that can lead to forced sex and gang rape. "What they teach is this kind of behavior is criminal—and real men don't put a seal of approval on it," explains Mitzi Vorachek, the center's director of community education.

The vital importance of such messages from the older to the younger is underscored by Tom Winstone, an Irish Protestant convicted of murdering two Catholics in 1974. After his release from prison, Winstone turned to helping Protestant youths stay away from violence: "When I was fifteen, sixteen, seventeen, I had no one to say, 'I went up a certain path; it didn't work; and it was wrong.' "

The power of delegitimizing violence should not be underestimated. Consider the history of dueling, for centuries an honorable, popular, and violent way of settling interpersonal disputes. Laws passed against dueling in many European countries failed to stop the entrenched practice. It required the force of community opinion, the third side, to bring dueling to an end. Dueling came to appear not heroic but slightly absurd and undignified. From something that was "just done," it became something that was "just not done." If the practice of dueling fell victim to the ridicule of the third side, one wonders if the same fate could one day befall the institution of war.

Teach Tolerance

The alternative to violence is tolerance. Tolerance does not mean agreeing with the other or remaining indifferent in the face of injustice, but rather showing respect for the essential humanity in every person.

In 1992, thousands of people died in Hindu-Muslim riots triggered by the destruction of a mosque at Ajodhya by a group of Hindu militants, yet in the state capital of Lucknow, only forty miles away from Ajodhya, there was not one casualty. The reason? In part, it was the influence on the local culture of the largest private school in the world, the City Montessori School. Founded in 1959, the school has over twenty thousand students from kindergarten through twelfth grade. Influenced by the teachings of Mahatma Gandhi, it seeks to imbue its Hindu, Sikh, and Muslim students with the value of religious and cultural tolerance.

During daily reflection time, teams of students use stories and texts from the world's religions to engage their fellow students in conversations about virtues like love and truthfulness. Students also visit India's holy places—Hindu, Sikh, Buddhist, Muslim, Christian, Jewish, Baha'i, and Jain—in order to learn understanding and respect for other faiths. Classroom activities center around collaborative problem-solving, and teachers go out of their way to commend and reward students for consideration of others. The school actively encourages parents and grandparents to be involved in designing the school curriculum and to reinforce the principles of tolerance and cooperation at home.

Perhaps not surprisingly, then, during the 1992 conflict, thousands of students and parents responded by marching through Lucknow, singing songs of unity and carrying posters with slogans like "The name of God is both Hindu and Muslim" and "God is One, Mankind is One, All Religions are One." Meanwhile all the city's religious leaders met at the school and, addressing members of the community, spoke out for coexistence, surrounded by models of a Hindu temple, a Muslim mosque, and a Christian church. Such efforts helped Lucknow escape the violence.

Today, tolerance is beginning to be taught in schools around the world; age-old prejudices and stereotypes are being challenged. In Northern Ireland, most schoolchildren are exposed to a program called "Education for Mutual Understanding" to ensure that they learn about the traditions, history, and culture of both the Protestant and Catholic communities. The School for Peace at Neve Shalom/Wahat al-Salaam, a Jewish-Arab community in Israel, has organized "encounter" workshops and summer camps for over sixteen thousand Arab and Jewish children. In the United States, more than fifty thousand schools use a program on "Teaching Tolerance." Children in Boston public schools learn perspective-taking and empathy by writing their personal stories and reading them aloud in class. If peace proves elusive for this generation of adults, these programs inspire hope for the next one.

On an even larger scale, television and radio have enormous potential as tools for teaching tolerance and respect. The children's television program *Sesame Street*, now shown in a hundred countries around the world, illustrates friendships across groups. The Canadian version shows English-speaking children playing with French-speakers; in the Dutch version, Dutch, Moroccan, Turkish, and Surinamese children interact. The young viewers, research suggests, are more likely to reach out on their own and form friendships across differences. In Burundi, torn by ethnic violence, radio soap operas feature Hutu and Tutsi people living alongside each other, carrying on friendships, and intermarrying.

Teach Joint Problem-Solving

Tolerance is not enough; people need practical ways to deal with everyday tensions so that they do not escalate into harmful conflicts and violence.

When I was a child quarreling with my siblings, no one taught us to negotiate. If an adult intervened, it was to punish us for fighting or to lay down the law. Now I see changes among my contemporaries. In one family I know, when six-year-old Zander and four-year-old Aliza started arguing over who could play with a certain toy, the father took the children aside and asked them patiently, "What are three good ways to resolve this?"

"What if I go first and you go next?" said the little boy.

"We can play with it together," offered the little girl.

"Very good," said the father. "Any other ways?"

After a reflective pause, the little boy said, "We can flip a coin to decide who goes first."

And so it went. Pretty soon, the children learned to handle their conflicts by themselves.

In thousands of elementary and high schools all across the United States, programs have been established to teach children the vital skills of problem-solving, communication, empathy, anger management, and conflict resolution. To the three R's of Reading, 'Riting, and 'Rithmetic, a fourth "R" has been added: Resolution. "Why don't we try it this way?" children learn to ask. Through role-playing and discussion, they practice how to react in potentially volatile situations and to think twice about little things that could turn into nasty fights. As guidance counselor Cora Pearson explains, "We teach them to ask themselves, 'Did that person intentionally step on my foot?' 'Is this a reason to fight, to jeopardize my goals?' "

Children can also teach their peers. "For some little boys, who regularly see conflict and macho attitudes on television, peacemaking is a foreign language," says teacher Patricia Bloxham. "Their solution to problems is sock them, bop them, until they watch other children use the [conflict resolution] skills successfully." Four hundred youths from Detroit, including gang members and affluent teenagers, went through intensive training in conflict resolution at the Martin Luther King Center in Atlanta, then returned to their schools and proceeded to teach twenty-eight thousand high schoolers.

The programs work. One long-term systematic study involving second- and third-grade students in Washington State, for instance, showed that those classes whose members had been trained in violence prevention exhibited significantly fewer acts of aggressive behavior and many more acts of positive social behavior than those classes whose students had not been trained. Anecdotal evidence abounds as well. In the words of one New York high school student:

> As I went through the training I realized that nine out of ten times the most unlikely words could cause people to get very upset. I learned that the best way to avoid a fight is to talk out the problem. . . . I began getting better grades in my classes. I do not react in a violent way to people who are only out to bring everyone else down with them. At home I found that I did not argue with my family as much as before.

One day there may be universal education for children in joint problem-solving, anger management, and conflict resolution. Just as physical education has become a standard part of the curriculum, so too may social-emotional education.

Adults can learn problem-solving too. In the midst of a major reorganization of a hospital in St. Paul, Minnesota, conflicts among co-workers soared. Employees, labor leaders, and managers got together and organized a skills program called "Communication and Conflict in the Workplace" to teach employees how to handle conflict, stress, and interpersonal relationships with co-workers. Taught by fellow employees who volunteered their time, the program measurably improved productivity and quality of patient care as well as the workplace environment. Such courses on collaborative negotiation skills are multiplying in universities, in the workplace, and in community centers.

In the fall of 1995, on a little island off the coast of New Guinea, I happened by a bar where some inebriated locals spotted me and vociferously commanded me to come in.

"What are you doing here in New Guinea?" they asked.

"I've come to learn about clan war and how to stop it."

"Oh," exclaimed one man, "you mean 'conflict resolution'!"

Sure enough, the speaker had just been to a weekend training at his church about negotiation and mediation so that he, in turn, could teach others.

Everyone, everywhere, as I realized that day, is a potential learner and Teacher of ways to deal with differences. The goal of teaching is to help create a culture of collaboration and constructive conflict, a genuine "co-culture."

3. THE BRIDGE-BUILDER
FORGING RELATIONSHIPS ACROSS LINES OF CONFLICT

It is not easy to build bridging relationships, particularly in conditions of actual conflict. That did not deter Sidney Frankel, a Johannesburg businessman who, in August 1991, invited Cyril Ramaphosa, a prominent young black leader in the African National Congress, and Roelf Meyer, a young white leader in the ruling Nationalist Party government, to his country cottage for the weekend. As Meyer and his family arrived by helicopter, they discovered that Frankel's ten-year-old daughter had fallen and broken her arm; so Frankel, his wife, and his daughter took the helicopter to the hospital, leaving the Meyers and Ramaphosas awkwardly alone together. Meyer's two young sons insisted on going fishing, as their father had promised, and Ramaphosa offered to show them how. Meyer, a novice, promptly got a fishhook painfully caught in his finger. Ramaphosa's wife, a nurse, tried to get it out, but in vain. After an hour, with Meyer growing faint with pain, Ramaphosa intervened with a pair of pliers.

"Roelf, I've always wanted to hurt you Nats [National Party members]," he told Meyer as he yanked, "but never as much as this."

"Well, Cyril," muttered Meyer afterward, "don't say I didn't trust you."

That weekend began a personal relationship of trust and respect that eventually played an essential role in the subsequent negotiations between the white government and the African National Congress. When official negotiations were broken off in the middle of 1992, the relationship between the two men helped prevent a total breakdown that might have escalated back into civil war. Both men continued to meet secretly and frequently, developing a confidence, as Meyer once explained to me, that no matter how intractable the issue, the two of them could find a way to work it out. Ultimately, they fashioned a formula that produced the breakthrough to a negotiated agreement.

Create Cross-Cutting Ties

A cross-cutting tie is a relationship, like that between Ramaphosa and Meyer, that cuts across a line of potential or actual conflict. Such cross-cutting ties, as the South African example illustrates, can build trust and establish natural avenues for communication. The relationships operate like savings in the bank; whenever an issue arises, the parties can dip into their account of goodwill to help deal with it.

I found myself particularly struck by the power of cross-cutting ties to prevent the escalation of everyday tensions while making two mountain-climbing expeditions during successive summers in the early 1990s. Each expedition, a week in length, took place with a group of twenty people, divided into two teams of ten. The first year, as the two teams made the ascent in parallel, suspicions began to develop, starting in the form of petty jealousies and rivalries: "They got the better campsite" and "We'll make it up the mountain before them." After only a few days, to my amazement, the suspicions turned serious. When food and fuel supplies ran low, the teams refused to share and there was talk of making a raid on the other team's supplies. So, the following year, we adopted a different approach. In the evenings, each team would send two ambassadors, on a rotating basis, bearing gifts of food, to have dinner with the other team. Interestingly, when a few individuals voiced suspicions of the other team this time, their distrust was defused by teammates who took a third-side perspective and vouched for the other team. Any emergent hostility was quelled from the start.

As I learned from the first expedition, nothing can escalate conflicts faster than the absence of communication, trust, and relationship. Ignorance creates and exacerbates fears. Misunderstandings accumulate and stereotypes build up. People attribute the worst intentions to others' behavior. On the second expedition, I saw how the process of sharing food and talk wove a web of cross-cutting ties that helped prevent harmful conflict. The ties created a host of insider third parties, belonging to one side but with links to the other, who had a stake in everyone getting along and who thus worked hard to protect the valuable web of relationships from being torn. Cross-cutting ties, I learned, can serve as a safety net to catch escalating tensions.

As I reflected on the experience, I came to see how anyone, no matter what their occupation, can help build bridging relationships across natural divides. The Bridge-Builder is the one who invites two estranged family members who have not talked in years to the same celebration or who invites two business rivals for a golf game. Often not a discrete activity, bridge-building takes place all around us, sometimes without us even perceiving it—at family meals, on school projects, in business transactions, and at neighborhood meetings.

The Knowledge Revolution facilitates the process of building bridges on a global scale. As more and more young people spend time living as exchange students in other countries, as more and more businesspeople make deals across borders and visit partners in their homes, as more and more tourists travel to foreign lands, stereotypes are replaced by genuine understanding. The more bridges we build across the chasms of culture and distance, the harder it becomes to demonize others.

Develop Joint Projects

One intentional way to forge cross-cutting ties is to create joint projects. A manager faced with two rivalrous sales representatives can put them to work as a team on the same important account. Similarly, as parents know, telling two children to get to know each other can be an awkward proposition; but assign them a common task like washing the dishes, and soon they will be grumbling together about adults and carrying on a lively conversation. In a classic 1950s experiment with two groups of boys at a summer camp, psychologist Muzafer Sherif demonstrated that a common task, such as jointly pushing a truck to get its engine started, helps reduce negative stereotypes and build friendships—far more effectively, in fact, than simply bringing the boys together to socialize.

In communities around the United States, a growing number of people are getting together across ethnic, class, and ideological divides to tackle concrete problems of mutual interest. In Memphis, Tennessee, the city where Martin Luther King, Jr., was assassinated, black and white churches have created a common agenda to reform the schools and won the community's support. In Sonoma, California, Hispanic farmworkers and middle-class whites have learned to work together by supporting each other's favorite causes—from education to affordable housing. In southern Oregon and northern California, environmentalists and loggers, longtime foes, have forged partnerships to plant trees, protect streams, and start new forest-product businesses. "This is not about preservation vs. exploitation," declares Lynn Jungwirth, a member of a third-generation logging family. "This is about communities—forest communities and people communities."

Perhaps the most substantial exercise in bridge-building in the world is the joint project of European integration spearheaded by Jean Monnet after the two bloodiest wars in world history. Monnet, who started off his career selling his family's cognac in North America, was a quintessential thirdsider who singlemindedly pursued his vision of a united Europe for fifty years. After World War II, he managed to persuade two bitter and ancient enemies, France and Germany, and a half dozen of their smaller neighbors, to pool their coal and steel resources. Monnet reasoned that joint control of the resources most essential to industrial development and modern war would make it difficult for the participating nations to go to war once again. And history has proven him right. From this first step has evolved the European Economic Community, the European Parliament, the European Court of Justice, the European Central Bank—the institutions of a confederated Europe. Disputes within the European Community continue to spring up, but it has become unthinkable to use force to resolve them. Europe, the epicenter of war in the twentieth century, is becoming an experiment in coexistence and cooperation.

Foster Genuine Dialogue

"I'm really not that much of a dialogue person. As a trial lawyer, I prefer action," says attorney Andrew Puzder. "But I have seen this dialogue process have a profound effect on people. New groups keep popping up. . . . It's an idea that really works." Puzder is referring to dialogues that have taken place between people who strongly oppose abortion, like himself, and those who support a woman's right to choose.

Such dialogues aim not to convert others or to reach agreement on the issues, but rather to promote mutual understanding and build relationships that can prevent escalation into violence. They provide a safe atmosphere in which people can talk openly and deeply about their differences, and perhaps discover their underlying commonalities.

In the spring of 1996, I facilitated a private dialogue at a château outside of Paris between five Turkish and five Kurdish civic leaders whose peoples were trapped in a civil war that had taken twenty-five thousand lives and destroyed three thousand villages. The dialogue was confidential; people had been killed by their own side for talking to the other. Many of the participants had spent time in jail. One Turkish nationalist, Tarik, had been described to me by his friends as someone who would "just as soon shoot a Kurd as talk to one." The tensions were so high the first day that, when one Kurdish nationalist, Ali, talked about "self-determination," Tarik and a colleague rose to their feet, about to walk out. For them, the use of that phrase was treason because it implied the creation of a separate Kurdish state.

I stepped in to explain that this work of dialogue was the most difficult psychological work one could do: "It requires listening to points of view that you absolutely don't want to hear and that make you angry." Tarik and his colleague nodded in silent assent and sat down again. "Ali," I continued, "is talking about the wounds of the past, the suffering of his people, and their frustrated need for respect and autonomy."

"Yes," Ali responded, "Kurds do have the right to self-determination, but I believe that they should exercise this right by choosing to remain as equals in Turkey. In fact, I personally would defend Turkey against external threat with my blood."

The atmosphere in the room changed perceptibly.

At our next meeting, Tarik asked to speak. "If someone had told me a few months ago," he declared, "that I would be sitting here with a group of Kurds using words like 'Kurdistan,' I would have thought I was living in my worst nightmare. Now"—Tarik paused and looked around the room—"I think I'm living in a dream." And he went on to thank Ali for helping him understand the situation from a new perspective. While he remained a strong defender of Turkish national interests, Tarik acknowledged the Kurds' right to express their identity as they saw fit.

Dialogue is demanding. It is much easier to remain at a distance casting stones at the other. It takes courage to face the pain of human differences and to talk in a vulnerable fashion about what really matters. Yet, as I have often witnessed in conflicts large and small, dialogue has the power to change attitudes. While it may seem obvious to outsiders, the parties often are amazed to discover that their enemies are human like themselves, and sometimes end up concluding, like Tarik, that, placed in the same position, they might feel and act the same way.

If dialogue can work among warring Kurds and Turks, it can work among ethnic groups whose conflicts are less violent. In Los Angeles, the city sponsored a series of interracial discussions in all parts of the city to try to ease tensions after the O. J. Simpson murder trial. Churches, unions, and businesses became involved. "It's amazing how little we really know about each other," commented one participant, the Reverend Pedro Villaroya. "I've seen two riots in my life," declared administrator Avis Ridley-Thomas. "This is riot prevention work. It has more potential than anything I've seen."

Bridge-Builders can foster dialogue even on the streets. In Omaha, Nebraska, a small group of African-American fathers came together under the name "Mad Dads" to walk the streets and reconnect with young people involved in drugs and violence. "We just started talking with them," explains cofounder Eddie Staton. " 'What would you like to see change around here?' We listen to them. We get them engaged expressing themselves. Then we get into feelings. 'How do you feel about so and so? What about your father?' " Mad Dads has spread to twelve states across America—with tangible results. As Bill Patten, coordinator of substance abuse prevention for Ocala-Marion County, Florida, explains, "In 1990, there were sixteen people killed in one single neighborhood. This year there has been only one killing. . . . Mad Dads taught us that ours was not a black or white problem but a community problem. The only way to help a community is for the community to help itself—one house, one block at a time."

I have seen dialogue work, too, among traditional political adversaries to whom it might naturally seem anathema. In the wake of the bitter feelings engendered by the impeachment hearings of President

Clinton, almost two hundred members of the U.S. House of Representatives came together for a weekend in March 1999. In small groups, each led jointly by a Democrat and a Republican, they discussed how the poisonous atmosphere had made it virtually impossible to pass constructive legislation, and they brainstormed ways to improve their working relationship. One highlight for me, as one of the facilitators, was one Democrat's moving description of an ongoing dialogue with a Republican. Despite their strong political disagreements, they had continued to meet once a week for twenty years just to talk about their families and their personal struggles. When the Democrat's son was killed, the first person to call was his political adversary. "If there were twenty such friendships across the aisle, the atmosphere would change," he exclaimed.

Just as joint projects can create openings for genuine dialogue, so dialogue can lead to joint projects. Some dialogue groups on abortion have taken the next step and begun to collaborate on joint projects of mutual interest. They work together to reduce teen pregnancies and domestic violence, make adoption more acceptable and available, provide affordable quality day care, and teach males to be more responsible sexually. "So much time, money and human resources have been wasted fighting each other for the last twenty years," says Jayne Flowers, a pro-choice activist. "If we had spent that time fighting unplanned and unwanted pregnancies, we would be so much better off."

Indeed, joint projects may work better if preceded by a process of dialogue. In the workplace, it is becoming common for business partners about to engage in a joint project to get together first with a third-party facilitator for a three- or four-day dialogue session. Sometimes called "partnering," the process is coming into increasing usage on large complicated construction or manufacturing projects; it can also improve relations between unions and their employers. Typically, the partners devise a mission statement together, talk through their common venture, establish goals and objectives, and learn how to resolve issues quickly at the lowest possible level of management. "The outcome is very positive, developing a feeling of mutual understanding of the goals of various organizations," says Peter Jobs, president of a construction company in Hawaii. "It helps us get better acquainted with each other—[and helps] especially [by] establishing procedures for the dispute resolution process." Partnering makes projects run more smoothly, saves money, and avoids costly litigation. Dialogue need not be limited, then, to situations of existing enmity but can prove effective in preventing conflict between people who simply need to work with one another.

Genuine dialogue can take place every day between potential adversaries—husbands and wives, workplace rivals, or neighbors at odds. Acting as third parties, even if we say very little, we can foster dialogue by bringing the parties together in a comfortable and neutral place—a couples counselor's office, a conference room, or a friend's living room. If emotions threaten to explode, we can intervene to cool things down and keep the conversation going. We can serve, in short, as containers for contention.

PREVENTION: THE BEST INTERVENTION

Prevention is the best intervention. When people are able to meet their basic needs, thanks to the Providers among us; when people have skills for handling their everyday tensions, thanks to the Teachers; and when people know, understand, and trust one another, thanks to the Bridge-Builders, destructive conflict diminishes in quantity and intensity. Latent conflict may not become overt and people may not even think of it as conflict. What does become overt the parties can often handle by themselves.

Containment may be more urgent, like building a good roof to protect against the elements; resolving may be more apparent, like erecting the house itself; but preventing, though less visible, is more fundamental, like pouring the foundation on which both the house and roof rest.

Chapter 6

RESOLVE
Mediator, Arbiter, Equalizer, Healer

Jaw jaw is better than war war.
— Winston Churchill

I spent the spring and summer of 1980 working as a mediator at a strife-torn coal mine in eastern Kentucky. Angry miners had been striking almost weekly in violation of their union contract, and management had fired a third of the workforce in retaliation. A local judge had jailed another third for a night for disobeying his order not to strike. The mine was receiving bomb threats and miners were carrying guns to work. The national coal miners' union expressed fears that the situation could end up triggering a nationwide coal strike.

Every morning for weeks, I donned miner's clothes, a lamp, and a safety mask and descended into the coal mine to listen to the miners' grievances. They led a hard life, spending their working hours in pitch-black tunnels a mile under the earth. The ceilings were so low in most places that miners had to walk bent halfway over. They had no lights other than headlamps and no bathroom facilities. The dust hung so thick in the air that my face and saliva had turned black by the time I emerged at the end of the day.

When I asked why they were striking, the miners did not, however, complain about their working conditions, but focused instead on management's actions, the layoffs and jailings.

"What could management do?" I inquired.

"Fire the mine foreman!" replied the local union president.

"The troublemaker is the union president!" management countered. "If we can get rid of him and a couple of other bad apples, the problem will go away."

The basic pattern of conflict was finger-pointing, personal animosity, and tit-for-tat retaliation. The principal problem seemed to reside less in the nature of individual grievances than in the *way* differences were handled.

Interests, Rights, Power—and Relationship

Upon investigation, my colleagues Stephen Goldberg, Jeanne Brett, and I came to realize that a miner who felt he had been unjustly treated had but three ways to respond: try to talk it out with his foreman, file a contractual grievance with the union, or turn his water bottle upside down and walk out on strike with his fellow miners. The first option led nowhere, the miners felt; the foremen never did anything to fix the problem. The second, filing a grievance, converted the problem into incomprehensible legal jargon, took forever, and rarely produced any satisfaction. The third, walking out, was the easiest and most direct; even if it produced no change, it felt good to strike back at injustice and make the company pay. Hence the constant walkouts followed by the retaliatory layoffs, lawsuits, and jailings.

My colleagues and I set to work, together with the union and management, to change the way disputes were handled. We sought to restore the miners' option of talking out their problems. Since employees had no specified person in management to whom they could bring their grievances, we recommended that management hire a full-time labor relations director. Similarly, since many of the strikes had begun on the midnight work shift when union officials were generally asleep, we asked the union to post an official on that shift to assist employees who had problems. To help both sides learn how to handle the inevitable tensions, I led a training workshop in joint problem-solving methods.

For three months, moreover, I worked at the mine as an informal mediator, listening to miners' grievances, bringing both sides together, and helping them find solutions. Surprised at their initial successes in grievance resolution, miners and managers began to develop confidence in their own ability to resolve their problems through negotiation. The result of all these changes: Both sides started to talk out even their most difficult issues and the strikes ceased.

As my colleagues and I reflected on this experience afterward, we came to realize that the three approaches at the miners' disposal for resolving disputes were, in fact, universal. Either one tries to reconcile the conflicting *interests* of each side through talking, or one takes the issue to a third party who determines the *rights* of each side, or one decides on the basis of *power*—by striking, for instance. Even though the interests approach is generally preferable, the rights and power approaches have an important role to play, if only as backups when talking alone does not succeed.

A fourth approach exists, parallel to the other three. It concerns the *relationship* between the parties. At the mine, for example, the accumulated distrust and hostility between miners and managers proved a huge obstacle to collaborative problem-solving. The fourth approach is to heal the strained relationship.

The third side can make a critical contribution to each of the four resolution approaches. As Mediators, we can help reconcile the parties' interests. As Arbiters, we can determine rights. As Equalizers, we can help balance the power between the parties. And as Healers, we can help repair injured relationships.

WHY CONFLICT ESCALATES		WAYS TO RESOLVE CONFLICT
Conflicting interests	→	4. The Mediator
Disputed rights	→	5. The Arbiter
Unequal power	→	6. The Equalizer
Injured relationships	→	7. The Healer

4. THE MEDIATOR
RECONCILING CONFLICTING INTERESTS

It was a family feud. Dan and Sally were in the middle of an acrimonious divorce. Sally's father, Jim, who had employed Dan in his business, refused to pay him for work he had done. Furious, Dan sued his father-in-law to recover his lost wages. The judge, however, suggested that they try talking with a volunteer mediator first. I was the volunteer; it was one of my first mediation cases twenty years ago.

Dan, Jim, and I sat in a little room in the courthouse. Clearly a little uncomfortable, they would not at first even look one another in the eye. I began by explaining the process.

"Mediation is very different from arbitration," I said. "As a mediator, I don't decide the case. You do. My job is to help you reach an agreement if possible. If we can't reach agreement, the case goes back to the judge."

I made it clear that anything they told me I would hold confidential, and then set out some ground rules for our discussion—no interruptions, no name-calling, keep to the point. "Any objections or additions?" I asked. They said no and we began.

"Why don't we start with you, Dan?" I asked. "Why don't you tell us what the problem is from your perspective?"

"Well, it all started when Jim—"

"That's not true!" Jim protested heatedly.

"Jim," I responded, "remember you agreed not to interrupt. You'll get your turn to speak in a moment. Okay?"

"Okay," Jim sighed.

After Dan finished telling his side of the story, I had a question.

"Dan, let me make sure I understand what you're saying. Your primary interest, as I hear it, is getting paid fairly for the work you did, is that right?"

"That's right."

"Okay, then, it's Jim's turn," I said.

Jim gave his account, which revolved around his dissatisfaction with Dan's frequent absences from work. It turned out that Dan, with Jim's consent, was working toward a business degree at the time.

"Okay, we're making progress here, at least in understanding each other's interests," I said. "Now, what are some ways to meet both your interests? Let's try to compile a list. I'm going to ask you to suspend your criticism for a bit while we try to come up with ideas. All right? And remember that these are just options, no one's committed to them. Now, anybody got an idea?"

"What if Jim pays me for my hours and I, in return, help train my replacement?" offered Dan.

"Good, that's one approach," I said. "What's another? Jim, you got an idea?"

The discussion was going well until somehow the subject of Sally came up.

"We were doing fine until her family started interfering," said Dan.

"What do you mean, you son of a gun? You were the one who left her in the dirt!" Jim fired back.

"Now, listen!" I interjected. "Remember, Dan, that Jim is the grandfather of your children. Jim, Dan is the father of your grandchildren. How do you want them to think of you—as bitter enemies or as men who dealt with their differences in a dignified fashion?"

In the end, after two and a half hours of discussion, Dan and Jim did reach agreement. They were pleasantly surprised, and I admit so was I. Jim agreed to pay Dan for the work he had done after deducting the health insurance payments Dan owed. Dan, in turn, agreed to drop the lawsuit and help train his replacement. We wrote up the agreement on the court form, specifying what the payment would be and when it would be paid.

"I'm sorry about what I said," Jim said to Dan as we were preparing to leave. "I'm sorry too," replied Dan. "I was rough with you. It wasn't necessary." They shook hands and left the room—together.

Not every mediation concludes so successfully, but one impressive statistic is that roughly three-quarters of all civil cases that go through mediation end up with a settlement. This remains true whether the parties are tussling schoolkids, neighbors quarreling about their boundary line, or businesses trying to resolve a contractual dispute. For international disputes, the proportion of successful attempts is lower but still substantial—more than four out of ten. While parties going into mediation are more open to agreement than those who refuse it altogether, the success rate is encouraging.

Everyone's a Mediator

My four-and-a-half-year-old nephew Jonah occasionally mediates between his two older brothers, ages eight and twelve. When an argument breaks out, he holds up his hands and says, "Okay, stop fighting!" He shuttles back and forth between them, explaining to each brother how the other one feels, and often brings about a reconciliation.

Like Jonah, each of us has a chance to mediate every day, at least in an informal sense. Parents can mediate among their children, and children between their parents. Supervisors can mediate among their employees, and employees between their bosses. Colleagues can mediate among their peers, managers among their teammates, and friends among their friends. We may not think of it as mediation, but that is what we are doing whenever we listen attentively to people in dispute, when we ask them about what they really want, when we suggest possible approaches, and when we urge them to think hard about the costs of not reaching agreement.

The Mediator does not seek to determine who is right and who is wrong, but rather tries to get to the core of the dispute and resolve it. The core is each side's interests—in other words, their needs, concerns, desires, fears, and aspirations. Splitting the difference between two opposed positions is not enough; a Mediator needs to help the parties meet the interests underlying those positions. One family dispute among the Bushmen, for example, concerned a certain betrothal gift from the bride's mother that the groom's mother had expected would go to her present husband but was given to someone else instead. Through a process of community mediation, the parties agreed a few days later that the stepfather would receive a gift, not the one in question, but a gift that satisfied everybody so that, as one Bushman put it, "they could all start again in peace." Even if the position, the particular item in question, was not obtained, the underlying interest in recognizing the stepfather and the community's interest in harmony were fulfilled.

Bring the Parties to the Table

The first step is to get people to sit down together. This is often the biggest challenge, as my colleagues and I discovered in trying to arrange a peace discussion in The Hague between the Chechen and Russian leadership in 1997. While the Chechens welcomed the chance to put their case in an international forum, they feared they would experience pressure to accept less than full independence. And while the Russians considered it useful for the Chechens to hear international views, they felt reluctant to have outsiders meddling in what they regarded as their internal affairs. Each side required a great deal of reassurance and encouragement, particularly from their peers, the presidents of Tatarstan and Ingushetia, who were convening the meeting.

After three or four postponements, everyone finally agreed on a date, but then, as the Chechen delegation took off from Grozny in a private plane headed to The Hague, several Russian MiGs suddenly appeared and forced them to land, on the grounds that they had not received Russian clearance to fly. Once this misunderstanding was cleared up, another promptly emerged; the Chechens insisted on using Chechen passports to enter the Netherlands, which did not recognize Chechnya. With the intervention of former Dutch prime minister Ruud Lubbers, we found a solution: The Dutch Foreign Ministry, knowing the Chechens had received visas in their Russian passports, agreed on a one-time basis to let them in without showing their passports. And all this—and more—took place before the Chechens and Russians even sat down to talk.

If the parties are not ready to meet, a Mediator can still help by using shuttle diplomacy. That is what Stephen Goldberg and I did in the first few months of our work at the coal mine mentioned earlier. Personal relationships were so strained and distrust so high that we felt it better to make some progress first in separate meetings with each side. Only when agreement seemed near, to the surprise of both sides, did we succeed in bringing them together for constructive talks.

Sometimes, the community can *require* the parties to go through the mediation process. Many American schools, for example, demand that students who have been suspended for violence—or other reasons—resolve any outstanding disputes with other students, teachers, or administrators before they can return. The mediation sessions include parents and other significant people in their lives who constitute the third side. "We are strict about not letting unresolved conflicts fester," explains one assistant principal Allan Lipsky. "The school has a different atmosphere than before we instituted the program."

Facilitate Communication

One of the Mediator's key functions is to help each side understand what the other is really saying or asking for. One union-management negotiation I facilitated became stuck on the issue of "attendance." Management complained that many employees were regularly absent; they wanted the union's help in improving attendance. The union officials refused even to discuss the subject. Upon questioning them closely, I discovered that much of their resistance came from the word "attendance." "People feel treated like schoolchildren, being reprimanded by the teacher for not showing up for class!" exclaimed one union leader. Interestingly, once we reframed the issue as "increasing worker participation," the union leaders became much more responsive. Participation was a positive issue they could support.

Simple ground rules can help. One rule that has helped prevent angry escalating exchanges is: Only one person can get angry at a time. The other person listens, knowing he or she will get a turn later. Another rule dates back at least as far as the Middle Ages, when theologians at the University of Paris used it to facilitate mutual understanding: One can speak only *after* one has repeated what the other side has said to that person's satisfaction.

Help People Search for a Solution

The next step is to help the parties generate creative options for agreement. "The students, not the mediators, make suggestions on how to solve the conflict," explains twelve-year-old peer mediator Stefanie Franson. "The mediator sums up the plan or the agreement that was reached." Franson is right; ideally, the solution comes from the parties themselves. Sometimes, however, a Mediator can advance the process by proposing solutions for the parties to consider. Because many people tend to distrust ideas offered by the other side, an option suggested by the Mediator may prove easier for both sides to accept.

The goal is a mutually satisfactory agreement. One dispute between a big department store in Johannesburg and the street vendors camped on the sidewalk outside had escalated into a bitter fight. The store wanted the vendors to move, but the vendors refused. The store then enlisted the help of the police, who, encountering fierce resistance, were reluctant to risk a violent confrontation. The deadlock was broken with the help of a community mediator, who began by probing for each side's interests. The store's managers, it turned out, feared that the vendors would scare away customers and damage its public image; the vendors just wanted a busy place to sell their wares. A creative brainstorming session resulted in a decision by the store to help the vendors set up proper booths, which enhanced the vendors' business as well as the street's appearance. In return, the vendors promised to keep the street clean and to look out for thieves, who had become a major problem for the store. Having begun as adversaries, the parties ended up as partners—thanks to mediation.

5. THE ARBITER
DETERMINING DISPUTED RIGHTS

When mediation doesn't work—or is not appropriate—the third side can usefully play the role of Arbiter. Whereas a Mediator can only suggest a solution, an Arbiter can decide.

The Arbiter is a familiar role, embodied in the judge in the courtroom or the arbitrator in a work setting. More informally, the Arbiter is the teacher deciding a dispute among two quarreling students, the parent ruling on a matter involving two children, or the manager determining an issue among two employees. In this sense, we are all potential Arbiters.

Peers Can Be Arbiters Too

To play the role of Arbiter, we need not necessarily be superior in status or power to the parties, as is traditional in hierarchically organized societies. As among the horizontally organized Bushmen and the Semai, we may simply be the parties' peers.

"Peer pressure seems to be the most important factor in whether a kid commits a crime," explained volunteer judge David Silverstein to the defendant, a thirteen-year-old boy who had stolen two packs of cigarettes from a Wal-Mart store. "Here you have a whole room of peer pressure, trying to turn you around."

Silverstein was referring to the six jurors in the case, all between the ages of ten and seventeen. After hearing from the boy, the six collectively decided on his "punishment": to perform twenty-eight hours of community service, make an apology to the store, and write two reports, one on the effect of stealing on the community's economy, and the other on the health hazards of smoking. They also directed him to serve as a juror himself on eight cases so that he could help the system that had helped him. Far from ostracizing him, then, they included him. "It's a second chance," the boy declared afterward.

"Since the inception of our youth court in 1983," reports police sergeant Gordon Ferguson, "our numbers [of juvenile crimes] have gone down drastically."

The Arbiter's goal, in such cases, is not just to determine who is right and who is wrong but to repair the harm to victims and to the community, and to reintegrate the offender as a constructive member of society. What works with teens works with adults as well. Hundreds of community courts have recently been established, part of a growing trend toward the restorative and compensatory justice long practiced in simpler societies. In Vermont, for example, citizen volunteers on Community Reparative Boards sentence nonviolent adult offenders to make amends to their victims and perform community service work. "They're trying to help, and not screw you over," explains one offender. "They have you think about what you did. I've learned a lot from it."

Replace Destructive Conflict

Adjudication stands as one of humanity's great social inventions if only because it provides an alternative to the violent resolution of conflicts. Its true value can best be appreciated from the perspective of societies that lack such a mechanism. Caught up in constant and costly clan wars, New Guinea tribesmen, for example, took with alacrity during the early contact years to the rough-and-ready adjudication of their land disputes by Australian field officers. Anthropologist Mervyn Meggitt writes:

> As expressed to me, the opinion of most men was straightforward: litigation appeared to be a speedy and effective way of achieving their individual and clan aims, one that was economical of time, energy, and blood, and that would permit them to get on with their gardening and exchanges without the annoying and painful interruptions posed by military mobilization, the evacuation of noncombatants and pigs, the rebuilding of burned houses and the replanting of ruined gardens.

Court, in other words, replaced war as a more sensible manner of fighting. Indeed, the disputing clans would often appeal the decision to the next roving field officer—just as in a war, they might retire only to fight again. The virtues of this speedy and flexible process were underscored when, during the 1960s, the Australians made the mistake of formalizing the procedure, rendering it slow, cumbersome, and inflexible. The unfortunate but illuminating result: Many clans gave up on the court system and reverted back to warfare.

Adjudication does not always require the intervention of the state, however, but can be arranged simply through the consent of the parties. They can agree in advance to accept the binding decision of a trusted third party, jointly selected, to whom they then present their case. This private form of adjudication—called arbitration—is widely used to resolve commercial disputes, both domestic and international, as well as employee grievances. Indeed, ninety-five percent of all collective bargaining contracts in the United States provide for arbitration of labor grievances.

Arbitration can also be employed to end wars. After Peru and Ecuador fought a brief but intense war in 1995 over their border, international mediators worked hard but proved unable to procure a complete agreement. Finally in 1998, under international prodding, the presidents of both countries agreed to seek arbitration by the four guarantors of a prior 1942 treaty: Brazil, Argentina, Chile, and the United States. To everyone's surprise, the legislatures of Peru and Ecuador consented in advance to accept the decision of the four guarantors. With nationalist passions still running strong, political leaders felt it easier to accept a ruling by others than to make direct concessions to the enemy.

Promote Justice

Peace is not the only aim of the Arbiter; so is justice. A ruling offers the community a chance to send a message about right and wrong. At the end of a Semai *bcaraa'*, for instance, writes anthropologist Clayton Robarchek:

> The headman gives voice to the group's consensus. Lecturing one or both parties concerning their guilt in the matter ... he instructs them in proper behavior, in the courses of action that they should have followed, and orders them not to repeat the offense or to raise this dispute again. The elders of the *waris* [extended families] of each of the disputants then lecture their own kinsman in the same vein.

Parents have a similar opportunity to reaffirm the principles of fairness when adjudicating among their children. In one case I know, seven-year-old Chip, who shared a bedroom with his five-year-old brother, Tony, announced one day that he would move to a separate bedroom. Terrified at the prospect of being left alone in the dark, Tony agreed to pay Chip his regular weekly allowance if Chip stayed. When their parents discovered the arrangement, however, they immediately stopped the transaction and used the occasion to teach both boys how wrong it was to use money in such a situation. They asked Chip to decide where he wanted to sleep without financial inducements. Chip chose to continue sharing the bedroom with Tony out of brotherly concern alone.

At a societal level, a court can use its rulings to establish critical principles protecting the rights of minorities, safeguarding the environment, and increasing safety in the workplace. If a dispute in Topeka, Kansas, in 1951 over the right of a little black girl named Linda Brown to attend the local all-white public elementary school had been resolved through negotiation, little Linda might have been granted permission to attend the school. As the dispute was adjudicated instead by the U.S. Supreme Court, the 1954 ruling in *Brown v. Board of Education* enabled millions of black children to attend formerly all-white public schools.

By promoting justice, courts might also one day help deter political violence. Domestic courts have already begun to extend their jurisdictions to hear cases involving crimes against humanity committed elsewhere in the world. One instance made worldwide headlines in the fall of 1998: Chilean ex-dictator Augusto Pinochet was arrested in Britain at the request of a Spanish magistrate for his involvement in the torture and murder of thousands of political opponents during the 1970s. Similarly in 1993, Bosnian Serb leader Radovan Karadzic was surprised in a New York hotel lobby by a man who shoved a sheaf of papers at him before being held back by Karadzic's security guards. Karadzic promptly found himself embroiled in a class-action lawsuit for rape, torture, and genocide. Thus far, no defendant has been brought to punishment, but if the trend continues and spreads to other nations, any individual who commits a crime against humanity will find it difficult to travel or do business without fearing arrest and the seizure of his assets.

Moreover, spurred by the massacres in Bosnia and Rwanda, and building on the precedent of the Nuremberg Tribunal, a hundred and twenty nations agreed in July 1998 to establish a permanent international criminal court in order to deter those who would commit genocide, aggression, and other crimes against humanity, such as mass rape and the forced recruitment of children as soldiers.

Eighteen judges from eighteen different countries will serve terms of nine years each. While the court's effectiveness remains to be seen, its establishment is a critical first step.

Encourage Negotiation

By deciding who is right and who is wrong, however, an Arbiter runs the risk of further straining the relationship among the parties. In the coal mine dispute, for example, the union and management initially expected my colleagues and me to act as Arbiters; they wanted to know who was wrong. But pointing fingers, we feared, would only compound the conflict; each side would take our report and use it to blame the other. Since any steps forward would need to have both sides' support, we resorted to mediation instead.

Paradoxically, then, the role of Arbiters is to encourage a negotiated settlement whenever possible and appropriate. Bosses can urge disputing employees who come to them for a decision to try first to resolve the matter by themselves, or a judge can take the parties into her chambers and instruct them to attempt mediation before returning. To assist the parties, the Arbiter can even suggest a standard or procedure of fairness to be employed in their settlement talks. A manager can specify the cost and quality criteria she wants met by two departments arguing about a product design. Or a parent can tell two children quarreling about a piece of cake: "Okay, Johnny, you cut the cake, and Mary, you get first pick."

 ## 6. THE EQUALIZER
DEMOCRATIZING POWER

Every conflict takes place within the larger context of power. Imbalance of power often leads to abuse and injustice. The strong refuse to negotiate with the weak or to submit their dispute to mediation or arbitration—why should they, they think, when they can win?

This is where the Equalizer has a contribution to make. Each of us holds a packet of power, a measure of influence over the parties around us. Individually, our influence may be small, but collectively, it can be considerable. We are capable of empowering the weak and the unrepresented so that they can negotiate a fair and mutually satisfactory resolution.

Help Bring the Powerful to the Table

Sally was faced with an alcoholic husband, John, who turned violent when drunk. John had repeatedly broken his promises to stop drinking and he absolutely refused to undergo treatment. In desperation, Sally resorted to an approach sometimes called an "intervention." She turned to others for help: his children, siblings, closest friends, and work colleagues. They called a meeting with John. One by one they told him how much he meant to them and recounted specific incidents of violent behavior, dangerous driving, and personal embarrassment. Collectively they insisted he seek help. To make his decision easier, they had already prepared a list of three treatment centers and made reservations at each. They left the choice of treatment center up to him. Faced with an outpouring of concern and peer pressure from the people he most cared about, John decided to accept the help being offered and underwent treatment.

Sally's effort would not have sufficed. It took the combined urging of the third side. "If one person tells you that you have a tail, you laugh," goes an old adage. "If a second person tells you, you laugh again. But if a third tells you, you turn around to look!"

Each of us has many such opportunities to use our influence to bring about productive negotiations. A parent can equalize the power between a younger and an older child, insisting that they reach an agreement fair to both. A boss can direct a more powerful department head to negotiate an even-handed resolution with a weaker rival. A chorus of newspaper editorials can promote talks between an unwilling company and its union, or vice versa. The neighbors of a country torn by civil war can exercise diplomatic peer pressure on that country's reluctant government to sit down with the rebels.

Ensuring that the weak and the unrepresented sits as equals at the table is just the first step, of course. As thirdsiders, we often need to remain involved so that the parties reach an equitable agreement—and carry it out. The job, for instance, of an organizational ombudsperson, who typically reports directly to the CEO, is to balance the power between a weaker employee (or customer) and someone more powerful inside the organization, such as a supervisor, so that the issue—racial discrimination, sexual harassment, or less serious matters—can be fairly addressed and a resolution fully implemented.

Build Collaborative Democracy

Stepping in to bring about a negotiation only temporarily equalizes the power balance. More sustainably, we as thirdsiders can build democracy and promote the fair sharing of power.

Democracy is fundamentally a mechanism for nonviolent conflict resolution. Historically in Europe, it evolved as a nonviolent power contest substituting for civil warfare among barons and kings. Political parties arose out of war parties, and parliaments replaced battlefields as the place to resolve political issues. On a visit to the English Parliament, I was struck to learn that the width of the corridor separating the seats of the governing party from those of the opposition is, not coincidentally, precisely two sword lengths. Intended to avert violence during the days when parliamentarians wore their weapons to work, the width of the corridor is a reminder of the times when force usually decided issues. In today's democracies, elections decide power. The ballot decides, not the bullet.

In working on mediation initiatives with former President Carter,

I have often admired his knack for persuading dictators like Daniel Ortega in Nicaragua to hold elections as a way to end a war. He plays on the conviction held by many dictators that they are genuinely popular and would actually win an election. Elections can also end dictatorships. Like Ortega, Augusto Pinochet in Chile and Ferdinand Marcos in the Philippines were dictators who mistakenly and fortunately believed they would emerge victorious from a democratic contest.

Voting is not only a nonviolent *power* contest, but a way to express the *interests* of the overall community. Families can vote about what movie they wish to see; work teams can vote about what schedule they want to adopt; and citizens can elect representatives who they think will represent their interests in legislative votes. Democracy is about much more than voting, however. It is about participating in decisions and negotiating agreements within a context of shared power. Voting can easily become divisive, ending in an outcome with winners and losers. In collaborative democracy, by contrast, people make every effort to reach a consensus that includes the full group. Voting becomes a last resort, not a first one.

Building democracy, moreover, extends beyond sharing power at the top; it involves devolving power from the top to the bottom. Families can give children increasing responsibility over their lives as they grow older. Companies can grant more authority to work teams on the shop floor. Nation-states can accord states, provinces, districts, and municipalities more power over issues like education, welfare, transportation, and taxation.

Creating a devolved and collaborative democracy helps handle difficult disputes, starting at home. Democratic family meetings can air contentious issues and allow creative agreements to be worked out. "We sit down maybe once a month, tears are shed, and we talk and air it out," explains Roger Atchison, father of a family of six. Parents and children participate as equals in such meetings, helping make decisions such as how to distribute chores fairly or where to go for a family vacation. It is not easy to share power, but it can work—if people learn to take the third side.

Collaborative democracy can be used in schools as well. The most effective strategy for preventing violence in American schools turns out not to be installing metal detectors but rather involving students in a problem-solving process. Adults frequently do not understand the depth of adolescent passions or what sets them off—the insults, the pressure to conform, the teasing in the school shower. Fellow students *can* understand and often have better ideas for what will work to resolve the problem. At one school cafeteria where fights were breaking out regularly on the lunch line, for example, students suggested creating two separate lines, one for pizza and the other for salad. The fighting stopped. There is a growing movement in the United States to place teenagers on the governing boards of organizations that address social problems such as teenage violence, job training for high school dropouts, and even food distribution to the poor and needy. "We know better than anyone what will keep us out of trouble," high school senior Diane Rondeau explains. "Everybody in the community benefits."

Collaborative democracy can be applied even among elementary school children. In over seventy-five schools in sixty-three American cities, children start each year by brainstorming about their hopes and dreams; they then discuss what rules will be necessary to realize their aspirations. Having made their own rules, the children tend to stick to them, freeing the teacher to teach. "You see an increase in cooperative behavior and a decrease in discipline referrals," reports educator Robert "Chip" Wood. In her "consensus classrooms," teacher Linda Sartor goes even further. Her students decide on homework requirements and classroom work needed to meet the established curricular standards. Decision making is sometimes slow and difficult, but "once a decision is made that everyone agrees to," says Sartor, "there is 100% participation with no opposition draining energy from the activity."

Collaborative democracy can also make the workplace more satisfying and productive. In one radical example, Ricardo Semler, chief executive of Semco, a Brazilian company, responded to resentment and unrest among his employees by calling a general meeting where he asked everyone to spell out their frustrations. The eventual result: a democratically managed company where the employees elected their bosses, set their own pay levels, and shared in the company's profits. "The interesting thing," says Semler, "is that, when given the chance to decide, employees make decisions that are as good or better than those of management. They judge their bosses fairly, and they know what is needed to make the company run." Within a few years, profits increased fivefold and productivity went up sevenfold. Critics may quibble about the explanation for this success and its long-term sustainability, but Semco's experiment serves to highlight the largely untapped potential of democracy in the workplace.

Building democracy can also help end wars. The more I have worked on ethnic conflicts in different parts of the world, the more convinced I have become of the value of sharing and devolving democratic power as strategies for defusing deadly differences. The violence ceased in Italy when the German-speaking minority was accorded autonomy in the 1970s. Malaysia, once torn by strife between ethnic Malays and Chinese in the 1950s and 1960s, learned to share power between the two communities and came to enjoy civil peace and prosperity in the 1970s and 1980s. At the time of this writing, a great experiment is under way to end the thirty-year civil war in Northern Ireland. In May 1998, the people of the entire island, North and South, voted together for the first time. Acting as thirdsiders, the great majority of them voiced their support for a peaceful solution through political power-sharing among Protestants and Catholics in the North. "The conflict isn't over," reflected one hopeful citizen on a radio talk show, "but the war is."

Support Nonviolent Action

Sometimes people resort to violence out of desperation, believing there is no other way to address their needs. Even in a democracy, the formal mechanisms of government may be insufficient to correct injustices. It is up to us as thirdsiders to show that nonviolent action can work instead. Indeed, community support is the key mechanism through which nonviolent action ultimately achieves its goals.

No one has done more to develop and popularize the tool of nonviolent action than Mahatma Gandhi. At the beginning of the twentieth century, Gandhi was determined to free India from centuries of British rule; he was equally determined to do so without using violence. At the time, most people thought his enterprise laughable. How could one man take on the British Empire, the largest empire on the face of the earth? How many battalions did Gandhi command? his opponents asked contemptuously. But over time Britain weakened and grew weary with the costs of empire, whereas Gandhi only grew stronger.

Gandhi carefully crafted a strategy for measuring power in terms of the willingness of people to suffer for their cause—without inflicting violent harm on their adversaries. Through such nonviolent actions as breaking unjust laws and flooding the jails of colonial India, boycotting English textiles, provoking the wrath of the occupiers, and accepting whatever violent punishment they meted out, he persuaded a nation infinitely more powerful in conventional military terms to withdraw peacefully from a country it had occupied for four hundred years.

Gandhi succeeded by mobilizing the community itself, millions of Indians from all walks of life. He also aroused widespread sympathy and support for his cause around the world, including Great Britain itself. The third side, both outside and inside India, served to hold in check those British officials who counseled using massive force to put an end to Gandhi and his followers.

Gandhi's efforts have inspired the use of nonviolent action around the world. During the 1960s, Martin Luther King, Jr., led the American civil rights movement in an effective nonviolent campaign to obtain equal rights for black Americans. During the 1980s, nonviolent protests in Poland, East Germany, and Czechoslovakia, orchestrated by labor unions, churches, and other civil institutions, helped bring an end to communist dictatorship. In all these cases, the wider public became engaged as thirdsiders and helped equalize the power between the weak and the strong.

Nonviolent action extends well beyond the political arena. It begins with babies; crying, after all, represents a nonviolent attempt to induce big, powerful adults to meet the baby's needs. In the workplace, employees use strikes and management resorts to lockouts when an impasse develops in contract negotiations. In schools too, students use nonviolent action. In one instance during the late 1960s, two hundred girls wore pants to a Massachusetts high school in violation of the dress code, confronting the principal with an unpleasant choice. He either had to suspend two hundred students or change the dress code; wisely, he chose to do the latter.

Whether the powerful negotiate with the weak usually depends on the rest of us. Whether or not we agree with the specific cause behind a nonviolent protest, an industrial strike or lockout, or a consumer boycott, we may choose as Equalizers to support nonviolence and assist the weaker party in bringing their stronger opponents to the table.

7. THE HEALER
REPAIRING INJURED RELATIONSHIPS

"I am aware," the retired Turkish general told a group of Kurdish and Turkish civic leaders during a dialogue I was facilitating, "that there has been much violence in the last forty years against the Kurds initiated by our political leaders. And last night I was horrified to hear about the specific abuses committed against the Kurds. I wish to apologize on behalf of the Turks for the suffering inflicted on the Kurds." The silence in the room was intense, then both Kurds and Turks broke out into spontaneous applause. The general's apology proved to be a turning point; tensions diminished and a genuine sense of solidarity began to emerge. While only one step along the journey, it built the trust necessary to go on to the next stage.

The general was playing the critical role of Healer. At the core of many conflicts, as in the civil war in Turkey, lie emotions—anger, fear, humiliation, hatred, insecurity, and grief. The wounds may run deep. Even if a conflict appears resolved after a process of mediation, adjudication, or voting, the wounds may remain and, with them, the danger that the conflict could recur. A conflict cannot be considered fully resolved until the injured relationships have begun to heal.

Each of us has a chance to heal the feuds in our families, in our workplaces, and in our communities. Sonia, a ten-year-old girl I know, once participated in a family meeting called by her father to discuss the rancorous conflict between her aunt and her grandparents. To everyone's surprise, the conversation took a healing turn; for the first time, people spoke from their hearts. All involved attributed the success to the presence of the little girl who had said nothing but who had silently reminded everyone of the importance of getting along. At the end of the meeting, when she proposed a family hug, none could resist. Like Sonia, anyone can play the role of Healer.

Healing is not limited to humans. On a visit to Yerkes Research Lab, I observed two chimpanzees, a male and a female, sitting together after a fight. The male groomed the female and then the female groomed the male. In this way, primatologist Frans de Waal explained, they repair their injured relationship. Chimps, he observed, are extremely sensitive to disruptions of their relationships, appearing to fear them as much as the physical effects of aggression. To initiate a reconciliation, chimps use gestures commonly considered human: They extend their hands to the other with an open palm, then kiss and hug.

Create the Right Climate

Healing ideally takes place not just at the conclusion of the process of dispute resolution, but at the very start. For talks to succeed, the right emotional climate must be set. That was the challenge faced at a meeting I facilitated between a group of American and Soviet policy advisers in 1984 at a time of high tension between the United States and the Soviet Union. Needing an icebreaker, a way to defuse the atmosphere of official hostility and mutual accusation, we decided to start the meeting with a New England lobster dinner. We figured that no one wearing a bib around the neck and trying to crack open lobster legs could remain aloof for long. Our hunch turned out to be correct—laughter and good-natured humanity broke through. That night, before retiring, our Soviet and American cochairs announced a special six A.M. session the next day entitled "Mutual Recriminations" for all those who wanted to show up. No one did.

A psychological wall of suspicion and hostility may separate the parties more definitively than any stone wall. Our task as Healers is to break through this psychological wall. "People would call me up angry," explains Timothy Dayonot, a community relations officer for the University of California at San Francisco. "There'd always be some tough issue—student noise, or traffic, or construction, or radiation from the labs. My approach was to listen to them calmly and then, when they paused for a second, I'd say, 'Do you have a pen and piece of paper handy?' 'Why?' they'd ask irritably. 'Because I want you to have my home telephone number. Any time you have a problem, day or night, feel free to give me a call.' They'd be so surprised—they were expecting some kind of bureaucratic runaround—that their tone would change. They'd begin to trust me, and we could then talk through their problem." In the five years Dayonot held the job, he reported that only once did he receive a call at home—and that was from a complainant who had been so impressed by Dayonot's open approach that he wanted to offer him a job!

Trust-building can take place not just between individuals but between nations. In May 1977, Egyptian President Anwar Sadat shocked the world and offered to fly to Jerusalem, the capital of his enemies, to talk peace. For the first time, he pierced the psychological wall dividing Arabs and Israelis. Up to that point, no Arab leader had publicly acknowledged the existence of the state of Israel, let alone even pronounced its name—it had always been the "Zionist entity." Overnight, Sadat's surprise trip to Jerusalem, undertaken within a week of his offer, seized the imagination of millions, both Israelis and Arabs, and created the atmosphere that led to the Camp David peace settlement between Egypt and Israel.

Listen and Acknowledge

One of the most powerful methods for healing a relationship is also the simplest. It is to listen, to give one's complete attention to the aggrieved person for as long as he or she has something to say. This is the key to the Semai *bcaraa'* [community dispute resolution meetings]. "A proper *bcaraa'* cannot end while anyone still has anything more to say," writes anthropologist Clayton Robarchek. "When the debate lags, the participants are asked by the elders of the *waris* [extended families] if they are still angry or if they have more to say. As long as anyone is willing or feels the need to talk, the *bcaraa'* continues."

Acknowledgment reinforces the effect of listening. "We have a lot of angry parents here," says Gina Shine, a school secretary in Riverside, California, who comes face-to-face every day with parents of suspended and expelled students. "Sometimes they come right over the counter." What works, she says, is to acknowledge their complaints and assure them that a school official will deal with their problem. "You validate their feelings of frustration," explains Dana Langley, a customer service representative for Bell Atlantic who deals daily with angry customers. In couples therapy and marriage workshops, husbands and wives learn to listen to and acknowledge each other's feelings. Indeed, sometimes what people really want most is a chance to have their grievance heard and acknowledged by others.

Healing can come from acknowledging the truth. In South Africa after apartheid, President Nelson Mandela established a Truth and Reconciliation Commission with a mandate to collect and investigate the accounts of the victims of apartheid, to offer amnesty for those who confessed their part in atrocities, and to make recommendations on reparations for the victims. The purpose was to use the healing power of the truth to help put the brutal past to rest. Limited by time and resources, the investigation could not possibly satisfy everyone's need for justice, but it did help many victims and their families. After testifying before the commission, one victim, Lucas Baba Sikwepere, who had been cruelly blinded by a police officer known as "Rambo," declared, "I feel what has been making me sick all the time is the fact that I couldn't tell my story. But now I—it feels like I got my sight back by coming here and telling you the story."

Encourage Apology

"I was part of a surgical team which made a mistake," the physician, a participant in one of my seminars, confided, "and we lost a child. I was in shock and didn't know what to say. I just went up to the child's mother and told her how very sorry I was. Three years later, the malpractice lawsuit finally came to court. Our lawyer just couldn't understand why I wasn't named when everyone else on the surgical team was. He asked me and I didn't know. Finally he couldn't contain his curiosity anymore so, during a deposition, he asked the child's mother why she wasn't suing me too. She replied, 'Because he was the only one who cared.' "

Apologies, sincerely offered, play a vital role in helping emotional wounds heal and restoring injured relationships. Recognizing this, the Bushmen, for instance, place great importance on apologies in their dispute resolution. The community encourages the "offender" to ask forgiveness in front of everyone. If the "victim" remains unable to forgive, "the community holds a dance in a circle," the Kua elder Korakoradue told me, "and they sing and ask the gods to remove the bitterness in the person's heart."

As third parties, we often don't need to do much except offer encouragement. "Our last meeting changed how we view our marriage," announced a husband to Paul Coleman, the therapist he and his wife had been seeing for some time. "For all that's been accomplished this past year with you, your question to us about whether we'd ever forgive each other might be the most important thing you've ever said." Coleman was surprised, scarcely remembering having asked the question. Yet it proved to be a turning point. While up until then the couple had made slow progress backing away from the brink of divorce, after that, Coleman reports, they were a "transformed couple." "Forgiveness was their goal, and they worked hard on it. Resentments really did wither, hope emerged healthy and vigorous, and they were in love again. Six months after we terminated, they were still going strong."

The surrounding community's reaction to violence can often make the difference between vengeance and reconciliation. When, in December 1997, the first teenager in more than two years was killed in Boston, the neighbors did not respond the way they had always done before by simply adding another lock and bolt to their doors. Instead, they came in great numbers to offer their condolences to the family and to express their concern about future violence. It was a genuine showing of the third side. The slain youth's friends talked of revenge, but at the funeral, the victim's cousin Carl Jefferson announced, "His blood is crying out to all of us. What will you do in regard to his life and legacy? Let's end this violence." No vengeance killing took place.

Forgiveness is not easy. "I've heard people say that forgiveness is for wimps," writes Marietta Jaeger. "Well, I say then that they must never have tried it. *Forgiveness is hard work.* It demands diligent self-discipline, constant corralling of our basest instincts, custody of the tongue, and a steadfast refusal not to get caught up in the mean-spiritedness of our times. It doesn't mean we forget, we condone, or we absolve responsibility. It does mean we let go of the hate, that we try to separate the loss and the cost from the recompense or punishment we deem is due. This is what happened to me," she explains as she recounts how she came to talk with and forgive the sick young man who murdered her seven-year-old daughter.

One person's act of forgiveness can sometimes move an entire nation. On Sunday, November 8, 1987, Gordon Wilson and his twenty-year-old daughter Marie were laying a wreath for the war dead at Enniskillen in Northern Ireland when a bomb exploded. Wilson lay buried under several feet of rubble, fumbling for his glasses, his shoulder dislocated. His daughter lay beside him, dying. Later that evening, in an interview with the BBC, Wilson described with anguish his last conversation with his daughter and his feelings toward her killers: "She held my hand tightly, and gripped me as hard as she could. She said, 'Daddy, I love you very much.' Those were her exact words to me, and those were the last words I ever heard her say." To the astonishment of listeners, Wilson went on to add, "But I bear no ill will. I bear no grudge. Dirty sort of talk is not going to bring her back to life. She was a great wee lassie. She loved her profession. She was a pet. She's dead. She's in Heaven and we shall meet again." As historian Jonathan Bardon recounts, "No words in more than twenty-five years of violence in Northern Ireland had such a powerful, emotional impact." In a few words, Gordon Wilson had spoken for all those on both sides who had lost family and friends—and he had furthered for many the slow painful process of healing.

The Goal Is Reconciliation

"Is there going to be a war?" my sons, aged nine and eleven, asked. I had been invited in the autumn of 1998 to facilitate a meeting of a group of community activists who had fallen out with one another.

"I don't know," I replied. As it turned out, each person spoke about his or her pain, about feeling disrespected or unappreciated by the others. Each person struggled to listen to the others, to acknowledge mistakes, to apologize, and to forgive. I did very little but listen. Later the boys asked me how the war went. "It went pretty well," I was able to say. "Each fought for their own truth in the best way possible—through dialogue and forgiveness."

As the Bushmen recognize, it is not enough simply to find a solution to the dispute. The community—the precious web of ties on which all depend—needs to be made whole again. One small way the company and union sought to achieve this at the strike-torn coal mine was to organize the first annual employees' picnic. Amid feasting and sporting activities, one of the mine foremen and his band played blue-grass and country music. The co-organizers of the event were the very men, the chief mine foreman and the local union president, who had initially blamed the conflict on each other. The wounds had begun to heal.

Chapter 7

CONTAIN

Witness, Referee, Peacekeeper

The best general does not fight.
—Sun Tzu

 Twenty-five hundred years ago during a period of terrible civil wars in China, the philosopher Mo Tzu roamed the country with his band of disciples, preaching the virtues of peace and teaching practical techniques for defense. When they heard of an imminent war, they would immediately travel to the place in order to dissuade the parties from fighting. If they found a city already under siege, Mo Tzu would offer his services as Mediator to the warring parties. If the attackers rejected his offer, he and his disciples would take the side of the defenders and fight the battle to a standstill—whereupon he would offer again to mediate a peace settlement.

As in Mo Tzu's time, much of the world is rent by sharply polarized conflicts. Many groups and individuals still believe that force is the only way to resolve serious conflicts. As Mo Tzu's experience illustrates, sometimes prevention and resolution alone may not stop escalation. The final challenge for the third side is whether, in these circumstances, it can *contain* the power struggle so that the parties may be brought back to the negotiating table.

As Mo Tzu understood, unresolved conflict escalates because no one is paying *attention* to the conflict or, even if someone is, because no one sets *limits* on the fighting, or, lastly, because no one intervenes to provide *protection.* Mo Tzu sought to perform all three functions; we as thirdsiders can learn to do the same. We can contain conflict by playing three successive, increasingly interventionary roles: as Witness, as Referee, and as Peacekeeper.

WHY CONFLICT ESCALATES		WAYS TO CONTAIN CONFLICT
No attention	→	8. The Witness
No limitation	→	9. The Referee
No protection	→	10. The Peacekeeper

 ## 8. THE WITNESS
PAYING ATTENTION TO ESCALATION

In the Amish farm country west of Philadelphia, the corrupt city police chief and his cronies had finally run down the honest cop in hiding who had uncovered their involvement in drug trafficking. After a dramatic cat-and-mouse hunt around a barn, the police chief caught up with the hero and forced him to give up his gun by threatening to kill the Amish woman he loved. The chief was about to dispatch the honest hero to his Maker—when suddenly, all around, there loomed a dozen solemn bearded faces of Amish farmers. They did not say a word but simply watched. A long moment elapsed as the police chief looked at them, realizing he could neither kill his intended victim in front of witnesses nor kill the witnesses. He reluctantly put down his gun.

This scene from the popular movie *Witness* captures the power of ordinary community members to contain violence. The Amish farmers were present as the third side in perhaps its most elemental form, seemingly doing nothing, but in fact playing the critical role of Witness. Like the Amish, we are all potential Witnesses.

Watch Out for Early Warning Signals

"We've got cops and clergy out there, visiting thirty-six schools and countless homes, trying to identify gang wannabes," says Boston Police Commissioner Paul Evans, speaking about community efforts to stop gang violence. "We didn't have to wait for three or four homicides before realizing we had a problem with the Bloods and Crips gangs."

As Commissioner Evans recognized, destructive conflict does not just break out but escalates through different stages, from tension to overt conflict to violence. By watching carefully, we can detect warning signals, which, if acted on, can save lives.

Early warning signals appear most clearly to those of us immediately around the disputants. "We all know everyone intimately," a Semai tribesman once told me. "We know everyone's personality. We can tell when they are angry and when trouble is brewing." In the days leading up to the fatal shooting of five students at a Jonesboro, Arkansas, school in March 1998, thirteen-year-old Mitchell Johnson and eleven-year-old Andrew Golden made their intentions clear to those around them. "I have a lot of killing to do," one of them remarked to a schoolmate. One of them even threatened a fellow student with a knife the day before the killing. Tragically, their friends and schoolmates did not pass on the information to those who might have headed off the impending massacre.

Perhaps the single most important action we can take is to pay attention to danger signals. "Hey, everyone knew he had a short fuse," a fellow postal clerk said about Thomas McIlvane, the mail carrier who killed three supervisors and wounded six others in a rampage at the Royal Oak, Michigan, regional postal center on November 14, 1991. "He told anyone who wanted to listen there'd be hell to pay if he wasn't reinstated. He even threatened some of the officials here over the telephone. The guy obviously had real problems."

On the largest scale as well, destructive conflict is often predictable. The war in Yugoslavia, for instance, was widely foreseen by analysts. And Saddam Hussein's 1991 surprise invasion of Kuwait should have come as no surprise. Here was a leader who had ruthlessly killed anyone who stood in his way, who had dropped chemical bombs on Kurdish villages in his own country, and who had previously attacked another neighbor, Iran, ten years earlier. If any more warning were necessary, Hussein ominously advanced his troops to the Kuwaiti border and left them there for a full week before invading. Unfortunately, the world ignored all these warning signals. Instead, during the decade before the invasion, it showered Hussein with advanced weaponry, and during the weeks before, it gave him mixed signals as to how it would react.

As a professional field, early warning remains in its infancy, but it is progressing. Police forces, which have traditionally aimed at arresting violent offenders *after* the fact, now develop "threat assessment" techniques to identify potential perpetrators *before* the damage is done. They have discovered that offenders typically have a traceable history of problems, disputes, and failures. Once they identify a person at risk of using violence, they can usually manage him or her by working with family, friends, neighbors, social service staff, and courts—in other words, by mobilizing the third side.

On the scale of nations, researchers are developing sets of indices which can help spot emerging ethnic conflict before it breaks out into violence. When human rights violations intensify, refugee flows increase, and governments turn more oppressive and unstable, ethnic war grows more likely. The United Nations, national governments, humanitarian agencies, and conflict-resolution groups are beginning to pool their knowledge, thus creating an effective early warning network.

Early warning is not enough, however. Early action must follow. After a promotions company in Los Angeles fired an employee, for example, co-workers reported that he had voiced threats against the manager, and security consultant David Smith was alerted. When the former employee came to the office the next day, Smith and a security guard met him and searched him for weapons. Finding none, Smith talked with him. In the end, the former employee decided to pray rather than confront the manager. Then Smith escorted him from the property. In the face of threatened violence, the co-workers and security people—the third side—had acted as an anti-violence network.

Go on Patrol

As Witnesses, we need not limit ourselves to watching; more actively, we can go on patrol. When two days of racial fighting in 1997 set off rumors of violent revenge at one middle school in Florida, United Colors, a student group formed earlier to counter racism and violence, started patrolling the halls and urged the principal to ban book bags and backpacks until fears about weapons died down. It worked. In thousands of violence-plagued schools across America, teachers and parents have come to rely on student groups like United Colors to help keep the peace by patrolling campuses and reporting incidents. "The heart of the philosophy is watching out for each other and helping each other, reporting crime because it's the right thing to do," says Betty Ann Good, the founder of Miami-based Youth Crime Watch of America.

At a neighborhood level, the Guardian Angels perform much the same role. Unarmed young people, they patrol the streets of many American cities in order to prevent robberies and violence. In Bloomington, Indiana, a group called Moms on Patrol walks the streets with cellular phones, looking out for dangerous gang activity, and reporting it to the police. On the global level, UN peacekeeping forces, armed only for self-defense, patrol hot spots around the world.

As in the movie *Witness*, the act of witnessing alone can often help prevent violence. During the Central American wars of the 1980s, church groups from North America and Europe went to "bear witness," spending time in villages threatened by paramilitary groups or the army. Similarly, during the violent transition to majority rule in South Africa, citizens from local peace committees, both white and black, would stay with people whose lives had been threatened.

Speak Out

"When there is gang warfare," explains Boston Police Commissioner Paul Evans, "we call [gang] members in for an open session with representatives from the District Attorney's office, the probation officers, social-service workers and neighborhood ministers and say, 'Look, the community is telling you that the violence has got to stop. If it doesn't, the whole system here is going to indict you, sentence you and send you to prison.'" Witnesses, in other words, need not limit themselves to watching; they can speak up to persuade the parties to cease fighting.

In the former Yugoslavia, I once asked a group of UN peacekeepers to describe their job. "It is 90 percent negotiation," they choroused. They explained how they spent most of their time trying to induce warring parties to withdraw to the agreed-upon lines, to respect the cease-fire, and not to shoot when provoked by a hothead on the other side or when someone's cow wandered over the line. The same opportunity to speak up against destructive conflict is available to each of us in the daily conflicts around us. "One of the kids from my class and a kid I didn't know were fighting," says six-year-old Jimmy Ellison, newly trained in conflict resolution, "until I told them, 'Maybe you guys should quit fighting, work the problem out together, and then play.'" It worked.

By speaking up, we as thirdsiders can actively delegitimize violence. In one extraordinary instance at the height of World War II, hundreds of Christian women turned out in the middle of Berlin to protest the arrest of their Jewish husbands, whom the Nazis were about to deport to the death camps. "Give us back our husbands," the women chanted. The Nazi police came out to disperse them with guns and fierce dogs. The women fled at first, but later regathered and continued their protest day after day before the eyes of ordinary Berliners, who served as Witnesses. Although the Nazi regime had no compunctions about massacring innocents, they were nonetheless reluctant to attack the women for fear of demoralizing the larger population. In the end, the Nazis gave up and released two thousand men, the great majority of whom went on to survive the war.

Get Help Fast

In the movie *Witness*, the Amish farmers come running because a little boy rings the barn bell for help. The Witness sounds the alarm to call the attention of other thirdsiders who can intervene as Mediators, Peacekeepers, or other Witnesses. For instance, at one New York school using a violence prevention program, a student who brought a knife was quickly reported by another student. School officials immediately confiscated the knife and suspended the student; only through a mediated agreement involving the community was he allowed to reenter the school.

One major reason why the incidence of street violence is so low in Japan is the widespread participation of citizens as Witnesses who report problems to the policeman stationed in the neighborhood. The lesson is catching on in the United States, where police forces are learning that, in order to reduce violence, they too must draw on local communities for information, early warning, and support. Called community policing, this approach is credited with decreasing violent crime all the way from New York City to Hawaii. In Spokane, Washington, for example, an armed robber called the "Bad Tooth Bandit" after his poor dental work, was nabbed nine blocks from the crime scene because the neighborhood immediately called in reports to the police substation. "The police are moving away

from a 'we do it for you' approach to where 'we're working with you,' "
explains Boston police captain Robert Dunford. "This requires citizens' taking responsibility."

The media play a key role in sounding the alarm. Their reporting
alerts thirdsiders around the world. When an artillery shell landed in
a Sarajevo marketplace in February 1994, the world community saw
the televised images of innocents slain, public revulsion was voiced,
and governments hitherto reluctant to act were spurred into action.
NATO bombers threatened to destroy Serb artillery in the hills over-
looking Sarajevo and the artillery attacks ceased for months. Just in
the course of doing their jobs, media professionals can serve as the
eyes and ears of the third side.

 ## 8. THE REFEREE
SETTING LIMITS TO FIGHTING

Susan and Rick's marriage was in trouble. They were fighting all
the time.

"You're wasting our money on trinkets!" he would shout.

"What about you, Mr. Showboat, buying drinks for all your
friends?"

"That was last year! I'm talking about yesterday."

"So what? All you're worried about is money when you ought to
worry about what kind of father you're being to our kids!"

And on it would go until he would threaten to move out and
she'd become frantic.

Their marriage counselor intervened, teaching them rules for carrying on an argument: to use "I" statements rather than "you" statements, to focus on one issue at a time, and to impose a "statute of
limitations" on old grievances. The next time Rick had an issue
about money, he began by asking if this was a good time to talk.
When Susan said okay, he announced, "Susan, I am really worried

about our finances. We agreed on a budget. And I feel angry, confused, and powerless when you go out shopping and come back with things that put us over budget that I don't think we really need."

"Rick," Susan countered, "I feel angry too. I feel blamed—and wrongly so. Let me explain what I was trying to do. . . ."

Some fighting can be salutary. In democratic politics, fair fighting can ensure that injustices are addressed, abuses stopped, and excesses kept in check. During my work as a mediator and arbitrator in the coal mines of Appalachia, I remember some old-time labor relations people arguing that, every once in a while, a mine needed a good strike in order to surface the suppressed resentments and exorcise the animosities. I have heard therapists say the same about some marriages; the couple needs a good fight. Fighting can serve the function of clearing the air and bringing suppressed problems into sharp focus.

If and when people do fight, it is important to reduce the harm. That is the role of the Referee, who sets limits on fighting. Parents and teachers know this role well: "Pillows are okay, but fists are not." "No blows above the neck or below the belt." As Referees, we can change the way people fight, replacing the more destructive weapons and methods with substantially less destructive ones. Just as we fireproof a house to protect against fire, we can think of "fightproofing" a relationship or situation to protect against destructive fights.

Establish Rules for Fair Fighting

"You on the 11th of May," went the hand-delivered note from one small business owner in Kansas City to a rival with whom he had fallen into a rancorous conflict, "left me a very insulting voice mail and viewed yourself in safety from the contempt I held you in. I hope, sir, your courage will be ample security to me that I will obtain speedily that satisfaction due me for the insults offered."

The reply came promptly: "I await satisfaction for the harm thou hast violated upon my person and my industry. We entreat thee for the day unless of course your pen hath more courage than thou."

Thus did two business rivals in Kansas City defuse their conflict— with paint guns in a costumed duel at sunrise witnessed by their friends drinking champagne. In a time-honored fashion for handling tensions, they fought with clearly understood rules and Referees.

During the Cold War, the United States and the Soviet Union evolved a code of conduct to contain their periodic conflicts around the globe. Rule number one was: Never use nuclear weapons, even against other parties. This rule turned into a taboo as strong as any tribal taboo. Rule number two was: Never put American and Soviet soldiers into situations where they would be firing directly at one another. Leaders feared that breaching either rule could all too easily escalate into a thermonuclear war. The rules may seem simple, but they helped avert World War III.

The same kind of rules apply on the streets. "If I can get them to have a fist fight, that's great," declares Ron Sinkler, a former gang member and prison inmate who now works for the city of Boston. His main priority, he says, is to persuade gang members to settle their disputes without guns. "I try to explain that if you use a gun, then you're going to prison. Kids aren't stupid. They listen, some of them anyhow."

The workplace too can benefit from rules for fair fighting. At one major corporation in the midst of a merger and acquisition wave, the executives explained to me how one of their principal tasks was "deconflicting," by which they meant reducing destructive competition between different parts of the newly merged businesses. Another giant company, in the telecommunications industry, was faced with the dilemma of how to continue to compete with its biggest competitor, who coincidentally was a major customer, a significant supplier, as well as a joint venture partner. Both companies decided, for example, not to engage in negative advertising campaigns that explicitly targeted the other. As for the labor-management area, labor laws explicitly spell out the rules for holding strikes; they allow pickets outside the factory grounds, for example, but only if they do not block others from entering and leaving the factory.

Referees have even arrived on the Internet. America Online, the world's largest Internet provider, has recruited nearly fourteen thousand volunteers to patrol over a hundred and eighty thousand continuing conversation groups to ensure that people do not harass, threaten, or deliberately embarrass others, a code of conduct accepted by subscribers when they sign up for the service. A further group of about a hundred, known as the Community Action Team, help determine when a comment crosses the line. While America Online was criticized, with good reason, when it suspended for three weeks a conversation about Northern Ireland that was getting belligerent, its initiative is an interesting large-scale experiment in the use of a code of conduct and Referees in a public forum.

Codes of conduct have a place in political campaigns as well. "We were frustrated by the personal attacks, one candidate calling the other one a liar," explained Nancy Koch of Rochester, New York. "People were getting angry and cynical." So a group of citizens—civic activists, campaign workers, former public officials, members of the media—devised a strategy called "Project Positive Campaign" that, through fliers and public service announcements in the media, urged voters to let their candidates know that they would support only those who ran positive, informative campaigns. As a start, candidates withdrew several negative "attack ads" after voters complained.

An old missionary in New Guinea told me about a battle he had witnessed in which a gun was used for the first time. All the warriors were fighting from a distance with their carefully orchestrated strategies for dodging arrows—and then a loud report was heard and a warrior dropped dead from a bullet. People were shocked. The elders felt outraged. "This is not fighting," they roared, "this is murder!" Like the tribal elders, the community can play a critical role as Referee. Each of us can serve as a potential Referee in the conflicts around us.

Remove Offensive Arms

During a house-to-house petition campaign in the Iowa country-side in the early 1980s, one woman farmer listened attentively to the campaigner's advocacy for a "freeze" on the testing and manufacture of nuclear weapons, thought about it for a while, and then pronounced slowly and reflectively, "It's time to take the toys away from the boys and tell 'em to come on in."

One way to stop people from using dangerous weapons against each other is to take them away. In Great Britain, the annual murder rate stands at one per hundred thousand people, while in the United States the rate is at least eight times higher. One powerful reason is that firearms, tightly controlled in Britain, are plentiful and easily available in America. The death rate among American children from firearms is nearly sixteen times higher than among children in twenty-five other industrialized countries combined. Far from "fight-proof," American society remains tragically "fight-prone."

To combat teen homicide in Boston in the 1990s, the Boston Gun Project sought to keep guns out of the hands of youths. Researchers at Harvard University provided information about the kinds of guns used by teenagers, and government officials then developed strategies for tracking down and arresting suppliers of these types of guns. The project also established a program to buy back guns from teenagers. Backed by the community, the police rigorously enforced firearms restrictions and the county imposed heavy sentences on offenders. The collaboration among researchers, government agencies, and the community worked. In 1996, no youths under seventeen died from handgun violence; and homicide rates for people under twenty-four had dropped by three-quarters from the 1990 numbers. The successful initiative has now spread to at least seventeen other cities. Hiding the poisoned arrows helps.

At the international level, the process of disarmament can seem maddeningly slow and frustrating. I remember participating in a meeting at Harvard in early 1981 of a group of scholars and peace activists on the subject of the "nuclear freeze." I felt sympathetic but skeptical about the possibility of success. But I was wrong. Those same activists later went on to create an effective public movement. Although the idea met official resistance at the time, within a few years, the United States and the Soviet Union had negotiated not merely a freeze but a substantial reduction in their nuclear stockpiles. Both nations began painstakingly to cut missiles up into iron scrap, dismantle atomic bombs, and neutralize deadly chemical agents. I have learned that, in a gradual process like disarmament, what seems impossible at the beginning can eventually come to seem almost natural.

Nations are more likely to enter into and abide by arms control and disarmament treaties if they have confidence that no one can secretly violate their provisions. Previously unimaginable, American teams have traveled around Russia inspecting plants, and Russian teams have done the same in the United States. Verification can also take advantage of the Knowledge Revolution. Already, satellites can capture pictures of tanks, artillery, missile silos, and production facilities anywhere on the planet. The American spy plane "Blackbird" can survey one hundred thousand square miles an hour, detecting objects from a distance of fifteen miles above the earth that are as little as twelve inches across. Infrared imaging systems can register the heat from objects and activities hidden from view; the United Nations used them to uncover hidden Iraqi weapons after the Gulf War. Radar can track objects from more than a thousand miles off, and seismic instruments can detect test explosions many thousands of miles away. Electronic signals of all sorts can be detected and decoded. And the technology grows more sophisticated every year.

Strengthen Defenses—Nonoffensively

It is not easy to persuade people to lay down their arms. Many efforts at disarmament in the twentieth century have failed in good part because the weapons themselves were treated as the primary problem instead of as an unfortunate response to a condition of insecurity. Once people feel safer through strengthened defenses, they become more willing to discard their offensive weapons. That is one reason why Mo Tzu devoted so much of his time to teaching city-states how to build stronger walls.

One promising approach advocated by British military strategist Sir Basil Liddell-Hart is simultaneously to strengthen defenses as one gets rid of weapons that could be used to attack. Building stronger castle walls works better if accompanied by efforts to eliminate the siege artillery that could destroy those walls. The aim is simultaneously to reduce the power of offensive weapons and strengthen defenses to the point where the advantage in any fight goes to the defender. Any would-be aggressor would then think hard before attacking.

Switzerland illustrates the approach at work. Centuries ago, it adopted a policy of armed neutrality, actively signaling its intention of threatening no one. Today, its armed forces have no nuclear weapons, no long-range aircraft, no heavy bombers, and no tanks capable of advancing deep into enemy territory. Its weapons consist instead of antiaircraft systems, antitank weapons, antitank traps, short-range aircraft, helicopters, and light vehicles suitable for mountain defense. Switzerland relies heavily on its own people. As a schoolboy living there, I remember my teachers disappearing for weeks for their yearly military training. Eighty percent of the active male population, a force of some six hundred and fifty thousand, can be mustered within forty-eight hours. Other citizens are trained to maintain essential economic activities, provide medical services to the wounded, and offer nonviolent resistance to the invaders. The entire community is thus mobilized to provide defense without offense.

Nonoffensive defense stretches into the schoolyard. "Your mother is nutty!" the ten-year-old bully shouts in a school skit. "So that's why she hangs out in trees so much," responds the hero. "Hey, Spike!" calls out another bully. "I know," comes the response, "I worked really hard on my hair this morning. I even used extra hair spray." This skit, written by ten-year-olds, is used to teach other children in school how to defend themselves against insult and provocation with humor, not counterattacks. The children learn that being a leader means going out of their way to befriend children who have no friends, thus putting would-be bullies on notice that these children will not prove easy targets. On a physical level, many children learn the defensive martial arts of judo, jujitsu, and aikido, all ways of protecting themselves without hurting others.

Nonoffensive defense can be used in the workplace as well. When a man was stalking his former girlfriend at the Los Angeles law firm where she worked, "We went out and got a restraining order, hired a guard and locked the doors," recalls her boss, George Dale. Thanks to the protective intervention of the employee's work community, the harassing calls and visits stopped and the crisis subsided.

Tramping around the desert near my home one day, I was struck by the power of the simple cactus. The cactus does not seek to prick you but silently lets you know that if you seek to hurt it, you will regret it. It has succeeded admirably in the art of nonoffensive defense. While peace is often depicted as a Garden of Eden filled with juicy vulnerable plants that need fear no living things, I would gladly settle, at this point, at least insofar as nations are concerned, for a garden of prickly cacti.

 ## 10. THE PEACEKEEPER
PROVIDING PROTECTION

May 20, 1961. A group of African-American civil rights protesters led by John Lewis had just arrived at the bus station in Montgomery, Alabama, where a hate-filled white mob awaited them. As the mob closed in to attack with heavy clubs, Lewis urged his people: "Stand together. Don't run. Just stand together!" The mob yelled, "Kill him. Kill him!" Murder might have ensued had not Floyd Mann charged into the bus station. Mann, Alabama's public safety commissioner, was a committed segregationist but tough on law and order. He fired his gun into the air and shouted, "There'll be no killing today!" A white attacker raised his bat for what would have been a final and probably fatal blow against young William Barbee. Mann put his gun to the assailant's head. "One more swing," he said, "and you're dead." The violence promptly ceased.

Rarely does the third side act so dramatically, but it is frequently called upon to play the role of Peacekeeper. When the rules are broken and the limits on fighting exceeded, the community needs to employ the minimally forceful measures necessary to stop harmful conflict in its tracks. Peacekeeping need not be limited to specialists like the police and UN peacekeepers; as Mo Tzu demonstrated, it is a community function that anyone may be called upon to play.

Interpose

At Yerkes Research Lab, I once watched two adolescent male chimpanzees chasing each other and tussling. As the fight started to get serious, an adult male chimp lumbered over and interposed his body between the two adolescents. The confrontation came to an abrupt end. Indeed, it often suffices, Frans de Waal explained, for an adult chimp to take a single step toward the disputants or merely raise an eyebrow and the fighting stops.

Interposing is perhaps the most obvious step a Peacekeeper can take to halt an escalating conflict. When two children fight, adults can step in the middle and, if necessary, physically pull the two apart. When two men brawl in a public place, their peers can drag them off each other. When rival gangs in Los Angeles started to eye one another, a group of mothers would regularly interpose themselves; after a gang member was killed, they shepherded his "brothers" from the funeral ceremony safely through the enemy gang's territory.

Neighbors can intervene as well. John Andrews, the owner of a small moving company in Lincoln, Nebraska, routinely fields emergency calls from the local Rape–Spouse Abuse Crisis Center. He promptly shows up with his truck and helps the victims of domestic violence escape with their possessions. It can be dangerous work. In one instance, he recalls, "We knew the husband carried guns and might be back soon. We were trying to hurry, but the rain delayed us. Finally, we told her son, 'Look, if you see your dad returning, you need to call the sheriff.' " Fortunately, they all got out before the husband came back.

Thankfully, there *is* the sheriff. When a fight breaks out, people can summon the police. "Okay, that's enough! Let's break it up!" is a familiar cry. To avert violence, police in New York and other cities patrol gang-troubled neighborhoods at night, working together with the community to ensure that teenagers on probation are off the streets. In hot spots around the world, interposing is perhaps the chief role for international peacekeepers, who establish and occupy buffer zones between hostile forces. From Africa to Central America, and from Europe to Asia, men and women from dozens of nations, many of whom are former enemies, work together as Peacekeepers, risking their lives so that others might survive.

Enforce the Peace

Sometimes the community needs to go further and use actual force to protect the innocent and stop the aggressor. An extreme instance of peace enforcement occurred among the Bushmen in the late 1940s. A Ju/'hoan Bushman named /Twi, possibly a psychotic, killed two people and threatened to kill more; after exhausting other remedies, the community finally ambushed and fatally wounded him. After he had died, all the men and women stabbed his body with spears, thus symbolically sharing responsibility for killing him.

While the Bushmen do not have prisons to contain killers on the loose, modern society does. Imprisonment is one of the tools of peace enforcement. "We can disrupt a gang," Boston police lieutenant Gary French points out, "by incarcerating the most aggressive player."

No matter how strong any single aggressor, the third side is potentially stronger. Consider how a group of young women freed another young woman being forcibly abducted by six youths in a working-class neighborhood in Mexico. "She was screaming and kicking," reports anthropologist Laura Cummings. "Then some of these young *cholos*, four or five girls, came along and were yelling at the fellows to let her go. All but one did. So the girls picked up stones and sticks and started pelting the guy who was dragging the girl. He let go of the girl. . . . The fellows who were with him stood in a circle and did not intervene." The power of numbers helped liberate the victim while the legitimacy of the young women's intervention helped neutralize the attacker's allies.

Experiments with peace enforcement are occurring on an international scale. When Saddam Hussein invaded Kuwait in August 1991 and refused to withdraw his troops, the forces of thirty-eight countries from around the world, operating under a mandate from the United Nations, expelled the Iraqi forces and liberated Kuwait. Not only did the world community establish a precedent for repelling aggression against another nation; it also set a bold and remarkable precedent for intervening to defend an endangered minority *within* a nation. For when Saddam Hussein dispatched his surviving army units to crush the Kurds who had risen up against him, the world community intervened a second time in order to create a protected zone for the Kurds in the north of Iraq. While both instances were exceptional and their success was mixed, together they point toward a possible day when genocide and clear aggression will be stopped by the armed will of a united world community.

Preempt Violence Before It Starts

However necessary at the time, a peace enforcement effort such as the Gulf War is always accompanied by tragedy. Much better than stopping an ongoing fight is preempting it before it breaks out. Adequate early warning makes this more than a hypothetical possibility.

Had international peacekeepers, for instance, been dispatched to the Kuwait-Iraq border during the week Iraqi troops stood poised for invasion, they might not have been able to physically stop the Iraqi troops from crossing the border, but they would have sent an unmistakable signal to Saddam Hussein of what he could expect if he proceeded with the invasion. Hussein, a ruthless but calculating man, might well have decided to call off his troops.

An even more dramatic failure to preempt came three years later in Rwanda. As Lieutenant-General Romeo Dallaire, the commander of the local United Nations assistance mission, has attested, and an international panel of senior military leaders has confirmed, an intervention within two weeks of the initial outbreak of violence could have stopped the bloodshed and provided a secure environment in which Hutu and Tutsi leaders might have reduced ethnic tensions. A mere *five thousand* properly trained and armed UN peacekeepers, General Dallaire insists, could have saved the lives of *five hundred thousand* innocent children, women, and men.

As a successful example of preempting violence, consider the case of the former Yugoslav republic of Macedonia in the six years immediately following its independence. Threatened from the start with annexation by its neighbors, and divided by internal ethnic strife, Macedonia did not collapse, thanks in good part to the proactive deployment of an international peacekeeping contingent in 1993. Their presence served to calm tensions and foster a sense of security. While Macedonia's future remains uncertain as of this writing, the success of the peacekeeping deployment during these years cannot be denied.

The lesson here comes straight out of Sun Tzu: The best Peacekeepers never fight. They never fight because they don't need to. They accomplish their ends by intervening early and using persuasion. American police forces have learned this lesson, sometimes painfully, over the past two decades. Their old approach when confronted by hostage-takers, for example, was the "John Wayne" method: Surround the place, pull out a bullhorn, give the hostage-taker an ultimatum, "You've got three minutes to come out with your hands up!" then lob in the tear gas canisters and charge. The result, more often than not, was dead hostages, dead police, and dead hostage-takers. The 1993 tragedy at Waco, Texas, in which FBI forces stormed the retreat of a religious group, the Branch Davidians, was all too predictable; twenty-one children and seventy-four adults died needlessly in the ensuing fire.

The alternative and more effective approach is to surround the place, toss in a phone, and talk with the hostage-taker. Talking may take hours, days, or even longer, but with patience, listening, and negotiation skills, the police are able to bring the overwhelming majority of hostage-taking situations to a peaceful end without casualties and with the surrender of the hostage-taker.

The New Warriors

International peacekeeping can be perilous work. Indeed, it takes more valor to expose oneself to fire on the ground, as peacekeepers routinely do, than to hurl bombs and missiles from the air. Ironically, peacekeeping may revive the martial virtues that derive from having to confront one's enemy face-to-face and hand-to-hand, virtues that modern warfare has eroded. Peacekeepers may thus prove to be the real warriors of the world. So, while soldiers are often considered part of the problem of destructive conflict, they in fact constitute part of the solution, with an essential role to play as police, peacekeepers, and peace enforcers.

Valor, however, is not limited to soldiers or police. Consider the story of nurse Joan Black. In August 1993, Sophelia White entered a hospital in southern California with a gun, proceeded up to the third-floor nursery, and wildly fired six shots at nurse Elizabeth Staten, whom she accused of stealing her husband and children. Wounded, Staten fled downstairs, but White caught up with her at the chart desk and told her, "Prepare to die. Open your mouth." As she took aim, Joan Black intervened. She crossed the room, wrapped her right arm around White. "I figured if she could feel my body, maybe she wouldn't kill me." Tightening the hug, she placed her left hand over the gun and began to talk softly: "You're in pain. I understand, and we can work it out." After five, perhaps ten minutes, Sophelia White finally gave up her gun.

Not everyone is called upon to be as heroic as Joan Black, but everyone is a potential Peacekeeper, whether as parents, managers, or citizens. As such, our job is to contain conflicts, stop them from escalating into the zone of force, and enable them to be peacefully resolved.

PUTTING IT ALL TOGETHER

I have presented each of the ten roles of the third side as if it were entirely distant from the others. Usually, however, the roles are blended in the same dispute and often played by the very same people. In a Semai *bcaraa*', for example, the community of friends, family, and neighbors acts as Mediator, seeking an outcome acceptable to each side; as Arbiter, determining which social rules have been broken; as Equalizer, ensuring that neither disputant wins simply by virtue of superior power or status; and as Healer, restoring the broken relationship among the disputants.

While each of the ten roles of the third side can make a real difference, it is together that they fulfill their real potential as a force for peace. Consider how the different roles can come into play at the level of a classroom fight, of an ethnically divided community, and of the world as a whole.

Stopping a Classroom Fight

In one situation I know firsthand, eleven-year-old James had bullied his classmate Mark for a long time, ragging him over his poor English and foreign origins. In chemistry class one day, James spilled a test-tube full of water on Mark's head; Mark retaliated with a test-tube full of water mixed with chemicals. The dispute threatened to escalate.

When conflict breaks out like this, the ten roles work in reverse sequence, beginning with containment and looping back to resolution and prevention. In this case, the teacher, acting first as Witness and then as Peacekeeper, intervened to stop the fight. He emphasized to the whole class the potential dangers and, serving as Referee, forbade them to play or fight with chemicals.

From containment, the focus turned back to resolution. The next day, the teacher and the school principal held separate meetings with both Mark and James, each with their respective parents. They asked about what had caused the fight in the first place. After Mark told them about James's bullying behavior, they—acting as Referees—explained to James that it had to stop. Later, the teacher—serving as Mediator and Healer—convened a meeting with both boys to help them resolve their differences. The boys apologized to each other and promised not to fight anymore. In order to send a strong message to the community about the importance of not fighting in chemistry class, the principal, acting as Arbiter, suspended both boys for a day.

Prevention then became key. The school counselor spent time with each boy. She sought to understand from James why he had bullied Mark, and brainstormed with him about other ways to get respect and feel powerful, thus acting as Provider. She then role-played with Mark effective techniques to handle his emotions when provoked, serving as Teacher. The bullying ceased and the boys developed a respectful relationship.

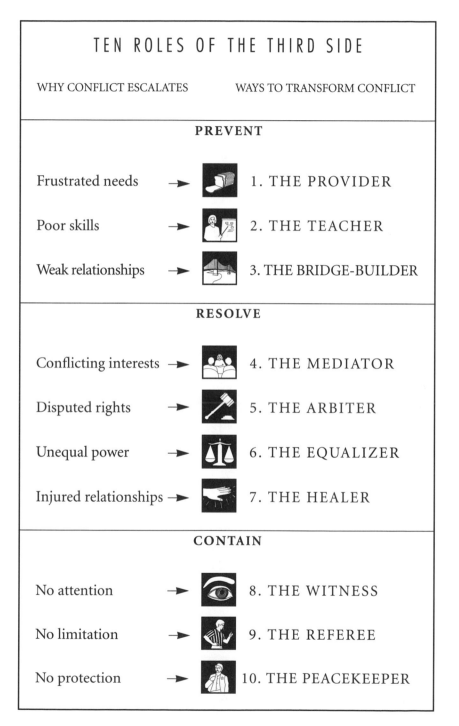

TEN ROLES OF THE THIRD SIDE

WHY CONFLICT ESCALATES   WAYS TO TRANSFORM CONFLICT

PREVENT

Frustrated needs   →   1. THE PROVIDER

Poor skills   →   2. THE TEACHER

Weak relationships   →   3. THE BRIDGE-BUILDER

RESOLVE

Conflicting interests → 4. THE MEDIATOR

Disputed rights → 5. THE ARBITER

Unequal power → 6. THE EQUALIZER

Injured relationships → 7. THE HEALER

CONTAIN

No attention → 8. THE WITNESS

No limitation → 9. THE REFEREE

No protection → 10. THE PEACEKEEPER

Preventing Ethnic Violence

Each of the third-side roles is like a single safety net. If one fails to catch destructive conflict, another stands ready. *The key is to line up all the safety nets in advance.*

Consider how this worked to prevent bloodshed in an ethnically divided community. The city of Bhiwandi in India was notorious for ethnic violence between Hindus and Muslims. Between 1970 and 1988, two major riots and several minor ones had left hundreds dead. In 1992, therefore, when Hindu extremists destroyed the Muslim mosque at Ajodhya, eight hundred miles to the northeast, people expected the worst to erupt in Bhiwandi, two-thirds of whose residents were Muslim. Yet, in sharp contrast to nearby Bombay, rocked by violent riots and police brutality, Bhiwandi remained peaceful.

The main reason Bhiwandi did not erupt into violence was that four years earlier, a farsighted police chief had undertaken a comprehensive community peace initiative in collaboration with local leaders. In the role of Bridge-Builders, they established, in each of the city's seventy neighborhoods, a peace committee, whose thirty members included everyone from teachers to tradesmen, and from factory owners to street vendors. Each committee met weekly with police to voice their concerns and discuss areas of tension in their neighborhood. No issue was considered irrelevant, even getting electricity properly connected. As one Bhiwandi leader put it, "The basic idea is that all these other problems eventually lead to a law and order problem." As Providers, then, the committees actively addressed their communities' frustrated needs. As Bridge-Builders, the committees helped build links between the different ethnic groups. And the police served as intermediaries—Mediators and Equalizers—between the communities and the often inefficient, sometimes corrupt city administration.

When tensions soared after the destruction of the Ajodhya mosque, the peace committees stood ready. Acting as Healers, they instantly sought to calm people's fear and anger. As Witnesses, they refuted the dangerous rumors that were spreading wildly and spoke out against violence. They also identified for the police individuals in their own communities who had incited violence and stockpiled weapons. These extremists found themselves temporarily detained by the police and their weapons confiscated. Police and peace committees thus ruled out the use of violence, serving together as Referees.

When the police found themselves attacked on several occasions, they refrained from opening fire, an action that in Bombay had only intensified the violence. Instead they sought assistance from the community, who helped them track down the violent offenders. The community effectively teamed up as Witnesses with the police, who acted as properly restrained Peacekeepers. Having worked hand in hand to prevent and resolve their underlying differences, the people of Bhiwandi were thus prepared to contain the conflict before it escalated into violence. While Bombay burned, Bhiwandi became a beacon for peace.

Preventing War

What works between individuals and between groups might also work between nations.

I once conducted a discussion on preventing war among a group of forty parliamentarians from twenty countries gathered at the United Nations. Since the gap was so large between the ideal of global security and the reality, I looked for a way to go beyond the usual cautious political speeches with their modest proposals and their calls to try harder. So I started the discussion with an imaginary newscast.

In the midst of a war between India and Pakistan, a reporter announced a nuclear bomb had been dropped on an Indian city. On television and radio, people around the world almost instantly learned about the devastation and started immediately clamoring for an end not just to the Indo-Pakistani war, but to nuclear weapons and to war itself. The political shock waves were intense. I asked the forty parliamentarians to imagine that they, as the leaders of their respective countries, were now meeting at the United Nations to decide what to do. A press conference had been scheduled two hours from then, so all eyes would be on them. Their task was to prepare a plan to reassure a panicking world.

Within two hours, forty parliamentarians from six continents devised a basic plan for global security and, to everyone's surprise, reached unanimous agreement. I was amazed by how excited normally stolid politicians became when able to free their imaginations. I was also struck by the similarity of each individual's vision of security—from the German's to the Gambian's and from the Mexican's to the American's. Perhaps I should not have been surprised. Devising a plan for global security is not rocket science. Each parliamentarian knew from the experience of his or her own country what security required: a police force able to stop and deter violence, the control and elimination of the most destructive weapons, a democratically elected legislative body able to resolve differences peacefully, a strong court able to bring justice and a new institution, a mediation service that would proactively seek to resolve conflicts before they escalated. In essence, the parliamentarians suggested mobilizing the world community to serve as Peacekeepers, Referees, Equalizers, Arbiters, and Mediators.

The world remains a long way from implementation of the parliamentarians' vision, but the direction is clear. None of the institutions they proposed could do the job alone, but all of them together, if supplemented by strong preventive measures and supported by the world community, might just suffice. As the Ethiopian proverb has it, "When spider webs unite, they can halt even a lion." The hope of humanity lies in weaving a series of spider webs in order to halt the lion of war.

Toward a Comprehensive System

Conflict today poses the same challenge that fire once did. Before the twentieth century, fire was one of people's greatest fears. In a few minutes, a fire raging out of control could destroy everything—houses, crops, and lives. Cities, with their closely placed buildings, posed the worst danger. When Mrs. O'Leary's cow kicked over a lantern in 1871, it began a fire that consumed most of Chicago. Yet, for all its evident danger, fire was long regarded as a natural and inevitable tragedy, part of human fate.

That is no longer true today in modern cities. Thanks to building regulations and fireproof materials, emergency exits and smoke detectors, and fire fighters and trucks—in short, a comprehensive fire prevention system—urban dwellers live largely free of fear of fire.

We have an analogous opportunity today when it comes to preventing destructive conflict. We can give up our belief in its inevitability, and learn step by step how to prevent, resolve, and contain it. The ten roles of the third side constitute a comprehensive system for transforming conflict into cooperation. Our challenge is to create such systems in every social domain—from our families to our organizations, from our neighborhoods to our nations, and from our interpersonal relationships to our world.

If we prove successful, schoolchildren may wonder one day why serious conflicts ever escalated to wars. They may be astonished why we did not take the simple precautions necessary to prevent conflagration. They may puzzle over why people did not see that whatever an effective system might cost in time and effort, its price is but a pittance compared to the exorbitant cost of destructive conflict.

Conclusion

TOWARD A CO-CULTURE

On a visit to Northern Ireland in March 1998, I was taken on an informal tour of the so-called "Peace Line" in Belfast. In the midst of an otherwise normal, bustling, and affluent European city, an ugly scar ran through the urban landscape, a boundary marked by high walls, barbed wire, security gates, and no-man's-land. It felt surreal, reminding me of the Berlin Wall. It served as the dividing line between Protestant and Catholic neighborhoods; so that no mistake could be made about which territory belonged to whom, even the sidewalk curbs and street lamp posts were identified—red, white, and blue in Protestant areas and green in Catholic districts.

That evening, I was taken to a restaurant in a little village across the international border in the Republic of Eire. Since the war ostensibly concerned whether Northern Ireland should remain part of the United Kingdom or should be united with the Republic of Eire, I expected the border to be a zone of tension. I could not have been more mistaken. We passed straight through the border without stopping; no one, in fact, was guarding the frontier. The real border, I suddenly realized, was not the border between states found on every map, but the border between Catholic and Protestant neighbors in Belfast.

That experience summed up for me the paradox of where humanity stands today. The world is changing fast. Boundaries grow increasingly porous everywhere—from international borders to interdepartmental boundaries at work. And yet borders remain, as in the city of Belfast, in the fearful minds of men and women. We are rapidly becoming a single global community, an interconnected body of peoples and nations, yet the erasing of boundaries seems, if anything, to increase conflict. The communications revolution gives us the ability to reach almost anyone on earth. Catholics can speak to Protestants, Israelis to Arabs, Tutsis to Hutus. But the question is: Do we know what to say?

No more daunting challenge faces us than learning to live together. How can we deal with our differences without either suppressing them or going to war over them? How can we create a co-culture of coexistence, cooperation, and conflict resolution?

THE OPPORTUNITY

If the challenge is great, so is the opportunity. As I hope this inquiry has shown, a constellation of favorable factors is in place. The conditions are ripe for learning.

A reexamination of the evolution of human conflict offers little cause for despair. For the great bulk of our time on earth, coexistence has been more the norm than coercion. Human beings are just as capable of living in peace as they are of living at war with one another. Getting along is perhaps even more rooted in human nature than is fighting to the finish. We are Homo Negotiator.

How we get along turns out to be heavily influenced by the conditions under which we live. When our main resource is an expandable pie, when relationships are horizontal, when governance is democratic, when the third side is strong and exit is an option, it is easier to learn to get along. Those conditions, absent for much of the planet during the last five thousand to ten thousand years—the period we know as history—are returning with the Knowledge Revolution.

The logic of conflict is shifting from win-lose toward a choice between lose-lose or both-gain, partly because knowledge is an expandable pie and partly because knowledge has made the weapons of destruction ever more terrible and available.

A key dilemma remains how to resolve serious differences without resorting to domination or force. As we have seen, the alternative to negotiation need not be destructive escalation; it can instead be the systematic use of the emergent will of the community. Other than take sides or do nothing at all, another option exists for those of us who surround the conflicting parties: to take the third side.

We know that the third side can work because it already does—some of the time. In Kenneth Boulding's words, "What exists is possible." The task remaining is to take the success stories and make them the norm. Plenty of obstacles remain but none are insurmountable. There is no longer any *good* reason for war.

So to return to the question with which I began this inquiry: Is it possible for human beings to prevent war at home, at work, and in the world? I am not saying that it will happen. I am not even saying that it is probable. I am simply saying that it is possible, *humanly* possible.

The answer to the question then is: "Yes *if*." "Yes if" we learn the lesson; "yes if" we seize the opportunity before us; "yes if" we do the hard work; "yes if" we take on the new responsibility of the third side. The "if," in other words, depends on us.

WHAT CAN I DO?

The "if" is not a little "if." It is a big "IF." Getting along does not mean harmony, after all, but rather a great cooperative struggle to resolve our differences with a minimum of harmful strife. Getting along is not the absence of conflict, but the strenuous processing of conflicting needs and interests.

It is not easy to face the pain of human differences. It takes courage to look into the mirror when finding fault rather than gazing into the telescope. It takes guts to forgive and to apologize. It requires patience to listen and to search for agreement. The peace we can aspire to is not a harmonious peace of the grave, nor a submissive peace of the slave, but a hardworking peace of the brave.

In the sheer magnitude and complexity of the challenge, the struggle for peace, ironically enough, most closely resembles nothing so much as war itself. Think of how much work goes into preparing for and engaging in wars. Consider how many young men and women serve in the armed forces. Weigh how much treasure, talent, and blood are poured into this gigantic venture. Reflect on the around-the-clock vigilance required by huge numbers of individuals. No less effort will be required for the sake of peace.

Think too about the virtues required for the successful conduct of war. Courage? Peace demands just as much; facing up to force nonviolently calls for perhaps even more bravery and self-control than fighting. Cooperation and discipline? Solidarity and altruism? All these ingredients are needed to get to peace. Ironically, in the end, war may have served as a great training ground for peace. For peace is harder than war.

Getting to peace may not be easy, but there are some simple steps any of us can take to begin to mobilize the third side:

1. Change the Story

Perhaps the principal obstacle to preventing destructive conflict lies in our own minds—in the fatalistic beliefs that discourage people from even trying. The story that humans have always warred, and always will, is spread unchallenged from person to person and from parent to child. It is time, in our everyday conversations, to question and refute this story and its embedded assumptions about human nature. It is time to give our children—and ourselves—a more accurate and more positive picture of our past and our future prospects. From realistic hope springs action.

2. Learn Some Skills

"Why do you feel this way?" said the student recently trained in conflict resolution to the youth pointing a gun at his head at a night-time basketball game. "Don't you understand that if anything happens to me, you'll get life?" The youth put the gun away.

Each of us can benefit from honing our joint problem-solving and conflict resolution skills. There are many ways: take a class, read a book, or get some coaching from a friend or colleague. The key lies in practice; the more, the better. As with sports, no matter how skilled you already are, there always remains room for improvement.

3. Start Close to Home

"You have to remember all the steps," reports third-grade mediator Ian Morton, "but when it's over, it makes you feel very happy to help a friend." We don't need to look far to find a place to practice our thirdsider skills. Daily occasions abound at home among our family and friends, at school, at work among our colleagues, and in the neighborhood. It may be to listen and hear the parties out. It may be to facilitate dialogue between those who do not understand one another. It may be to use peer pressure to stop a fight and urge constructive resolution. Each of us has a role to play.

4. Mediate Your Own Disputes

"This one kid came up to me and was pushing me," recalls fifth-grader Alexandria Ritch, "and I said, 'Don't push me.' He said, 'What are you going to do about it, hit me?' And I said, 'I would never hurt you. I'm a Mediator, and hitting others isn't right.' He started listening to me . . . and then he said he was sorry and we got on the bus. I felt better because I was being a bigger person."

Even closer to home are our own disputes, which often prove the most challenging. It may not be easy to gain perspective, yet, if we can, each of the ten thirdsider roles is available to us. We can attempt to build bridges, heal wounds, and resolve our differences by ourselves. In the absence of a Mediator, we can, in effect, mediate our own dispute. If our efforts falter, we can actively seek the help of others, mobilizing the third side around us.

5. Do What You Do Best

As you look around and wonder how you can contribute to the wider community, you don't need to start from scratch. Instead, begin with what you already do and add an extra third-side dimension. Parents can help their children learn how to deal with conflicts constructively. A teacher can weave a conflict resolution strand into the subject matter, whether it is history, social studies, or languages. A religious leader can help people apologize and forgive. A lawyer can facilitate the creative resolution of disputes by practicing "collaborative lawyering" or mediation. A journalist can spotlight emergent conflicts for public attention. A police officer can mediate domestic disputes informally. Some of us may have special talents as Providers, others as Bridge-Builders, and still others as Peacekeepers. The key is to identify your distinctive competence and incorporate it into what you do every day.

6. Volunteer Your Services

"In over two hundred cases [I mediated], I can think of only two that bogged down," says seventy-four-year-old volunteer community mediator Gail Robertson, speaking of her experience over the past ten years. "If they're willing to listen, speak, and follow the process, it works."

Like Gail Robertson, any one of us can volunteer our time and skills. Many communities have neighborhood justice centers that rely on volunteer mediators and staff. Schools have peer mediation programs. You can volunteer as a peer juror, as a neighborhood peace officer, or as a mentor or sports coach for needy teens. You can also teach others in the community about joint problem-solving and conflict resolution. Further afield, there exist volunteer opportunities as election monitor or humanitarian aid worker in conflicted societies. All these roles help build a strong third side.

7. Fill a Missing Role

The firm's strategic planning committee was paralyzed. Although the vice presidents disagreed with the senior vice president for administration, none of them wanted to confront him directly, nor did they intend to implement what he proposed. Finally Olivia Lane spoke up in exasperation, pointing out how they were skirting the real issues. As manager of executive training and development, she was not formally a member of the committee, but informally she had spent a lot of time listening individually to each of the participants. Once she brought the issues out in the open, the committee members began discussing them in earnest. For follow-up sessions, the committee appointed Lane as official facilitator. The result: the first strategic plan ever implemented at the firm.

Just as Olivia Lane spotted the conflicting interests and surfaced them as an informal Mediator, so each of us can identify the causes of escalation around us and then play—or find someone else to play—the appropriate thirdsider roles that address them. In this way, role by role, voice by voice, we can construct a comprehensive system for transforming conflict.

8. Create a Winning Alliance

"The deal we cut [with the police] was, 'Take this one off the streets, we can deal with him in prison ministry,' " explained the

Reverend Jeffrey Brown. The police, in turn, depend on the ministers to work with the more winnable kids. "Right now," said the Reverend Eugene Rivers, "any cop in Dorchester can dump a kid off in Baker House [a neighborhood recreation center and parish house run by Rivers] and say, 'Look, I'm gonna crack this kid's skull, take him.' So we have taken the pressure off the police to play heavies." The ministers and the police have created a winning alliance against teenage violence.

Don't fall into the trap of thinking you need to do it all yourself. Recruit help. Take a lesson from the Bushmen and speak to all the disputants' friends and relatives. Keep on strengthening the third side until it becomes more powerful than any aggressor.

9. Urge Your Organization to Take the Third Side

Most of us belong to organizations—businesses, professional associations, unions, civic clubs, cultural affinity groups, or political parties—that can greatly magnify our thirdsider efforts. We can leverage our membership, turning our organizations into thirdsiders. On the issues that divide the wider community, our organization can take a stand for constructive discussion. They can serve as Bridge-Builders, for example, offering public fora for dialogue, or as Equalizers, providing weaker parties with information and support.

10. Support the Third Side in the Wider Community

"As long as we the citizens let [negative political campaigning] be effective, it will continue," says Becky Cain of the League of Women Voters. "We are the only ones with the power to stop it." Even where you are unable to assume a direct role in the wider conflicts surrounding us, you can still lend your voice to the third side. You can speak out and cast your vote against harmful conflict and violence.

When even a single person takes a stand, the ripple effect can result in surprising change.

11. Help Build Thirdsider Institutions

Programs and institutions are the backbone of the third side. Each of us can champion the teaching of tolerance and conflict resolution to children of all ages as a standard part of the school curriculum. We can promote the establishment of community justice centers. In the wider world, we can support the development of international mediation services, the strengthening of the International Criminal Court, and the creation of standing peacekeeping units that can act promptly to prevent genocide and war.

12. Help Create a Social Movement

For some, serving as part of the third side may mean nothing more than putting a new label on what they have been doing all the time. For others, it may mean engaging in new activities. For all, it may mean a new awareness of themselves as part of the larger human community engaged in the historic project of learning to live and work together. Just as the environmental movement addresses the relationship between human beings and nature, so a coexistence movement would deal with the relationship between human beings and other humans. In coalition with other great social movements like those for human rights, women's rights, and democracy, such a movement could help raise awareness and mobilize a powerful third side.

Such a movement needs a new vocabulary. In my wilder flights of imagination, I visualize a prefix like "co" (from the Latin "with") starting to be attached to names in the way that "eco" is for environmental terms. "Co-democracy" would mean the practice of democracy through consensus-building and collaboration rather than by destructive combat. "Co-history" would mean the history of how humans have gotten along together. "Co-culture" would mean a culture of conflict resolution and cooperation.

These are but a few of the possible steps any of us can take. Peace is a process that begins with each of us and radiates out from there.

LEARNING TO LIVE TOGETHER

This past century has been full of atrocities inflicted by human beings on other humans. Tragically, it remains entirely possible that the coming century could be equally if not more hellish. In the midst of the horror, however, lies the hope that we can learn to live together.

Learning, after all, is the human specialty. Throughout our evolution, humanity has faced challenges that have wiped out other species—and survived by learning new ways to subsist. Accustomed to a warm climate, our ancestors adapted to the cold of the Ice Age by learning to use fire and clothing. When the great hoofed animals perished with the sudden warming, humans survived by learning new ways to hunt and new eating habits. Confronted by growing population and scarce game, our ancestors learned to subsist on plants they could grow and animals they could domesticate.

The eighteenth-century philosopher Voltaire expressed the widespread beliefs of his time when he pronounced that "slavery is as ancient as war and war as human nature." What has happened to the institution of slavery can now happen to the institution of war. From dueling to the divine right of kings, human history is littered with ways of relating to one another, each believed in its time to be fixed in the very order of things and each now relegated to the history books. It is time now for war to follow the same path.

In the space of a century, humanity has succeeded in making technological breakthroughs of evolutionary importance. We have put humanity in touch through instant communication, split the atom, and traveled to the moon. The challenge now is to learn to make social breakthroughs of similar proportions. People at the beginning of the past century would have found it difficult to imagine the changes that have taken place since. The lesson is clear: Future reality extends far beyond what is now deemed realistic. In this new millennium, much is possible. Why not the age-old dream of peace?

A Chinese nobleman once asked his gardener to plant the seed of a rare and beautiful tree. When the gardener protested, "But sir, that tree will take a hundred years to flower," the nobleman replied, "Then we'd better plant it this afternoon." Because the task of creating a genuine co-culture may take a generation or more, there is no better time for us to begin than now.

A ROAD MAP TO
Getting to Peace

Author's Note   viii

Acknowledgments   x

Introduction: Can We All Get Along?   xv

I.   THE MISSING KEY

1.   *The Third Side*   *3*

Reimagining conflict as three-sided   4

   Conflict resolution in simpler societies   5

   The challenge in modern societies   6

From the nuclear family to the human family   8

   In the family   8

   In the workplace   9

   In the community   10

   In a warring world   12

   Across domains   13

What exactly is the third side?   14

   People from the community   14

Using the power of peers   15
From a perspective of common ground   16
Supporting a process of dialogue and nonviolence   16
Aiming for a product of a "triple win"   17
Who is the third side?   18
    Outsiders   18
    Insiders   19
    An inner third side?   20
    All together   22
The third side is us   22
The potential of the third side   24

II.   A BRIEF HISTORY OF CONFLICT

2.   *From Coexistence*   **29**

The archaeological puzzle   31
    The startling absence of evidence   33
    The puzzle   36
The cooperative ape   38
    Cooperating to compete   38
    An expandable pie   39
    The most successful way of life—yet   40
The logic of coexistence   41
    Cooperation does not exclude conflict   41
    Little place for coercion   42
    Learning the logic   44
A conflict management system   47
But isn't violence human nature?   51
    False polarities   51
    What about the chimps?   52
    Capable of war, capable of peace   54
Homo Negotiator   55

3.   To Coercion   *57*

A revolution in human life   59
   Humans settle down and start farming   59
   The population grows   60
The consequences for conflict   61
   The expandable pie becomes fixed   62
   "Too many people in the same place"   63
   "The fight follows you around"   65
   The third side weakens   65
   Conditions, not certainties   66
The pyramids of power   67
   From cooperation to compulsion   67
   Power becomes a prize   69
   From horizontal to vertical relations   69
The logic of war   70
   States breed wars as wars breed states   70
   Orders to kill   71
   War is contagious   73
   Force makes sense   73
The deadliest century   74
   The world wars   74
   The specter of mass destruction   75
   A rash of ethnic wars   76
   Yet signs of peace   78
Which way humanity?   80

4.   And Back Again?   *81*

A shift in the logic   83
   From a fixed pie back to an expandable one   84
   From arrows to guns   86
   From win-lose toward lose-lose   87
   From win-lose toward both-gain   89
   The example of South Africa   90

Back to the network		92
	The flattening of the pyramids	92
	The return of the network	95
The Ingathering		98
	More conflict	99
	More vulnerability	100
	A potentially stronger third side	101
The Negotiation Revolution		101
	Negotiation becomes ubiquitous	103
	Negotiation becomes a necessity	105
The Recurrence		106

III. THE TEN ROLES OF THE THIRD SIDE

5.	**Prevent:** *Provider, Teacher, Bridge-Builder*	*114*
	Needs, skills, and relationships	115
1.	The Provider: enabling people to meet their needs	117
	Share resources, share knowledge	118
	Protect	120
	Respect	120
	Free	123
	Open doors	124
2.	The Teacher: giving people skills to handle conflict	125
	Delegitimize violence	125
	Teach tolerance	127
	Teach joint problem-solving	129
3.	The Bridge-Builder: forging relationships across lines of conflict	131
	Create cross-cutting ties	132
	Develop joint projects	134
	Foster genuine dialogue	135
	Prevention: the best intervention	139

6. Resolve: *Mediator, Arbiter, Equalizer, Healer*   ***140***

   Interests, rights, power—and relationship   141
4. The Mediator: reconciling conflicting interests   143
   Everyone's a Mediator   145
   Bring the parties to the table   146
   Facilitate communication   147
   Help people search for a solution   148
5. The Arbiter: determining disputed rights   149
   Peers can be Arbiters too   149
   Replace destructive conflict   150
   Promote justice   152
   Encourage negotiation   154
6. The Equalizer: democratizing power   154
   Help bring the powerful to the table   155
   Build collaborative democracy   156
   Support nonviolent action   159
7. The Healer: repairing injured relationships   161
   Create the right climate   163
   Listen and acknowledge   164
   Encourage apology   165
   The goal is reconciliation   167

7. Contain: *Witness, Referee, Peacekeeper*   ***169***

8. The Witness: paying attention to escalation   170
   Watch out for early warning signals   171
   Go on patrol   173
   Speak out   174
   Get help fast   175
9. The Referee: setting limits to fighting   176
   Establish rules for fair fighting   177
   Remove offensive arms   180
   Strengthen defenses—nonoffensively   181
10. The Peacekeeper: providing protection   183
   Interpose   184

Enforce the peace   185
Preempt violence before it starts   186
The new warriors   188
Putting it all together   189
Stopping a classroom fight   189
Preventing ethnic violence   192
Preventing war   193
Toward a comprehensive system   195

Conclusion: Toward a Co-Culture   **196**

The opportunity   197
What can I do?   198
1. Change the story   199
2. Learn some skills   200
3. Start close to home   200
4. Mediate your own disputes   200
5. Do what you do best   201
6. Volunteer your services   201
7. Fill a missing role   202
8. Create a winning alliance   202
9. Urge your organization to take the third side   204
10. Support the third side in the wider community   204
11. Help build thirdsider institutions   205
12. Help create a social movement   205
Learning to live together   206

End Notes   214

END NOTES

INTRODUCTION: CAN WE ALL GET ALONG?

For research on marriage and the critical ability to handle conflict, see J. M. Gottman and L. J. Krokoff, "Marital Interaction and Satisfaction: A Longitudinal View," *Journal of Consulting and Clinical Psychology* 57 (1989): 47–52. For further reading, see Howard Markman, Scott Stanley, and Susan L. Blumberg, *Fighting for Your Marriage* (San Francisco: Jossey-Bass, 1994).

For the relationship between conflict resolution in hospitals and the quality of health care, see W. A. Knaus, D. P. Wagner, J. E. Zimmerman, and E. A. Draper, "An Evaluation of Outcome from Intensive Care in Major Medical Centers," in *Annals of Internal Medicine* 104 (1986): 410–18.

The statistics about domestic abuse come from National Coalition Against Domestic Violence, "Facts about Domestic Violence," January 12, 1999, p. 1. For an excellent discussion of domestic abuse, see K. J. Wilson, *When Violence Begins at Home* (Alameda, CA: Hunter House, 1997), p. 8.

The statistics about the numbers and costs of lawsuits and the numbers of homicides come from National Research Council and the Kennedy School of Government, Harvard University, *Violence in Urban America: Mobilizing a Response* (Washington, DC: National Research Council, 1994), p. 5.

In 1994, the Stockholm International Peace Research Institute (SIPRI) identified thirty-one "major armed conflicts." SIPRI defines a major armed conflict as one involving the armed forces of at least one government, and incurring at least one thousand battle-related deaths per year. See *SIPRI Yearbook 1995: Armaments, Disarmament and International Security* (Oxford: Oxford University Press, 1995), pp. 21–35.

The dangers of nuclear terrorism are described in Graham T. Allison, Owen T. Cote, Jr., Richard A. Falkenrath, and Steven E. Miller, *Avoiding Nuclear Anarchy* (Cambridge, MA: MIT Press, 1996). See p. 1 for the World Trade Center scenario.

Our common ancestry is posited in Rebecca L. Cann, Mark Stoneking, and Allan C. Wilson, "Mitochondrial DNA and Human Evolution," *Nature* 325 (January 1, 1987): 31–36.

The figure of fifteen thousand ethnic groups comes from David Maybury-Lewis, *Millennium: Tribal Wisdom and the Modern World* (New York: Viking, 1992), p. 262.

I. THE MISSING KEY

1. The Third Side

The quote from Freud comes from *Why War? A Correspondence between Albert Einstein and Sigmund Freud*, translated by Stuart Gilbert (Geneva: International Institute of Intellectual Cooperation, League of Nations, 1933), p. 10.

Reimagining conflict as three-sided

Since the appellation "Bushman" was often a term of denigration in southern Africa, many anthropologists have come to use the term "San." But unfortunately "San" is also unsatisfactory, meaning "rascal" in Khoi-Khoi. Besides, the Bushmen themselves don't use the term "San"; according to the anthropologist Megan Biesele, the Ju/ho'ansi, at least, think the term "Bushman" as a general appellation is just fine. The other linguistic issue is the term "!Kung," used extensively in the ethnographic literature for the Ju/'hoansi. At the risk of some confusion, I will use the term "Ju/'hoansi" wherever possible since that is the name they use themselves, and the term "!Kung" only when I am referring to the work of Richard Lee and others who use the term "!Kung."

The two groups I visited were a Kua (or Baqwa) group near Bothapatiou in Botswana and a Ju/'hoansi group around Gautscha, Namibia. The visits took place in April and May 1989.

The quote from /Twi!gum about the headmen comes from Richard B. Lee, *The Dobe !Kung* (New York: Holt, Rinehart, and Winston, 1979), p. 89.

Conflict resolution in simpler societies

The description of Bushman decision-making comes from Megan Biesele, "Sapience and Scarce Resources: Communication Systems of the !Kung and Other Foragers," *Social Science Information* 17 (1978): 939–40.

For more on the way the Semai resolve their conflicts, see Robert K. Dentan, *The Semai: A Nonviolent People of Malaya* (New York: Holt, Rinehart, and Winston, 1968), particularly chapter 6. Also see the numerous works on the subject by Clayton A. Robarchek, beginning with his doctoral dissertation *Semai Nonviolence: A Systems Approach to Understanding*, unpublished, University of California, Riverside. Some writers have sought to refute the nonviolence of the Semai by quoting out of context a quote from Dentan about "blood drunkenness" among Semai soldiers during the Malaysian insurgency in the 1950s. Dentan and Robarchek set the record straight in "Blood Drunkenness and the Bloodthirsty Semai: Unmaking Another Anthropological Myth," in *American Anthropologist* 89 (1987): 356–65. As they point out, the military unit in which the Semai served managed to kill one person every other year—and most of that killing was done by British and Malay regulars and officers. "Blood drunkenness," moreover, does not connote any pleasure but disorientation and nausea from seeing large quantities of blood.

The group of Semai I visited live in Bare Chee, which means "elephant's plain," in the Tenlop River basin. My visit took place in July 1996.

From the nuclear family to the human family

In the family

The story of Marquise Johnson comes from Tamar Lewin, "Student Disputes Become Mediation Lessons," *New York Times*, June 15, 1997, p. 12.

For more on the changes in public attitudes toward spousal abuse, see Nancy Fraser, *Unruly Practices* (Minneapolis: Minnesota University Press, 1989), and Susan Schechter, *Women and Male Violence: The Visions and Struggles of the Battered Women's Movement* (Boston: South End Press, 1982).

Jane's story comes from Frances Gibb, "Calming Family Conflict," *Times of London*, September 29, 1998, p. 43.

In the workplace

The quote from Michael Rosenberg comes from Morey Stettner, "How to Mediate On-the-Job Conflicts," *Investor's Business Daily*, December 31, 1998, p. 1.

Statistics about the use of mediation in business come from a survey carried out by Cornell University and Price Waterhouse, "The Use of ADR in U.S. Corporations," 1997, quoted in *Consensus*, October 1998, p. 12.

In the community

The account of Boston's approach to fighting teenage crime comes from Blaine Harden, "Boston's Approach to Juvenile Crime Encircles Youth, Reduces Crime," *Washington Post*, October 23, 1997, p. A3.

The quotes from Judge Seeliger and Hal Rives, Georgia Department of Transportation commissioner, refer to the settlement of the Presidential Parkway dispute in Atlanta. The quotes come from *World Mediation and Arbitration Report*, 1991, pp. 258–59.

Alisha's story is from Tamar Lewin, "Student Disputes Become Mediation Lessons," *New York Times*, June 15, 1997, p. 12.

The school in Oakland, Melrose Elementary School, is described by Sharon Massey, "Schools Find Pupil Mediators Cut Violence," *Wall Street Journal*, February 2, 1994, p. 1.

For a description of the Hawaiian mediation practice of *ho'oponopono*, see James A. Wall, Jr., and Ronda Roberts Callister, "Ho'oponopono: Some Lessons from Hawaiian Mediation," *Negotiation Journal* 11:1 (January 1995). For more on the Palestinian tradition of *sulha*, see Elias J. Jabbour, *Sulha: Palestinian Traditional Peacemaking Process* (Montreat, NC: House of Hope, 1993).

In a warring world

For a discussion of the Oslo negotiations, see Amos Elon, "The Peacemakers," *New Yorker*, December 20, 1973, pp. 77–85. Also see David Makovsky, *Making Peace with the PLO: The Rabin Government's Road to the Oslo Accord* (Boulder, CO: Westview, 1996), and Jane Corbin, *The Norway Channel* (New York: Atlantic Monthly Press, 1994).

For an analysis of the Vatican's mediation of the Beagle Channel dispute, see Thomas Princen, "International Mediation—The View from the Vatican: Lessons from Mediating the Beagle Channel Dispute," *Negotiation Journal* 3 (1987): 347–66.

Across domains

Makita Moore is quoted in Tamar Lewin, "Student Disputes Become Mediation Lessons," *New York Times*, June 15, 1997, p. 12.

For the effect of labor negotiation experience on the political process in South Africa, see Patti Waldmeir, *Anatomy of a Miracle* (New York: Norton, 1997), pp. 28–29.

What exactly is the third side?

Using the power of peers
The story of the North Wind and the Sun can be found in *The Fables of Aesop and Others: With Designs on Wood by Thomas Bewick* (London: Methuen, 1903), pp. 325–26.

For an excellent discussion of the effects of the mere presence of a third party on conflict, see J. Rubin and B. Brown, *The Social Psychology of Bargaining and Negotiation* (New York: Academic Press, 1975), pp. 54–57.

Tsamko, a member of the Ju/'hoan group, is quoted in Megan Biesele, "Learning a 'New' Language of Democracy: Bushmen in an Independent Namibia," mimeographed article, 1989, p. 13.

From a perspective of common ground
The quote from the New York high school students comes from Linda Singer, *Settling Disputes* (Boulder, CO: Westview, 1994), p. 156.

Supporting a process of dialogue and nonviolence
The story of the monks in battle is told by David Busch in "Culture Cul-de-Sac," *Arizona State University Research*, Spring/Summer 1994. I am indebted to Daniel Goleman for bringing the story to my attention. He quotes it in *Emotional Intelligence* (New York: Bantam, 1997), p. 114.

Aiming for a product of a "triple win"
The Presidential Parkway dispute is described in *World Mediation and Arbitration Report* (1991): 257–59.

Who is the third side?

Outsiders
The quote from Archbishop Desmond Tutu comes from a speech he made in New Orleans to the Council on Foundations on April 18, 1999.

Insiders
For more on the concept of pairs of insider third parties, see Paul Wehr and John Paul Lederach, "Mediating Conflict in Central America," *Journal of Peace Research* 28:1 (February 1991): 85–98.

For an excellent description and analysis of the South African National Peace Accord, see Peter Gastrow, *Bargaining for Peace* (Washington, DC: United States Institute of Peace Press, 1995).

An inner third side?
The data about the reaction of U.S. Army riflemen in battle and the quote come from S. L. A. Marshall, *Men Against Fire: The Problem of Battle Command in Future War* (Gloucester, MA: Peter Smith, 1978 [1947]), p. 78.

The potential of the third side

The story of Le Chambon and the quote from Major Schmehling come from Philip Hallie, *Lest Innocent Blood Be Shed* (New York: Harper and Row, 1994 [1979]), p. 245.

The quotes from Pastor Roger Darcissac and the elderly peasant from Le Chambon are taken from a film written, produced, and directed by Pierre Sauvage, *Weapons of the Spirit* (Chambon Foundation and Greenvalley Productions, 1989).

The phrase "the banality of evil" comes from Hannah Arendt, *Eichmann in Jerusalem: A Report on the Banality of Evil* (New York: Viking, 1963).

II. A BRIEF HISTORY OF CONFLICT

2. From Coexistence

The opening quote from Demi is taken from Lorna Marshall, "Sharing, Talking, and Giving: Relief of Social Tensions Among !Kung Bushmen," *Africa* 31:3 (July 1961): 231–49.

The quote from Hobbes comes from Thomas Hobbes, *Leviathan,* edited by Richard Tuck (Cambridge, England: Cambridge University Press, 1991 [1651]), pp. 88–89.

The quote from Freud comes from *Why War? A Correspondence between Albert Einstein and Sigmund Freud,* translated by Stuart Gilbert (Geneva: International Institute of Intellectual Cooperation, League of Nations, 1933), p. 11.

The archaeological puzzle

The quote about the shocking specimen comes from Raymond A. Dart, "Cultural Status of the South African Man-Apes," *Smithsonian Report* 4240 (1956): 325–26.

The quote about the blood-bespattered archives of human history comes from Raymond A. Dart, "The Predatory Transition from Ape to Man," *International Anthropological and Linguistic Review* 1 (1953): 207–8.

Bob Brain's research project is described in detail in C. K. Brain, *The Hunters or the Hunted: An Introduction to African Cave Taphonomy* (Chicago: University of Chicago Press, 1981), pp. 136 and 269.

The startling absence of evidence

See Lawrence H. Keeley, *War Before Civilization: The Myth of the Peaceful Savage* (New York: Oxford University Press, 1996). An even more recent archaeological compilation, to which Keeley has contributed, is Debra L.

Martin and David W. Fayer (eds.), *Troubled Times: Violence and Warfare in the Past* (Amsterdam: Gordon and Breach, 1997). Intended to compile evidence of prehistoric war, it shows that violence is indeed clearly detectable in archaeological remains and surprisingly suggests that it is exceptional and certainly rarer than surveys of the far more recent ethnographic record have indicated.

The quote from archaeologist Marilyn Roper comes from Marilyn Roper, "Evidence of Warfare in the Near East from 10,000 to 4300 B.C.," in M. Nettleship, R. D. Givens, and A. Nettleship (eds.), *War, Its Causes and Correlates* (The Hague: Mouton, 1975), p. 260. See also Marilyn Roper, "A Survey of the Evidence for Intrahuman Killing in the Pleistocene," *Current Anthropology* 10 (October 1969): 427–59.

The information about White and Toth's survey comes from a phone interview by Lara Olson, March 14, 1994. It should be noted that Drs. White and Toth were unable to fully complete their survey owing to problems of access to certain European collections. For examples of their work, see Timothy D. White and Nicholas Toth, "Engis: Preparation Damage, Not Ancient Cutmarks," *American Journal of Physical Anthropology* 78 (March 1989): 361–67, and also Timothy D. White and Nicholas Toth, "The Question of Ritual Cannibalism at Grotta Guattari," *Current Anthropology* 32 (April 1991): 103–24.

For an excellent survey of archaeological evidence of prehistoric violence, see Debra L. Martin and David W. Fayer (eds.), *Troubled Times: Violence and Warfare in the Past* (Amsterdam: Gordon and Breach, 1997). Brian Ferguson's overview, entitled "Violence and War in Prehistory," can be found on pp. 321–55. Also see Brian Ferguson, "Anthropological Perspectives on War," November 1998, to be published in Triangle Institute for Security Studies "Study of War" volume.

The quote from Philip Tobias comes from personal communication, March 1, 1995.

Archaeologist Bar-Yosef's explanation of the walls of Jericho is in O. Bar-Yosef, "The Walls of Jericho: An Alternative Interpretation," *Current Anthropology* 27 (April 1986): 157–62. The more traditional explanation of the walls as defenses can be found in Kathleen M. Kenyon, *Digging Up Jericho: The Results of the Jericho Excavations 1952–1956* (New York: Frederick A. Praeger, 1957).

For description and analysis of scenes of violence in prehistoric rock art, see Antonio Beltrán Martínez, *Rock Art of the Spanish Levant*, translated by Margaret Brown (Cambridge, England: Cambridge University Press, 1982), and Lya Dams, *Les Peintures Rupestres du Levant Espagnol* (Paris: Picard, 1984). Also see Paul Taçon and Christopher Chippingdale, "Australia's Fighting Warriors: Changing Depictions of Fighting in the Rock Art of

Arnhem Land, N.T.," *Cambridge Archaeological Journal* 4:2 (1994): 211–48. The argument that such figures might be depictions of combat in the spiritual world is made in J. D. Lewis-Williams and J. H. N. Loubser, "Deceptive Appearances: A Critique of Southern African Rock Art Studies," *Advances in World Archeology* 5 (1986): 253–89. Spiritual depictions or not, the art suggests a familiarity with the phenomenon of combat.

The puzzle

The curious incident of the dog is told in Sir Arthur Conan Doyle, "Silver Blaze," *The Memoirs of Sherlock Holmes*, edited by Christopher Roden (Oxford: Oxford University Press, 1993), p. 23.

The cooperative ape

Cooperating to compete

For more on the role of cooperation in our early ancestors' lives, see Richard E. Leakey and Roger Lewin, *Origins: What New Discoveries Reveal About the Emergence of Our Species and Its Possible Future* (New York: E. P. Dutton, 1977).

The quote about the !Kung's boundaryless network is described in Richard B. Lee, *The !Kung San: Men, Women, and Work in a Foraging Society* (London: Cambridge University Press, 1979), p. 335.

The estimate for how much time the Bushmen spend visiting comes from Richard B. Lee, "What Hunters Do for a Living, or How to Make Out on Scarce Resources," in Richard B. Lee and Irven DeVore, *Man the Hunter* (Chicago: Aldine, 1968), p. 31.

An expandable pie

The Bushman quote about the mongongo nuts comes from Lee, "What Hunters Do for a Living," in Lee and DeVore, *Man the Hunter*, pp. 37–38.

The logic of coexistence

Little place for coercion

The quote from Robert Ardrey comes from *Aggression and Violence in Man: A Dialogue between Dr. Louis Leakey and Mr. Robert Ardrey*, Munger Africana Library Notes, no. 9 (Pasadena: California Institute of Technology, 1971), p. 12.

For a discussion of the average population density of hunter-gatherers, see "Introduction," in Lee and DeVore, *Man the Hunter*, p. 11. Also see Fekri Hassan, *Demographic Archaeology* (New York: Academic Press, 1981). Hassan estimates an average of 0.33 people per square kilometer, or 0.85 people per square mile.

The Bushman quote about wanting to hunt antelope rather than man comes from Lee, *The !Kung San*, p. 391.

The quote from the Semai man comes from anthropologist Lye Tuck-Po, personal conversation, August 2, 1996.

The story of the Hadza exercising the exit option comes from James Woodburn, "Discussion, Part III," in Lee and DeVore, *Man the Hunter*, p. 156.

Learning the logic

For an excellent discussion of the Prisoners' Dilemma and the emergent logic of cooperation, see Robert Axelrod, *The Evolution of Cooperation* (New York: Basic Books, 1984).

The British World War I soldier is quoted in S. Gillon, *The Story of the 29th Division* (London: Nelson and Sons, n.d.), p. 77, cited in Axelrod, *Evolution of Cooperation*, p. 81. "Mr. Bosche" was a nickname used for the Germans by Allied troops during World War I.

The incident of the German apology for the surprise salvo is recounted in Owen Rutter (ed.), *The History of the Seventh (Services) Battalion: The Royal Sussex Regiment 1914–19* (London: Times Publishing, 1934), p. 29, cited in Axelrod, *Evolution of Cooperation*, p. 85.

A conflict management system

The Ju/'hoansi description of themselves as the "owners of argument" comes from Megan Biesele, "Learning a 'New' Language of Democracy: Bushmen in an Independent Namibia," unpublished draft, 1989, p. 12.

The Bushman's description of the aftermath of an impulsive homicide comes from Lee, *The !Kung San*, p. 395.

The !Kung homicide data are from Lee, *The !Kung San*, pp. 382–400.

The Washington, DC, homicide rate is sixty-nine per hundred thousand people per year. For a comparative survey of homicide rates of major American and European cities, see the London police Web site http://www.met.police.uk/police/mps/mps/press/pub1908.htm.

Some scholars have suggested that the relative peacefulness of the Bushmen and the Semai comes from the fact that they are defeated refugees, driven into remote places. Richard Lee refutes this notion for the !Kung with strong archaeological evidence and the oral traditions of the !Kung themselves. See Lee, *The !Kung San*, p. 76. In any case, it has not been explained why defeated refugees should necessarily be any less violent. As contemporary counterexamples, consider the Palestinians, and the Hutus and the Tutsis, when exiled and out of power in Central Africa.

For a comparative study of war in tribal and state societies, see Keith Otterbein, *The Evolution of War: A Cross-Cultural Study*, 3rd ed. (New Haven, CT: HRAF Press, 1989). Otterbein's results show that the simplest form of political organization and the simplest form of subsistence economy (hunting-gathering) are correlated with the lowest frequency of warfare.

Di//Xao=Toma's answer to those who say the Bushmen have no government is quoted in Megan Biesele, "Learning a 'New' Language of Democracy: Bushmen in an Independent Namibia," unpublished draft, 1989, p. 1.

But isn't violence human nature?

False polarities

I owe the analogies about eating and sex to Professor Bruce Knauft of Emory University.

What about the chimps?

For a description of the murderous attacks of the Gombe chimpanzees, see Jane Goodall, *The Chimpanzees of Gombe* (Cambridge, MA: Harvard University Press, 1986), pp. 503–34.

Margaret Power presents her arguments about the artificial feeding conditions in *The Egalitarians—Human and Chimpanzee* (Cambridge, England: Cambridge University Press, 1991).

Jane Goodall's quote about the effect of the constant feeding comes from *In the Shadow of Man* (Boston: Houghton Mifflin, 1971), p. 143.

For more about the behavior of the bonobos, see Frans de Waal and Frans Lanting, *Bonobo: The Forgotten Ape* (Berkeley: University of California Press, 1997), and Takayoshi Kano, *The Last Ape: Pygmy Chimpanzee Behavior and Ecology* (Stanford: Stanford University Press, 1986).

The observation about three bonobo females lining up comes from zookeeper Gale Foland at the San Diego Zoo, personal communication, January 18, 1996.

Frans de Waal's research about peacemaking among chimpanzees and other primates is detailed in his book *Peacemaking Among Primates* (Cambridge, MA: Harvard University Press, 1989). For more on this subject, see James Silverberg and J. Patrick Gray, "Violence and Peacefulness As Behavioral Potentialities of Primates," in James Silverberg and J. Patrick Gray (eds.), *Aggression and Peacefulness in Humans and Other Primates* (New York: Oxford University Press, 1992).

Capable of war, capable of peace

For a fascinating comparison between the Waorani and the Semai, see Clayton A. Robarchek and Carole J. Robarchek, "Cultures of War and Peace: A Comparative Study of Waorani and Semai," in Silverberg and Gray (eds.), *Aggression and Peacefulness*, pp. 189–211.

3. To Coercion

The Sumerian inscription is quoted in Bruce Chatwin, *The Songlines* (New York: Penguin Books, 1988).

A revolution in human life

Humans settle down and start farming

For more on the origins of agriculture, see Mark Nathan Cohen, *The Food Crisis in Prehistory: Overpopulation and the Origins of Agriculture* (New Haven: Yale University Press, 1977).

For a discussion of the dangers inherent in the transition to agriculture, see Mark Nathan Cohen and George J. Armelagos, "Editors' Summation," in Mark Nathan Cohen and George J. Armelagos (eds.), *Paleopathology at the Origins of Agriculture* (Orlando, FL: Academic Press, 1984), pp. 585–601. See also Jared Diamond, *The Third Chimpanzee* (New York: HarperCollins, 1992), pp. 180–91.

The population grows

For an interesting discussion of birth spacing, see Melvin Konner and Carol Worthman, "Nursing Frequency, Gonadal Function and Birth Spacing Among !Kung Hunter-Gatherers," *Science* 207 (February 15, 1980): 788.

For archaeological estimates of human population, see Fekri A. Hassan, *Demographic Archaeology* (New York: Academic Press, 1981). Also see Edward S. Deevey, Jr., "The Human Population," *Scientific American*, September 1960.

For more on El Amarna, see B. J. Kemp, *Amarna Reports*, vols. 1–5 (London: Egypt Exploration Society, 1984–89).

The consequences for conflict

The expandable pie becomes fixed

The information about the Northwest Coast Indians such as the Ahousaht and the Clayoquot comes from Carleton S. Coon, *The Hunting Peoples* (Boston: Little, Brown, 1971), p. 263.

"Too many people in the same place"

I heard the Bushman quote about too many people in the same place from John Marshall and Megan Biesele. Personal communication, May 1989.

The research on the Sika deer is described in John J. Christian, Vagn Flyger, and David E. Davis, "Factors in Mass Mortality of a Herd of Sika Deer (*Cervus nippon*)," *Chesapeake Science* 1 (June 1960): 79–95. I am grateful to Edward T. Hall for bringing Christian's and Calhoun's research to my attention.

The experiments with Norway rats are described in John B. Calhoun, "Population Density and Social Pathology," *Scientific American* 206 (February 1962): 139–46.

The correlation between crime and population density is suggested by the research of Paul Chombart de Lauwe, *Famille et Habitation* (Paris: Editions du Centre National de la Recherche Scientifique, 1959). The work is discussed in Edward T. Hall, *The Hidden Dimension* (New York: Anchor, 1981): 171–73.

My interview with Aki Tumi, Director, Enga Cultural Centre, at Par, Enga Province, Papua New Guinea, took place on November 16, 1995.

"The fight follows you around"

The Ju/'hoan quote about the fight following you around comes from John Marshall. Personal communication to the author, May 1989.

Conditions, not certainties

For a discussion of peacefulness of early agricultural societies in southeastern Europe, see Marija Gimbutas, *The Goddesses and Gods of Old Europe, 7000–3500 B.C.* (Berkeley and Los Angeles: University of California Press, 1982).

The pyramids of power

From cooperation to compulsion

The Sumerian inscription is quoted in Chatwin, *The Songlines,* p. 189.

The definition of the state in terms of its monopoly on the use of force comes from Max Weber, *The Theory of Social and Economic Organization*, translated by A. M. Henderson and Talcott Parsons (London: Collier-Macmillan, 1947).

The idea of the state as "protection racket" is developed in Charles Tilly, "War Making and State Making As Organized Crime," in Peter Evans, Dietrich Rueschemeyer, and Theda Skocpol (eds.), *Bringing the State Back In* (Cambridge, England: Cambridge University Press, 1985), pp. 169–88.

The logic of war

States breed wars as wars breed states

Sir Richard Burton's observation about wars in Africa is quoted in Montgomery of Alamein, *A History of Warfare* (Cleveland, OH: World Publishing, 1968), p. 30.

Orders to kill

I am indebted for the "kill or be killed" definition of the state to Professor R. Brian Ferguson of Rutgers University.

Robert Renaldo's conversation with the Ilonget headhunters appears in "Discussion," in Robert G. Hamerton-Kelly (ed.), *Violent Origins: Walter Burkert, Rene Girard and Jonathan Z. Smith on Ritual Killing and Cultural Formation* (Stanford: Stanford University Press, 1987), p. 255.

Ashurbanipal is quoted in Gwynne Dyer, *War* (New York: Crown, 1985), p. 29.

War is contagious

For a fascinating exposition of the contagiousness of war, see Andrew Schmookler, *The Parable of the Tribes: The Problem of Power in Social Evolution* (Boston: Houghton Mifflin, 1984).

Force makes sense

For a masterful analysis of the multiple causes of war, see Brian Ferguson, "Violence and War in Prehistory," in Debra L. Martin and David W. Fayer (eds.), *Troubled Times: Violence and Warfare in the Past* (Amsterdam: Gordon and Breach, 1997), pp. 321–55. For a more recent and comprehensive version, see Brian Ferguson, "Anthropological Perspectives on War," November 1998, to be published in Triangle Institute for Security Studies' "Study of War" volume.

The deadliest century

The casualty statistics come from Ruth Leger Sivard, *World Military and Social Expenditures 1996* (Washington, DC: World Priorities, 1996), pp. 18–19.

The world wars

The young Frenchman's story is recounted in Barbara Tuchman, *The Guns of August* (New York: Ballantine, 1994 [1962]), p. 439.

The specter of mass destruction

The commonly accepted date for the discovery of fire is six hundred thousand years ago. The earlier date at the Swartskrans cave in South Africa comes from Professor Lee Berger of the University of Witwatersrand. Personal communication, March 5, 1995.

A rash of ethnic wars

For statistics comparing World War I casualties and warfare in the 1980s, see Sivard, *World Military and Social Expenditures 1996*, p. 7.

Yet signs of peace

For more on the changes in the pattern of war, see John Mueller, *Retreat from Doomsday: The Obsolescence of Major War* (New York: Basic Books, 1989).

The French Foreign Legionnaire is quoted in Chatwin, *The Songlines*.

4. And Back Again?

The quote from British Prime Minister Tony Blair comes from a press release by the British Embassy in Washington, DC.

The Cuban Missile Crisis is described in Robert F. Kennedy, *Thirteen Days: A Memoir of the Cuban Missile Crisis* (New York: Norton, 1969), p. 61. Also see

Elie Abel, *The Missile Crisis* (Philadelphia: J. B. Lippincott, 1968), p. 203. For more recent accounts, see James G. Blight and David A. Welch, *On the Brink: Americans and Soviets Reexamine the Cuban Missile Crisis* (New York: Hill and Wang, 1989), and James G. Blight, Bruce J. Allyn, and David A. Welch, *Cuba on the Brink: Castro, the Missile Crisis, and the Soviet Collapse* (New York: Pantheon, 1993).

President John F. Kennedy's reflection on the steps to nuclear war is quoted in Robert F. Kennedy, *Thirteen Days*, p. 76.

A shift in the logic

From a fixed pie back to an expandable one

The point about there being no limits to learning I owe to James Botkin. For more on this subject, see James W. Botkin, Mahdi Elmandjra, and Mircea Malitza, *No Limits to Learning: Bridging the Human Gap* (Oxford: Pergamon Press, 1979).

For the idea of a shift from "power over" to "power to," I am indebted to Marilyn French, *Beyond Power: On Women, Men and Morals* (New York: Summit Books, 1985).

The story of Netscape is described in Victor Keegan, *The Guardian Weekly*, July 28, 1996. News of Netscape's sale is from "America Online Profits Triple," *AP Online*, January 27, 1999.

From win-lose toward lose-lose

The quote from Voltaire comes from Herbert Mayes (ed.), *An Editor's Treasury: A Continuing Anthology of Prose, Verse, and Literary Curiosa* (New York: Atheneum, 1968), p. 1032. I am grateful to Professor Martha Minow for bringing this quote to my attention.

For the point about how the best scientific minds could not find a way to win a nuclear war, I am indebted to Professor Martin van Creveld. Personal communication, March 1995.

The number of Chechen fighters comes from an interview with Chechen Vice President Vasya Arsanov, May 1997.

For an excellent account of the Chechnya war, see Carlotta Gall and Thomas De Waal, *Chechnya: Calamity in the Caucasus* (New York: New York University Press, 1998).

From win-lose toward both-gain

For an explanation of how Benetton works for "cooperative advantage," see Werner Ketelhohn, "What Do We Mean by Cooperative Advantage?" *European Management Journal*, March 1993.

The example of South Africa

The quote from Nelson Mandela comes from *Long Walk to Freedom* (Boston: Little, Brown, 1994), p. 533.

The views of Roelf Meyer, former Minister of Provincial Affairs and Constitutional Development, were expressed in a personal interview in Johannesburg, March 1995.

Back to the network

The flattening of the pyramids

UN Secretary-General Kofi Annan is quoted in Max Frankel, "A More Perfect Future," *New York Times Magazine*, January 24, 1999, p. 18.

The return of the network

The information about the spread of democracy comes from *Freedom in the World 1995–6* (Washington, DC: Freedom House, 1996). See also Tina Rosenberg, "Overcoming the Legacies of Dictatorship," in *Foreign Affairs*, Spring 1995.

For a discussion of the long peace among liberal democracies, see Michael Doyle, "Liberalism and World Politics," *American Political Science Review* 80 (December 1986): 1151–69, and "Kant, Liberal Legacies and Foreign Affairs," *Philosophy and Public Affairs* 12 (1983): 205–35. For a different view, see Nils Petter Gleditsch, "Democracy and Peace," *Journal of Peace Research* 29 (November 1992): 369–76.

The information about Asea Brown Boveri comes from Wally Wood, "How Big Should a Head Office Be?" *Across the Board* 32 (May 1995): 24. Percy Barnevik is quoted in John Naisbitt, *Global Paradox: The Bigger the World Economy, the More Powerful Its Smallest Players* (New York: William Morrow, 1994), p. 14.

The ingathering

More vulnerability

For the impact of the GM strike, see "Despite GM Strikes, Jobless Rate Holds at 4.5%," *Buffalo News*, August 7, 1998, p. 9A. Also see Beth Belton, "Impact Will Add to Growth," *USA Today*, July 29, 1998, p. 3B.

The Negotiation Revolution

Negotiation becomes ubiquitous

Howard Markman of the University of Denver is quoted in Kevin Merida and Barbara Vobejda, "Battles on the Home Front," *Washington Post*, March 25, 1998.

The quote from Arnie Klayman comes from Tim Diering, "Teachers, School District Work On 'Getting to Yes,' " *Hamilton-Wenham Chronicle*, February 22, 1995, p. 18.
The quote from Denny Morris comes from personal communication, October 1993.

Negotiation becomes a necessity
The quote from General Lebed comes from Gall and De Waal, *Chechnya: Calamity in the Caucasus*, p. 361.

III. THE TEN ROLES OF THE THIRD SIDE

The quote from William Shakespeare can be found in *Henry VI, Part III*, Act 4, Scene 8.

5. Prevent: Provider, Teacher, Bridge-Builder

The quote from Lao Tzu comes from Stephen Mitchell (trans.), *Tao Te Ching* (New York: Harper, 1991), p. 63.
My interview with Korakoradue took place near Bothapatiou, Botswana, on May 5, 1989.

Needs, skills, and relationships
The story of sharing meat and the quote about lions come from Lorna Marshall, "Sharing, Talking, and Giving: Relief of Social Tensions Among !Kung Bushmen," *Africa* 31:3 (July 1961): 236.
My interview with Purana took place near Bothapatiou, Botswana, May 6, 1989.
The !Kung Bushman's quote about *hxaro* can be found in Richard B. Lee, *The !Kung San: Men, Women, and Work in a Foraging Society* (London: Cambridge University Press, 1979), p. 98.

1. The Provider: enabling people to meet their needs
The story about Eugene Rivers is taken from Joe Klein, "In God They Trust," *New Yorker*, June 16, 1997, pp. 40–41.
My understanding of basic human needs owes much to Abraham Maslow and John Burton. Maslow posited five sets of needs: physiological, safety, belonging, esteem, and self-actualization. See Abraham Maslow, *Motivation and Personality* (New York: Harper & Row, 1954). John Burton was the first to apply basic human-needs theory systematically to the field of conflict resolution. See John Burton, *Resolving Deep-Rooted Conflict* (Lanham, MD: University Press of America, 1987), and John Burton (ed.), *Conflict: Human Needs Theory* (London: Macmillan, 1990).

Share resources, share knowledge

For more on the Semai view of the world, see Clayton A. Robarchek and Carole J. Robarchek, "Cultures of War and Peace: A Comparative Study of Waorani and Semai," in James Silverberg and J. Patrick Gray (eds.), *Aggression and Peacefulness in Humans and Other Primates* (New York: Oxford University Press, 1992), pp. 189–211.

The correlation between social equity and low crime is discussed in Melvin and Carol R. Ember, "Facts of Violence," *Anthropology Newsletter*, October 1998, p. 14.

Deborah Hernandez is quoted in James V. O'Connor, "Citizens Put the Community in Community Policing," *American News Service*, July 12, 1996.

Protect

The phrase "common security" was first popularized by the Palme Commission on Disarmament and Security Issues, *A World at Peace: Common Security in the 21st Century* (Stockholm: The Palme Commission on Disarmament and Security Issues, 1989). The phrase appears to have been coined by the eminent Danish physicist Niels Bohr. See Niels Bohr, "Memorandum to FDR, July 3, 1944," quoted in Richard Rhodes, *The Making of the Atomic Bomb* (New York: Simon and Schuster, 1986), p. 534.

Respect

The story of Steven Spielberg is quoted in *Time*, July 15, 1985. I am grateful to Arthur Kanegis for bringing it to my attention.

Robert Earl Mack is quoted in S. Anthony Baron, *Violence in the Workplace: A Prevention and Management Guide for Businesses* (Ventura, CA: Pathfinder Publishing of California), p. 44.

For more on Milwaukee's midnight basketball league, see Walter C. Farrell, Jr., et al., "Redirecting the Lives of Urban Black Males: An Assessment of Milwaukee's Midnight Basketball League," *Journal of Community Practice* 2:4 (1995): 95–107.

The Florida town is Ocala. See Jane Braxton Little, "After-School Programs: Young People Are Choosing Homework over Drugs and Crime," *American News Service*, article 101, 1997.

Louis G. Lower II is quoted in Pamela Schaeffer, "Workplace Diversity Programs Work Best When They Expand Beyond Race," *American News Service*, article 170, 1997.

The quote from Mayor Selim Beslagic comes from an interview in ECHO News no. 10, March 1996. ECHO is a publication of the European Community Humanitarian Organization in Brussels.

The quote about Mauritius comes from "Mauritius: Celebrating Differences," a video program of Franklin Covey Co. I am grateful to Stephen Covey and Boyd Craig for bringing it to my attention.

Free
The story of Tatarstan and the quote from President Mintimer Shaimiev come from a conference held in The Hague in February 1994.

Open doors
The story of the woman making the bamboo chair comes from an interview with Muhammad Yunus in Rushworth Kidder, *Shared Values for a Troubled World* (San Francisco: Jossey-Bass, 1994), pp. 143–44.

2. The Teacher: giving people skills to handle conflict
The story of Heavy comes from an interview with Michael Lewis, May 14, 1987. It is cited in William L. Ury, Jeanne M. Brett, and Stephen B. Goldberg, *Getting Disputes Resolved* (San Francisco: Jossey-Bass, 1988), p. 79.

The prospective husband, John Swanson, is quoted in Kevin Merida and Barbara Vobejda, "Battles on the Home Front: Couples in Conflict over Roles," *Washington Post,* March 25, 1998.

Delegitimize violence
The Veterans Education Project is described in Paul Bush, "When Vietnam Veterans Talk About Violence, Even Tough Teens Listen," *American News Service,* February 7, 1997.

The work of the Women's Center in Houston is depicted in L. C. Nojechowicz, "Enlisting Men to Stop Domestic Violence Spreads Across the Country," *American News Service,* November 29, 1996.

Tom Winstone is quoted in David Lynch, "Ex-Prisoners Speak Up for Peace," *USA Today,* May 22, 1998, p. 13A.

For a good history of dueling, see Robert Baldick, *The Duel: A History of Dueling* (New York: Potter, 1965).

Teach tolerance
The story of Lucknow and the City Montessori School comes from Carolyn Cottam, "A Bold Experiment in Teaching Values," *Educational Leadership International,* May 1996, pp. 54–57. I am grateful to Sunita Gandhi for bringing this example to my attention.

The information about the School for Peace at Neve Shalom/Wahat as-Salaam comes from its home page listed at www.ourworld.compuserve.com.

For more on the programs on teaching tolerance in schools, see Sara Bullard, *Teaching Tolerance: Raising Open-Minded, Empathetic Children* (New York: Doubleday, 1996).

The programs in Boston public schools are described in Ken Gewertz, "Voices Against Violence," Harvard University *Gazette*, May 2, 1996, p. 11.

The research on the effects of television programming on children is cited in David Hamburg, *Annual Report Essays 1983–1996*, Carnegie Corporation of New York 1997, p. 186.

The radio programs in Burundi are produced by Search for Common Ground, a conflict resolution organization based in Washington, DC.

Teach joint problem-solving

Cora Pearson is quoted in Sharyn Kane and Richard Keeton, "Racial Tensions Spark School Conflict Resolution," *American News Service*, article ED28, 1997.

The quote from Patricia Bloxham comes from Patricia Squires, "Class Learns to Cope with Conflict," *New York Times*, December 17, 1989.

The story of the four hundred Detroit students comes from Kane and Keeton, "Racial Tensions Spark School Conflict Resolution."

The long-term study of violence prevention curricula in Washington State schools is presented in David Grossman et al., "Effectiveness of a Violence Prevention Curriculum Among Children in Elementary School— A Randomized Controlled Trial," *JAMA* (*Journal of the American Medical Association*) 277 (1997): 1605–11. In classes which had been trained, students exhibited approximately thirty fewer acts of aggression per day and approximately eight hundred more acts described as neutral or positive.

The New York high school student is quoted in Linda Singer, *Settling Disputes*, 2nd ed. (Boulder, CO: Westview, 1994), p. 156.

For more on the spread of social-emotional education, see Daniel Goleman, *Emotional Intelligence* (New York: Bantam, 1995).

3. The Bridge-Builder: forging relationships across lines of conflict

The story of Meyer and Ramaphosa is told in Alistair Sparks, "Letter from South Africa: The Secret Revolution," *New Yorker*, April 11, 1994, pp. 76–77.

Develop joint projects

The Sherif experiment, called the Robbers Cave experiment, is described in "Experiments in Group Conflict," *Scientific American* 195:5 (1956): 54–58.

The cross-racial cooperation in Memphis and Sonoma is described in William Bole, "Citizens Cross Racial Divide to Tackle Concrete Problems," *American News Service*, April 4, 1997.

Lynn Jungwirth is quoted in Jane Braxton Little, "Saving Trees and Jobs, Longtime Foes Find Common Ground," *American News Service*, October 13, 1995.

Foster genuine dialogue

Andrew Puzder is quoted in Jeannette S. Keton, "Beyond Talk, Opponents in the Abortion Debate Join Forces Against a Common Enemy," *American News Service*, March 8, 1996.

The dialogue between Turks and Kurds is accurate, but I have disguised the names of the participants to protect them.

The Days of Dialogue in Los Angeles are described in Jack Crowl, "Some Try a Deceptively Simple Strategy to Defuse Racial Tension—Talking," *American News Service*, article 21, January 12, 1996.

The story of Mad Dads comes from Frances Moore Lappé, "The Drug War at Home—Citizens' Success in the Streets," *American News Service*, January 28, 1996.

Jayne Flowers is quoted in Keton, "Beyond Talk," *American News Service*, March 8, 1996.

Partnering is described in Linda McCrerey, "Win-Win Partners: Partnering Is a New Approach to an Old Concept of Problem-solving Outside the Courtroom," *Hawaii Business*, September 1, 1996 19.

6. Resolve: Mediator, Arbiter, Equalizer, Healer

Interests, rights, power—and relationship

For more on the case of the coal mine and on the theory and practice of designing dispute resolution systems, see William L. Ury, Jeanne M. Brett, and Stephen B. Goldberg, *Getting Disputes Resolved* (San Francisco: Jossey-Bass, 1988).

4. The Mediator: reconciling conflicting interests

For statistics on the success rate of mediation of civil cases, see Jeanne M. Brett, Zoe I. Barsness, and Stephen B. Goldberg, "The Effectiveness of Mediation: An Independent Analysis of Four Major Service Providers," *Negotiation Journal* 12:3 (July 1996): 259–70. For the figures on international mediation, I am indebted to Professor Jacob Bercovitch of the University of Canterbury, Christchurch, New Zealand.

Everyone's a Mediator

The dispute about the groom's mother's husband's gift is recounted in Lorna Marshall, "Sharing, Talking, and Giving: Relief of Social Tensions Among !Kung Bushmen," *Africa* 31:3 (July 1961): 233–34.

Bring the parties to the table

Assistant Principal Allan Lipsky is quoted in Les Kozaczek, "School Violence Reduced When Students Participate in Problem-Solving," *American News Service*, article 437, March 30, 1998.

Help people search for a solution

The quote from Stefanie Franson comes from Mary Knapp, "Schools Address Conflict," Tampa *Tribune*, November 3, 1996, p. 1.

For the story of the Johannesburg department store negotiation, I am indebted to Stephen Covey, personal communication, March 1995.

5. The Arbiter: determining disputed rights

Peers can be Arbiters too

Judge David Silverstein and Sergeant Gordon Ferguson are quoted in Nancy Weil, "In Teen Courts, Young People Set Their Peers Straight," *American News Service*, August 23, 1996.

The Community Reparative Boards in Vermont are described in Mark Lewis, "A New Approach to Nonviolent Crime: Communities Help Determine Justice," *American News Service*, article 18, January 10, 1997.

Replace destructive conflict

The reaction of New Guinea warriors to the introduction of courts is described in Mervyn Meggitt, *Blood Is Their Argument* (Mayfield Publishing Company, 1977), p. 153.

The statistics about the prevalence of arbitration in collective bargaining contracts can be found in Stephen B. Goldberg, Eric D. Green, and Frank E. A. Sander, *Dispute Resolution* (Boston: Little, Brown, 1985), p. 189.

Promote justice

The description of the Semai *bcaraa'* comes from Clayton Robarchek, "Conflict, Emotion, and Abreaction: Resolution of Conflict Among the Semai Senoi," *Ethos* 7:2 (Summer 1979): 110.

The information on *Brown v. Board of Education* comes from the Internet site www.law.cornell.edu/supct/cases/historic.htm.

Information on the Karadzic lawsuit comes from *The Economist*, March 22, 1997, pp. 31–32.

6. The Equalizer: democratizing power

Build collaborative democracy

For an analysis of how democracy evolved in Europe from civil war, see Ralph M. Goldman, *From Warfare to Party Politics: The Critical Transition to Civilian Control* (Syracuse, NY: Syracuse University Press, 1990).

For more on building collaborative democracy, see David D. Chrislip and Carl E. Larson, *Collaborative Leadership: How Citizens and Civic Leaders Can Make a Difference* (San Francisco: Jossey-Bass, 1994).

Roger Aitchison is quoted in Diane Eicher, "Living 'Stepmom' Scenario Doesn't Have to Rule," Denver *Post*, December 28, 1998, p. F1.

Strategies for preventing violence in schools are described in Les Kozaczek, "School Violence Reduced When Students Participate in Problem-Solving," *American News Service*, article 437, March 30, 1998.

The movement to include teenagers on governing boards of social service agencies is discussed in Gus Spohn, "Social Agencies Give Youth a Seat at the Table," *American News Service*, October 12, 1995.

Diane Rondeau is quoted in Paul Bush, "Youths Gain Voice in Government," *American News Service*, May 19, 1997.

The account of democratic classrooms and the quote from Chip Wood come from Mark Lewis, "Teachers Lick Discipline Problems When Students Make the Rules," *American News Service*, article ED 126, February 9, 1996. Also see the Web site of The Responsive Classroom, www.responsiveclassroom.com. The quote from Linda Sartor comes from the Web site www.co-intelligence.org. I thank Tom Attlee of the Co-Intelligence Institute for bringing it to my attention.

The story about Semco is taken from Peter Larson, "Democracy Reaches the Workplace," Ottawa *Citizen*, July 2, 1994, p. F3. A fuller treatment of the story can be found in Ricardo Semler, *Maverick: The Success Story Behind the World's Most Unusual Workplace* (New York: Warner, 1993).

Support nonviolent action

The story of the high school girls' nonviolent protest is reported in *The Third Alternative* 13 (Fall–Winter 1997): 8.

7. The Healer: repairing injured relationships

Create the right climate

Timothy Dayonot's story comes from personal communication, June 14, 1998.

Listen and acknowledge

The description of the Semai *bcaraa'* comes from Clayton Robarchek "Conflict, Emotion, and Abreaction: Resolution of Conflict Among the Semai Senoi," *Ethos* 7:2 (summer 1979): 110.

Gina Shine is quoted in Mary J. Pitzer, "Taking Steps to Protect Employees Amid Rising Workplace Violence," Los Angeles *Times*, March 23, 1997.

Dana Langley is quoted in Matthew Mariani, "Peacemakers" *Occupational Outlook Quarterly*, U.S. Department of Labor, June 1, 1996, pp. 38ff.

The testimony of Lucas Baba Sikwepere to the Human Rights Committee of the South African Truth and Reconciliation Commission is quoted in Antiji Krog, *Country of My Skull* (Johannesburg: Random House, 1998), p. 31. I thank Martha Minow for bringing it to my attention. For an in-depth analysis of Truth Commissions, see Martha Minow, *Between Vengeance and Forgiveness: Facing History after Genocide and Mass Violence* (Boston: Beacon Press, forthcoming).

Encourage apology

Paul Coleman's story comes from Robert D. Enright and Joanna North (eds.), *Exploring Forgiveness* (Madison: University of Wisconsin Press, 1998), p. 75.

Carl Jefferson is quoted in Peter S. Canellos, "Street Soldiers' Peaceful Call to Arms: Many in Project Foster Calm After Slaying," Boston *Globe*, December 16, 1997.

Marietta Jaeger's account is from Enright and North (eds.), *Exploring Forgiveness*, p. 12.

Jonathan Bardon, *A Shorter Illustrated History of Ulster* (Belfast: Blackstaff Press), pp. 276–77.

7. Contain: Witness, Referee, Peacekeeper

For more on Mo Tzu, see Burton Watson (trans.), *MoTzu: Basic Writings* (New York: Columbia University Press, 1963).

8. The Witness: paying attention to escalation

Watch out for early warning signals

Boston Police Commissioner Paul Evans is quoted in *Newsweek*, June 1, 1998, p. 25.

The story of the school shootings in Arkansas is told in Les Kozaczek, "School Violence Reduced When Students Participate in Problem-Solving," *American News Service*, article 437, March 30, 1998.

The quote from a co-worker of Thomas McIlvane comes from S. Anthony Baron, *Violence in the Workplace: A Prevention and Management Guide for Businesses* (Ventura, CA: Pathfinder Publishing of California), p. 49.

For more on how police forces are beginning to use threat assessment, see Robert Fein, Bryan Vossejil, and Gwen A. Holden, "Threat Assessment: An Approach to Prevent Targeted Violence," *Research in Action*, National Institute of Justice, September 1995.

For further reading on the emerging field of early warning, see Kumar Rupesinghe and Michiko Kuroda (eds.), *Early Warning and Conflict Resolution* (New York: St. Martin's, 1992). One network of nongovernmental organizations is the Forum for Early Warning and Early Response (FEWER). Their initial focus is on the Caucasus and the Great Lakes area of Africa.

The story of the angry ex-employee comes from Mary J. Pitzer, "Taking Steps to Protect Employees Amid Rising Workplace Violence," Los Angeles *Times*, March 23, 1997.

Go on patrol

The story of United Colors and the quote from Betty Ann Good come from Nancy Weil, "Thousands of Teens Join Fight Against Crime," *American News Service*, February 21, 1997.

The work of Moms on Patrol is described in *The Economist*, May 25, 1996, p. 30.

Speak out

Commissioner Paul Evans is quoted in *Newsweek*, June 1, 1998, p. 25.

The story of Jimmy Ellison is recounted in Patricia Squires, "Class Learns to Cope with Conflict," *New York Times*, December 17, 1989.

The protests of the Christian wives to save their Jewish husbands is told in Nathan Stoltzfus, "Dissent in Nazi Germany," *The Atlantic* 270 (September 1992): 86–94. For further reading, see Nathan Stoltzfus, *Resistance of the Heart: Intermarriage and the Rosenstrasse Protest in Nazi Germany* (New York: Norton, 1996).

Get help fast

The story of the New York student reported by a fellow student for bringing a knife to school is recounted in Les Kozaczek, "School Violence Reduced When Students Participate in Problem-Solving."

The story of the Bad Tooth Bandit and the quote from Captain Robert Dunford of the Boston Police Department come from James V. O'Connor, "Citizens Put the Community in Community Policing," *American News Service*, July 12, 1996.

9. The Referee: setting limits to fighting

Establish rules for fair fighting

The story of the duel by paint pistols comes from Rhonda Chriss Lokeman, "Conflict Resolution via Paint Pistols: Other Businesses Could Take a Lesson from These," Kansas City *Star*, June 7, 1998, p. L3.

The growing taboo on the use of nuclear weapons is an idea I owe to Professor Thomas Schelling of the University of Maryland. Personal communication, March 1997.

The quote from Ron Sinkler comes from Blaine Harden, "Boston's Approach to Juvenile Crime Encircles Youths, Reduces Slayings," Washington *Post*, October 23, 1997, p. A3.

The story of America Online comes from an article by Amy Harmon in *The New York Times*, January 31, 1999, p. 1.

The story of Project Positive Campaign comes from Kim A. Lawton, "Sick of Mudslinging, Civic Groups Say No to Negative Campaigning," *American News Service*, article 49, April 19, 1996.

Remove offensive arms

I owe the quote from the woman farmer to Shirley Anderson.

The figures comparing death rates among children from firearms come from *The Economist*, April 4, 1998, p. 16: "A 1997 study found that the firearm-related death rate among American children under fifteen years old was nearly sixteen times higher than among children in twenty-five other industrialised countries combined."

The Boston Gun Project is described in Robert Peer, "Boston Anti-Gun Initiative Becomes National Model, Gets NRA Endorsement," *American News Service*, 1997.

The capabilities of the American spyplane "Blackbird" are described in Charlie Cole, "Our Spy on High: The Air Force's SR-71 Shows an Eye for Detail," *New York Times Magazine*, May 10, 1987, pp. 32–34.

Strengthen defenses—nonoffensively

The concept of reducing offensive weapons while leaving defensive weapons untouched is sometimes called "qualitative disarmament." The idea is credited to Sir Basil Liddell Hart and was first introduced by Lord Robert Cecil at the 1932 Geneva Disarmament conference. See Harry B. Hollins, Averill L. Powers, and Mark Sommer, *The Conquest of War* (Boulder, CO: Westview, 1989), pp. 64–65.

The story about the skit comes from Mary Knapp, "Schools Address Conflict," Tampa *Tribune*, November 3, 1996, p. 1.

The story of the stalker comes from Mary J. Pitzer, "Taking Steps to Protect Employees Amid Rising Workplace Violence," Los Angeles *Times*, March 23, 1997.

10. The Peacekeeper: providing protection

The story of John Lewis and Floyd Mann is described in David Halberstam, *The Children* (New York: Random House, 1998).

Interpose

The story about mothers of gang members is described in Geoffrey Mohan, "Mothers Rally to Halt Gang Killings," Los Angeles *Times*, October 8, 1995, p. B1.

The story of John Andrews comes from L. C. Nojechowicz, "Men Get 'Off the Sidelines' to Fight Domestic Violence," *American News Service*, November 29, 1996.

Enforce the peace

The story of the execution of /Twi can be found in Richard B. Lee, *The Dobe !Kung* (New York: Holt, Rinehart and Winston, 1979), p. 96.

The quote from Gary French comes from *Newsweek*, June 1, 1998, p. 23.

The quote from anthropologist Laura Cummings comes from "Does Society

Limit Women's Aggression? Studies Conclude That the Way Women Deal
with Aggression Has Less to Do with Genes Than Culture," Orlando *Sentinel-Tribune*, April 22, 1992, p. E1.

Preempt violence before it starts

For a sobering discussion of the Rwanda tragedy, see Scott R. Feil, *Preventing Genocide: How the Early Use of Force Might Have Succeeded in Rwanda* (New York: Carnegie Corporation, 1998). On p. vi, the report quotes Lieutenant-General Romeo A. Dallaire: "The killings could have been prevented if there had been the international will to accept the costs of doing so even after the politically difficult losses of peacekeepers in Somalia and the ad hoc confusion of April 1994." An international panel of senior military leaders, convened by the Carnegie Commission on Deadly Conflict, the Institute for Study of Diplomacy at Georgetown University, and the United States Army, generally agreed with General Dallaire's assessment. See Carnegie Commission on Preventing Deadly Conflict, *Preventing Deadly Conflict* (New York: Carnegie Corporation, December 1997), p. 6.

The case of Macedonia is discussed in Alice Ackermann and Antonio Pala, "From Peacekeeping to Preventive Deployment: A Study of the United Nations in the Former Yugoslav Republic of Macedonia," *European Security* 5:1 (Spring 1996): 83–97.

For more on Waco, see Dick J. Reavis, *The Ashes of Waco: An Investigation* (Syracuse, NY: Syracuse University Press, May 1998).

The new warriors

The story of nurse Joan Black comes from *Time*, August 23, 1993, p. 11.

Putting it all together

Preventing ethnic violence

The story of Bhiwandi comes from "Why Bombay Burned . . . and Bhiwandi Didn't," *India Today*, January 13, 1993, pp. 42–43. I am grateful to Steven Wilkinson for bringing this example to my attention.

Conclusion: Toward a Co-Culture

What can I do?

The story of the student's response to the gun pointed at him comes from Massachusetts Attorney-General Scott Harshbarger. It is cited in Mary McGrory, "Program Helps Kids Head Off Violence," St. Louis *Post-Dispatch*, October 6, 1994, p. 7B.

Ian Morton is quoted in Elise T. Chisolm, "With Resolve Aplenty, Community Mediators Give Peace a Chance," Baltimore *Sun*, June 20, 1995, p. 3D.

The quote from Alexandria Ritch, a student in Mrs. Gaye Baca's class at Sweeney Elementary in Santa Fe, comes from Arthur Kanegis, personal communication, February 18, 1998.

Gail Robertson is quoted in Paul Bush, "Forgoing the Courtroom, More Americans Try Do-It-Yourself Approach to Justice," *Hope*, October 1997, pp. 11–12.

The case of Olivia Lane, a disguised name, comes from Cynthia J. Chataway and Deborah M. Kolb, "Working Behind the Scene: Gender and Power in Informal Conflict Management," in A. Taylor and Judi Bernstein (eds.), *Conflict and Gender* (Cresskill, NJ: Hampton Press, 1994).

The quotes from Reverend Brown and Reverend Rivers are from *Newsweek*, June 1, 1998, pp. 22–23.

The story of Project Positive Campaign is told in Kim A. Lawton, "Sick of Mudslinging, Civic Groups Say No to Negative Campaigning," *American News Service*, article 49, April 19, 1996.

INDEX

Abel, 61
Abu Alaa, 12
acknowledgment, healing and, 164–65
active listening, 115
Adam, 61
adjudication, 150–51
Aesop, 15
Afghanistan, 87
Africa, 96
African National Congress, 19, 20, 91, 131–32
Age of Force, 80
Agricultural Revolution, 40, 59–61, 83
agricultural societies, 58, 59–61, 64, 65–66
Aki Tumi, 64
alliances, 89, 202–4
Allstate Insurance Company, diversity at, 122
Allyn, Bruce, 93
America Online, code of conduct and Referees of, 179
Andrews, John, 184–85
Annan, Kofi, 94–95
apartheid, xx, 13, 18, 21, 165
apologies, 161–62, 165–66
Arab countries, *see* Middle East conflict

Arafat, Yasser, 12
arbitration, 10, 142, 143, 149–54, 189, 194
Ardrey, Robert, 31, 43
Arendt, Hannah, 2, 25
Argentina, 12, 152
Army, U.S., 21
Arnhem Land, 34, 36
Asea Brown Boveri (ABB), 96–97
ASEAN, 99
Asfour, Hassan, 12
Ashurbanipal, 72, 74
Assyrian empire, 71, 72
Atchison, Roger, 157
Atlanta, Ga., 11, 17, 51, 130
Australia, 34, 36
australopithecines, 30, 31–33, 35

Babylonian empire, 71
"Bad Tooth Bandit," 175
"banality of evil," 25
Bangladesh, 124
Barbee, William, 184
Bardon, Jonathan, 167
Barnard, Isak, 48–49
Barnevik, Percy, 97
Batek society, 50
bcaraa' 6, 7, 152, 164, 189

Beagle Channel islands, 12
Belfast, Protestant vs. Catholic
    neighborhoods in, 196
Bell Atlantic, 164
Benetton, 89–90
Berger, Lee, 29, 30, 32
Berlin, 174–75
Berlin Wall, 196
    collapse of, 92, 97
Beslagic, Selim, 122
Bhiwandi, 192–93
Black, Joan, 188–89
"Blackbird" spy plane, 181
Blair, Tony, 81
Bloomington, Ind., Moms on Patrol in, 173
Bloxham, Patricia, 129
bonobo chimpanzees, 53
Bosnia, xviii, 13, 77–78, 122, 153
Boston, Mass., 10–11, 119, 128, 171, 174,
    175–76, 180, 185
Boston Gun Project, 180
"both-gain" logic, 89–90, 107, 198
Boulding, Kenneth, 198
Brain, Bob, 32–33, 75
Branch Davidians, FBI storming of, 188
Brazil, 152
Brett, Jeanne, 141
Bridge-Builder, third side as, 116, 131–39,
    192, 201
British Empire, 87, 94, 160
Brown, Jeffrey, 204
Brown, Linda, 153
Brown v. Board of Education, 153
Burke, Edmund, 23
Burton, Sir Richard, 71
Burundi, tolerance taught in, 128
Busch, David, 17
Bushmen, 8, 28, 42, 63, 98, 114, 125
    agriculture and, 60
    conflict resolution system of, 4–6, 7, 9,
        17, 47–50, 65, 114, 115–16, 146,
        165–66, 168, 185, 204
    cooperation among, 38–39, 106
    Ju/'hoan, 15, 48, 50, 185
    Kua, 5–6, 48, 49
    !Kung, 4, 29, 39, 40, 49–50, 116
    modern management ideas practiced
        by, 106–7
    own name for, 115
    sharing and gift-giving among, 115–16

Cain, 61
Cain, Becky, 204
Calhoun, John, 64
California, 134, 188
Camp David peace accords, 164
Canada, 44, 96, 128
Carter, Jimmy, 156
Catal Huyuk, 36
Caucasus, mediation among peoples of,
    12
cave paintings, 36
Center for Conflict Resolution, 11
Central America, 173–74
Chechnya, 88, 106, 146–47
chiefs, 71
children:
    deaths from firearms of, 180
    disputes among, 6, 11–12, 145–46, 174,
        182–83, 189–90
    fairness and, 152–53
    in Semai culture, 6
    teaching problem-solving to, 129–30
    see also family disputes
Children of the Arbat (Rybakov), 93
Chile, 12, 152, 153, 157
chimpanzees, 51, 52–54, 162, 184
China, 78, 169–70
Christian, John, 63
churches, 119, 134
Churchill, Sir Winston, 140
city-states, 65, 70–71
civilization, beginnings of, 33
civil rights movement, 160, 183–84
Cleveland, Ohio, 8
Clinton, Bill, 137–38
coal mines, 140–42, 168, 177
"co-culture," 55–56, 131, 196–207
"co-democracy," 205–6
coercion, 42–44, 57–80
    agricultural societies and, 58, 59–61,
        64, 65–66
    power structures and, 67–70
    state power and, 68, 70–73, 74, 79
Cold War, xx, 43, 76, 78, 82, 87, 178
Coleman, Paul, 166
Colombia, 54, 97, 105
colonial powers, 94, 96
Columbine High School, xvi
combat fatigue, 21–22
common ground, 16

communication, 147–48
"Communication and Conflict in the
    Workplace" program, 130
communications technology, 93–94, 95,
    100, 101
community, 125, 168
    conflict resolution role of, 4–7, 8–13
    third side as, 14, 204–5
Community Action Team, 179
community policing, 175–76
Community Reparative Boards, 150
conflict, xvi, xviii, xx–xxi
    "both-gain" logic in, 89–90, 107, 198
    among chimpanzees, 51, 52–54
    coercion and, 42–44, 57–80
    containment of, 113, 139, 169–95
    cooperation and, 38–47, 55–56
    early warning signs of, 171–73
    history of, 27–109
    human nature and, 30–38, 51–55, 73
    importance of, 112
    increased interdependence and,
        99–100
    "lose-lose" logic in, 87–88, 107, 198
    management system for, 47–50
    prevention of, 113, 114–39
    three types of, 41–42
conflict resolution, xix, xx–xxi, 101, 113,
    129–30, 140–68, 190
    by Bushmen, 4–6, 7, 9, 17, 47–50, 65,
        114, 115–16, 146, 165–66, 168, 185,
        204
    at Ford, 101–3
    importance of, xv
    interests, rights, power, and
        relationship in, 141–43
    in Semai culture, 6, 7, 17, 23, 47, 55,
        152, 164, 171, 189
    see also third side
conflict-resolution groups, 172
consensus classrooms, 158
containment, 113, 169–89
    through Peacekeepers, 170, 183–89,
        190
    through Referees, 170, 176–83
    three ways of, 170
    through Witnesses, 170–76, 190
cooperation, 38–47, 55–56, 67, 85
corporations, 89–90, 96–97, 101–3
Costa Rica, 119–20

crime, 64, 119
Croatia, 13, 77–78
cross-cutting ties, 132–34
Cuban Missile Crisis, 81–83, 88
Culpepper, Patrice, 11
Cummings, Laura, 186

Dale, George, 183
Dallaire, Romeo, 187
Darcissac, Roger, 25
Dart, Raymond, 31–33, 35
Dayonot, Timothy, 163
"deconflicting," 178
deer, 63
Defense Department, U.S., 23
defenses, strengthening of, 181–83
de Klerk, F. W., 18, 19, 20–21, 90, 91
Demi, 29
democracy, 95–96, 105–6, 112
    collaborative, 156–59, 205–6
Des Noyers, Nanette, 101–2
destructive conflict, see conflict; wars,
    warfare
Detroit, Mich., 130
de Waal, Frans, 51, 53, 54, 162, 184
dialogue, 135–39
dinosaurs, 75
Di//Xao-Toma, 50
domestic violence, 8
dueling, 126–27, 177–78
Dunford, Robert, 176

East Africa, 44, 71
Eastern Europe, 92, 160–61
Ecuador, 54, 151–52
Eden, Garden of, 61
"Education for Mutual Understanding"
    program, 128
Egypt, 90, 164
Egypt, ancient, 36, 61, 66, 68, 71, 97
Ellison, Jimmy, 174
empires, 71, 87, 94
employment, for teenagers, 119
Engel, Herman, 3, 4
Enoch, 61
equalizing, 142, 143, 154–61, 189, 192,
    194
Ethiopian proverb, 194
ethnic conflict, xvii, 76–78, 121, 128, 159,
    192–93

ethnic groups, number of, xvii, 122
Europe, 87, 99, 100, 120, 156
European Union, 99, 135
Evans, Paul, 10, 171, 174
Eve, 61
exit option, 48, 49, 65, 74

family disputes, 13, 155, 164–65
    community role in, 8–9
    healing in, 162
    mediation of, 143–46
    setting limits in, 176–77
family power structure, 96
Ferguson, Brian, 34
Ferguson, Gordon, 150
fire, human mastery of, 75
Fletcher-Howell, Gordon, 126
Florida, 122, 173
Flowers, Jayne, 138
food supply, 41, 53, 115, 119
Ford Motor Company, 101–3, 106
Ford 2000, 102–3
forgiveness, healing and, 167
Fort Worth, Tex., 119
France, 24–26, 96, 135
Frankel, Sidney, 131
Franson, Stefanie, 148
Frayer, David, 34
freedom, 123–24
French, Gary, 185
Freud, Sigmund, 30
Fujitsu, 89

Galbraith, John Kenneth, xix, xx
Gandhi, M. K. (Mahatma), 88, 127, 160
Garden of Eden, 61
General Dynamics, 121
General Motors, 89, 100, 123
Genesis, 61
Georgia Department of Transportation,
    17
Germany, European unity and, 135
Gladysvale site, 29–30, 31
glasnost, 93
Goldberg, Stephen, 141, 147
Golden, Andrew, 171
Good, Betty Ann, 173
Goodall, Jane, 52, 53
Gorbachev, Mikhail, 93
Grameen Bank, 124

Great Britain, 54, 96, 120, 153, 180
Guardian Angels, 173
Gulf War, 181, 186–87
guns, 86, 179, 188–89

Hadza group, 44
Harrington, Michael, 125–26
Harvard University, 180
Hawaii, 12, 175
healing, 142, 143, 161–68, 189, 190, 192
help, speed in getting, 175–76
Hernandez, Deborah, 119
hierarchies, pyramidal, 96–98
Hindu-Moslem violence, 127–28, 192–93
Hiroshima, 75, 78
Hirschfeld, Yair, 12
Hitler, Adolf, 74
Hobbes, Thomas, 30, 47, 50
"homework clubs," 121–22
Homo habilis, 30, 35
Homo Negotiator, 56, 103, 197
Homo sapiens sapiens, 35
ho'oponopono, 12
House of Representatives, U.S., 138
Houston, Tex., 126
humanity:
    cooperation as key to survival of,
        38–39
    evolution of, xvii, 29–30, 31, 206
    ingathering of tribes of, xvii
human nature, conflict and, xvii, xviii,
        30–38, 51–55, 73
humor, 115–16
hunters-gatherers, 58, 106–7, 119
    agriculture's displacement of, 60
    cooperation among, 38–40, 46
    warfare among, 43–44, 62–63
    see also Bushmen; Semai people

IBM, 89
Ilonget tribesmen, 71–72
immune system, 7
India, 78, 127–28, 160, 192–94
individual action, 198–206
Industrial Revolution, 84
Ingushetia, 146
interdependence, 98–100
interests, conflicts of, 41–42, 142, 143
International Criminal Court, 153–54,
    205

International Monetary Fund, 99
Internet, xvi, 85–86, 95, 97, 101, 179
interventions, 155, 184–85
Iran, 172
Iraq, 172, 181, 186–87
Ireland, Northern, xx, 81, 126, 128, 159, 167, 179, 196
Ireland, Republic of (Eire), 196
Iron Age, 30
Israel, xx, 12, 90, 128, 164
    see also Middle East conflict
Italy, 159

Jaeger, Marietta, 166
Japan, 175
Jebel Sahaba, 34
Jefferson, Carl, 166
Jericho, 36
Jerusalem, Sadat's visit to, 164
Jews, 24–26, 174–75
Jobs, Peter, 138–39
Johannesburg, 148–49
Johnson, Marquise, 8
Johnson, Mitchell, 171
joint problem-solving, 129–31
joint projects, 134–35, 138
joint ventures, 89
Jonesboro, Ark., 171
Ju/'hoan Bushmen, 15, 48, 50, 185
Jungwirth, Lynn, 134
justice, 152–54
Juul, Mona, 12

Kalahari Desert, Bushmen of, see Bushmen
Karadzic, Radovan, 153
Keeley, Lawrence, 33–34
Kennedy, John F., 81–83
Kentucky, 140–42
KGB, 93
kgotla, 5, 7
Khrushchev, N. S., 82
King, Martin Luther, Jr., 134, 160
kings, 71, 94
Klayman, Arnie, 104–5
Knowledge Revolution, 83–92, 100, 101, 108–9, 119, 133, 181, 197
Koch, Nancy, 179
Korakoradue, 5, 48, 114, 166
Kosovo, 28

Kua Bushmen, 5–6, 48, 49
!Kung Bushmen, 4, 29, 39, 40, 49–50, 116
Kurd, Maher el, 12
Kurds, 121, 136–37, 161–62, 172, 186
Kuwait, 172, 186–87

labor disputes, 140–42, 151, 178–79
lagom, 118
Lamech, 61
land, 64, 74, 84, 85, 118
Lane, Olivia, 202
Langley, Dana, 164
Lao Tzu, 114
Larsen, Terje Rod, 12
lawsuits, annual number and cost of, xvi
League of Women Voters, 204
Leakey, Louis, 43
Le Chambon, Jews rescued by people of, 24–26
Lee, Richard, 4, 39, 40, 49, 50, 116
Le Forestier, Roger, 25
Lévi-Strauss, Claude, 40
Lewis, John, 183
Lewis, Michael, 125
Lewis-Williams, J. D., 36
Liddell-Hart, Sir Basil, 182
Lincoln, Neb., 184–85
listening:
    active, 115
    healing and, 164–65
Littleton, Colo., xvi
loans to poor people, 124
Los Angeles, Calif., 137, 172, 184
"lose-lose" logic, 87–88, 107, 198
Loubsher, J.H.N., 36
Lower, Louis G., 122
Lubbers, Ruud, 147
Lubowski, Anton, 18
Lucknow, 127–28

Macedonia, 187
McIlvane, Thomas, 171–72
Mack, Robert Earl, 121
McNamara, Robert Strange, 82
"Mad Dads," 139
Malaysia, 159
    see also Semai people
Mandela, Nelson, 18, 19, 23, 90, 91, 165
Mann, Floyd, 183–84
Marcos, Ferdinand, 157

Markham, Howard, 104
Marshall, Lorna, 115, 116
Marshall, S.L.A., 21–22
Martin, Debra, 34
Martin Luther King Center, 130
Martin Luther King High School, 11
Massachusetts, 126, 161
Mauritius, 122
mediation, 9–10, 11, 140–42, 143–49,
    169, 189, 190, 192, 194, 200–201
Meggitt, Mervyn, 151
Melrose Elementary School, 12
Memphis, Tenn., 134
Mercosur, 99
Mexico, 186
Meyer, Roelf, 91, 131–32
Miami, Fla., 173
Middle East conflict, 12, 90, 100, 128, 164
Milwaukee, Wisc., 121
Moms on Patrol, 173
monarchy, 71, 94
Monnet, Jean, 135
Montgomery, Ala., 183–84
Moore, Makita, 13
Morris, Denny, 105
Morton, Ian, 200
Mo Tzu, 169–70, 182, 184
mountain climbers, cross-cutting ties of,
    132–33
Mozambique, 13
murder rates, xvi, 49–50, 120, 180
Muslims, 13

NAFTA, 99
Nagasaki, 75
Namibia, 63
National Peace Accord, 20
Nazis, 24–25, 174–75
Neanderthals, 35
needs, 115, 118, 121
negotiation, 154
negotiation revolution, 101–6
Netherlands, 128, 147
Netscape, 85–86
network structure, 95–98
Neve Shalom/Wahat al-Salaam, 128
New Guinea Highlands, clan warfare in,
    36, 57–58, 62, 64, 86, 131, 151, 179
New York, N.Y., 175, 185
Nicaragua, 157

nonviolent action, 159–61
Northern Ireland, see Ireland, Northern
Northwest Coast Indians, 62–63
Norway, 12
nuclear weapons, xvi–xvii, 22–23, 75–76,
    78, 81–83, 86, 87, 100, 178, 180–81,
    193–94
Nuremberg Tribunal, 153

Oakland, Calif., 12
Ocala-Marion County, Fla., 137
Omaha, Neb., 137
ombudspersons, 9, 156
Oregon, 134
organizational structures, 6, 69–70, 74,
    92–95, 101–3, 105, 108
"origin myth," 28
Ortega, Daniel, 157
Oslo Accord (1993), 12

Pakistan, 78, 193–94
Palestine Liberation Organization (PLO),
    12
Palestinians, sulha tradition of, 12
parents, see family disputes
Paris, University of, 148
partnering, 138–39
patrolling, 173–74
Patten, Bill, 137
peace:
    enforcement of, 185–86
    as natural, xviii–xix, 54–55
    signs of, 78–79, 80
peacekeepers, containing conflict
    through, 170, 183–89, 190, 193,
    194, 201
Pearson, Cora, 129
peer mediators, 13, 148
peers, 15, 149–50
Peru, 151–52
Philippines, 72, 157
Pinochet, Augusto, 153, 157
policing, 175–76, 185
population, xvii, 40, 43, 60–61, 63–65,
    73
positions, conflicts of, 41–42
power, 41–42, 67–70, 77, 84, 92–95, 108
    equalizing of, 142, 143, 154–61
Power, Margaret, 53
preempting violence, 186–88

prevention, 114–39, 190
    bridge-building in, 116, 131–39
    needs, skills, and relationships in,
        115–16
    providing in, 116, 117–24
    sharing in, 115, 118–20
    teaching in, 116, 117–24
Prisoners' Dilemma, 44–47, 66, 73
problem-solving, 129–31
"Project Positive Campaign," 179
Provider, third side as, 116, 117–24, 192,
    201
proxy wars, 78
Pundik, Ron, 12
Purana, 49, 115
Puzder, Andrew, 135
pyramidal hierarchies, 96–98

Rabin, Yitzhak, 12
race, 137, 173
    see also South Africa, Republic of
radio, 128
Ramaphosa, Cyril, 131–32
Ramones (Kua elder), 5–6
rape, xvi
Rape-Spouse Abuse Crisis Center, 184–85
rats, 63–64
reconciliation, 167–68
Referees, containing conflict through,
    170, 176–83, 194
relationships, 116, 142, 143
Renaissance, 83
Renaldo, Robert, 71–72
respect, 4, 120–22
Rice University, 126
Ridley-Thomas, Avis, 137
rights, 94, 142, 143
Rio de Janeiro, 119
Ritch, Alexandria, 200
Rivers, Eugene, 117, 118, 204
Rives, Hal, 11
Robarchek, Clayton, 152, 164
Robertson, Gail, 201
Rochester, N.Y., 179
Rondeau, Diane, 158
Roper, Marilyn, 34
Rosenberg, Michael, 9
Rousseau, Jean-Jacques, 37
Royal Oak, Mich., 171–72
Russian Federation, 123–24, 146–47

Rwanda, xviii, 76, 77, 153, 187
Rybakov, Anatoly, 93

Sadat, Anwar, 164
Saddam Hussein, 172, 186–87
St. Paul, Minn., 130
San Diego Zoo, 53
San Francisco, University of California at,
    163
Sant'Egidio, 13
Sarajevo, media role in, 176
Sartor, Linda, 158
Saturn Corporation, 123
Scandinavia, 118
School for Peace, 128
science, 83, 85
security, common, 120
Seeliger, Clarence, 11
Semai people, 8, 11, 28, 43, 50, 54, 118
    conflict resolution system of, 6, 7, 17,
        23, 47, 55, 152, 164, 171, 189
Semler, Ricardo, 158–59
separatist movements, 100
Serbia, 13, 77–78
Sesame Street, 128
sex, tensions diffused by, 53
Shaimiev, Mintimer, 123
Shakespeare, William, 112
sharing, 115, 118–20
Sherif, Muzafer, 134
Shine, Gina, 164
shuttle diplomacy, mediation through,
    147
Sikwepere, Lucas Baba, 165
Silverstein, David, 150
Simpson, O. J., trial of, 137
Sinkler, Ron, 178
Six-Day War, 90
Sketch, Ed, 101–2
skills, 115–16, 200
slavery, abolition of, 94
Smith, David, 173
South Africa, Republic of, xx, 13, 18–21,
    22, 29–30, 31–32, 35, 75, 76, 90–92,
    131–32, 165, 174
Soviet Union, 14, 22–23, 78, 81–83, 87,
    88, 92–94, 95, 163, 178, 181
speaking out, 174–75
Spielberg, Steven, 120–21
Spokane, Wash., 175

spy planes, 181
state, 68, 70–73, 74, 79
State Department, U.S., 23
Staten, Elizabeth, 188
Staton, Eddie, 139
Sterkfontein site, 35
Strategic Air Command (SAC), 22–23
strategic alliances, 89
street vendors, department store conflict
    with, 148–49
Sudan, 34
sulha, 12
Sumeria, 36, 57, 68, 71
Sun Tzu, 169, 187
Supreme Court, U.S., 17
Swartkrans cave, 75
Switzerland, 182

Tatarstan, 123–24, 146
Teacher, third side as, 116, 125–31, 139
teenage violence, xvi, 10–11, 119, 121–22,
    158, 171, 175, 180, 184, 185
television, 128
terrorism, xvi–xvii, 77
third side, 3–26, 28, 48, 49
    as Arbiter, 142, 143, 149–54, 189, 194
    as Bridge-Builder, 116, 131–39, 192, 201
    in community disputes, 10–12
    conflict resolution roles of, 3–7, 8–13,
        14–17, 53–54, 111–207
    containment mode of, 113, 169–95
    definition of, 14
    as Equalizer, 142, 154–61, 189, 192, 194
    as everybody's responsibility, 22–24
    in family disputes, 8–9
    as Healer, 142, 143, 161–68, 189, 190,
        192
    inner, 20–22
    insiders as, 19–20
    make-up of, 18–22
    as Mediator, 142, 143–49, 169, 189,
        190, 192, 194, 200–201
    motto of, 113
    outsiders as, 18–19
    in peace negotiations, 12–13
    as Peacekeeper, 170, 183–89, 193, 194,
        201
    potential of, 24–26
    prevention mode of, 113, 114–39
    as Provider, 116, 117–24, 192, 201

putting the roles together, 189–95
    as Referee, 170, 176–83, 194
    resolution mode of, 113, 140–68
    strengthening of, 101, 204–6
    as Teacher, 116, 125–31
    ten roles of, 111–207
    ten voices of, 203
    weakening of, 65–66, 73–74
    as Witness, 170–76, 192–93
    in workplace disputes, 9–10
Third World, xvii, 79
threat assessment techniques, 172
Time, 44
Tobias, Philip, 34–35
Tokyo, 64
tolerance, 127–28
Topeka, Kans., 153
Toth, Nicholas, 34
Toyota, 89
triple wins, 10, 17
Trotman, Alex, 102
Troubled Times (Martin and Frayer, eds.),
    34
trust-building, 163–64
Truth and Reconciliation Commission,
    165
Tsamko, 15
Tsumkwe, 63, 65
Tuchman, Barbara, 74
Turkey, 121, 136–37, 161–62
Tutu, Desmond, 18
/Twi, 185
/Twi!gum, 4

United Colors, 173
United Nations, 18–19, 99, 172, 173, 181,
    184, 186, 187, 193, 194
U.S.S.R., *see* Soviet Union

Varagnac, André, 74–75
Vatican, 12
Vermont, 150
Veterans Education Project, 126
Vietnam War, 16–17, 87
Villamizar, Alberto, 97
Villaroya, Pedro, 137
violence, delegitimizing of, 125–27
Voltaire, 87, 206
volunteering, 201–2
Vorachek, Mitzi, 126

Waco, Tex., 188
Waorani people, 54
War Before Civilization (Keeley), 34
waris, 164
wars, warfare:
  agricultural societies and, 61–62, 64–66
  alternatives to, xviii, 2, 106
  contagion of, 73, 74
  cooperation in, 46–47
  current number of, xvi, 77
  between democracies, 96
  doing away with, 206–7
  ethnic, xvii, 76–78, 121, 122, 128, 159, 192–93
  human nature and, xvii, xviii, 30–38
  inner resistance to, 21–22
  logic of, 70–74
  prevention of, 193–94
  reasons for, 42–43, 62–63, 74, 77, 121
  signs of peace and, 78–79
  third side and, 12–13, 16–17, 22–23
Washington, D.C., 50
Washington, George, 95
Washington State, 130
weapons, 4, 35–36, 43, 58, 86, 87–88, 175, 179, 180–81
  see also nuclear weapons

Webster, David, 18
Wendorf, Fred, 34
West Africa, 71
White, Sophelia, 188–89
White, Timothy, 34
Wilson, Gordon and Marie, 167
"win-lose" logic, 104, 198
Winstone, Tom, 126
Witness, 170–71, 173, 175
witnesses, containing conflict through, 170–76, 190, 192–93
Witswatersrand, University of, 32
women, 96
  rates of assault and rape of, xvi
  rights of, 94
Women's Center, 126
Wood, Robert "Chip," 158
World Trade Center bombing, xvi–xvii
World War I, 46–47, 74–75, 77, 87
World War II, 2, 21–22, 24–26, 72, 74, 75, 135, 174–75

Yerkes Primate Research Lab, 51, 162, 184
Youth Crime Watch of America, 173
Yugoslavia, former, xvi, 13, 28, 76, 77–78, 79, 122, 153, 172, 174, 176, 187
Yunus, Muhammad, 124

ABOUT THE AUTHOR

William Ury is co-founder of the Program on Negotiation at Harvard Law School, where he directs a research project on the prevention of war. He is co-author of *Getting to YES* and author of *Getting Past No.*

He works with business, government, and community leaders around the world on transforming adversarial relationships into mutually beneficial partnerships. Over the last two decades, he has mediated between quarreling corporate divisions, battling unions and management, and warring ethnic groups. Ury was actively involved in the creation of nuclear risk reduction centers in Washington and Moscow, serving as a consultant to the Crisis Management Center at the White House. Working with former President Jimmy Carter, he helped found the International Negotiation Network, which seeks to end civil wars around the world.

Trained as an anthropologist, with a B.A. from Yale and a Ph.D. from Harvard, he has carried out his research not only at the bargaining table and the boardroom, but also among the Bushmen of the Kalahari and the clan warriors of New Guinea.